DREAMBOATS & PETTICOATS

BRINGING ON BACK THE GOOD TIMES!

by Brian Southall

THIS DAY
IN MUSIC BOOKS
www.thisdayinmusicbooks.com

Text © Brian Southall 2016
ISBN: 978 1 9196 1654 4
Printed in the UK

Layout by Gary Bishop
Production Liz Sánchez and Neil Cossar

This Day in Music Books
Unit 6 Swindells Yard
Arden Street
New Mills
SK22 4NS

THIS DAY IN MUSIC BOOKS

www.thisdayinmusicbooks.com

Email: editor@thisdayinmusic.com

Exclusive Distributors:
Music Sales Limited
14/15 Berners St London
W1T 3JL

Acknowledgements: The author would like to thank all those good people who gave their time and, more importantly, their memories plus – courtesy of the British Library - a selection of back issues of national newspapers and copies of Melody Maker and New Musical Express music papers. Also thanks to go Brian Berg for his persistence and Neil Cossar and all at This Day In Music Books for taking over the reins.

For Maurice and Carol who heard it all and danced to some of it …

Contents

Introduction

If the Sixties were swingin' in oh so many ways, the Fifties were sort of left dangling, in the aftermath of a war. It began as a drab colourless decade with nothing of note to excite a new generation of youngsters, their young lives still blighted by rationing and shortages. But it slowly emerged as the era in which a new rebellious attitude took hold and eventually erupted, as the youth of the 1950s discovered their own music, cinema and fashion – they found their own identity.

The austerity and hardships of the Forties was slowly eroded and replaced by an up-beat attitude. Comedies and musicals hit the cinema screens while snappy new outfits, man-made fibres and make-up arrived to liven up the way people dressed and looked – although the wartime motto of 'make do and mend' was still at the heart of the nation's fashions. But, arguably, it was music that went through the most obvious change in the Fifties as the establishment's interest in jazz and big bands was gradually replaced with an obsession for all things American. And that meant rock 'n' roll and everything that went with it: fancy outfits, wild dance routines, smoky coffee bars, angry parents, public protests and even the odd punch-up. Three decades on from the Roaring Twenties and just a few years before the Sixties began to swing, the Fifties – which arrived with as much relief as hope – finally set things rockin' and rollin'.

While rock 'n' roll set the pace, the new front runners in the Sixties were British groups who launched a successful takeover of the pop world. But, not to be outdone, America rallied and came back with a new sound and hopeful message of peace and love. It didn't last but thankfully music, as it has done for generations, carried on although like the times, it was a-changin'.

Brian Southall

Chapter 1

1950-54: Life before rock 'n' roll

Two things happened in Britain in the early years of the 1950s, which played a huge part in shaping the future of what we now call pop music – even though, at the time, nobody grasped their true significance. Firstly a long-established radio station began broadcasting on a new wavelength and then a newly re-launched music paper came up with the idea of listing the bestselling records of the day.

Radio Luxembourg began broadcasting in 1933 and was one of the first commercial radio stations which could be heard in the United Kingdom, thanks to its transmission on the European long-wave band alongside the BBC Light Programme and radio stations in Warsaw, Prague and Oslo.

In July 1951 the powers that be decided to switch Luxembourg (known officially as Radio Television Luxembourg or RTL) to the less powerful medium wave – on 208 metres – which served Germany, Netherlands and Belgium, plus Britain where the signal was far from perfect.

Despite broadcasting under the banner 'Your Station of the Stars', Luxembourg's service to Britain was affected by the weather and by night-time conditions over the UK, which led to the station broadcasting from 6pm, when reception was supposedly improved

– especially if you lived in Scotland or the north of England. Even so, the shows faded in and out and radio sets needed to be constantly re-tuned as stations based in Strasbourg, Athens, Brussels, Cork and even Tirana in Albania interrupted the programmes broadcast from the Grand Duchy.

With the launch of Radio 208 (as Radio Luxembourg was often referred to) in 1951, listeners in Britain could enjoy such gems as adventure shows featuring 'Pilot of the Future' Dan Dare and detective Perry Mason, entertainment from Leslie 'Memory Man' Welch, religious moments with the 'Old Fashioned Revival Hour', the quiz programme 'Chance Of A Lifetime' (with comedian Dick Emery) and, at 11pm on a Monday night, Pete Murray hosting 'The Top Twenty Show'. As there were no actual hit parades at the time, this was based on the top-selling songs and sheet music of the day – until the first chart arrived.

At the same time, a show called 'Smash Hits' was also on Radio Luxembourg. But this one had a difference: it featured the most hated records around. Listeners wrote in with the titles of the discs they liked least and, after hearing them played one last time, they could enjoy the moment when the records were destroyed live on air.

The second major step forward for Britain's growing audience of pop music fans was the introduction of the UK's first ever sales chart by the *New Musical Express* on November 14, 1952. The music paper had only been launched a year earlier, when publisher Maurice Kinn bought the title *The Musical Express & Accordion Weekly* for £1000 and re-branded it as *New Musical Express* in March 1952.

Aware of the growing interest in popular music – particularly the records and artists coming out of America – Kinn printed the Billboard list of bestselling records in a September issue of the *NME*. The chart, which only ran from one to five, had 'You Belong To Me' in the top spot and, bizarrely, it was credited to J. Stafford. She was followed by 'Auf Wiederseh'n Sweetheart' by V. Lynn; 'Wish You Were Here' from E. Fisher; 'I Went To Your Wedding' by P. Page and finally 'Half As Much' from R. Clooney. There were no Christian names listed or record company credits given; for the record, Jo Stafford was on Columbia, Vera Lynn on Decca, Eddie Fisher on RCA, Patti Page on Mercury and Rosemary Clooney on Columbia.

Two months later, page eight of the *NME* carried Britain's first history-making chart under the banner heading: 'Announcing The First RECORD HIT PARADE'. It was accompanied by a story which explained that a 'An authentic weekly survey of the bestselling 'pop' records has been devised and instigated.' It went on to credit the 'willing co-operation of the largest gramophone record retailers in all parts of the country'.

The chart, which the *NME* claimed would be of the 'greatest interest and benefit to all our readers' was a

Top 12 listing, which in practice featured 15 records as some titles were tied at numbers 7, 8 and 11.

While Al Martino's 'Here In My Heart' (Capitol) took the historic debut top spot, he was followed by: 'You Belong To Me' by Jo Stafford (Columbia); 'Somewhere Along The Way' by Nat King Cole (Capitol); 'Isle Of Innisfree' by Bing Crosby (Brunswick); 'Feet Up' by Guy Mitchell (Columbia); 'Half As Much' by Rosemary Clooney (Columbia); 'Forget-Me-Not' by Vera Lynn (Decca) and 'High Noon' by Frankie Laine (Columbia) both in joint seventh place; 'Sugar Bush' by Doris Day & Frankie Laine (Columbia) and 'Blue Tango' by Ray Martin (Columbia) both tied at number eight; 'Homing Waltz' by Vera Lynn (Decca); 'Auf Wiederseh'n Sweetheart' by Vera Lynn (Decca); 'Cowpuncher's Cantata' by Max Bygraves (HMV) and 'Because You're Mine' by Mario Lanza at number 11; and 'Walkin' My Baby Back Home' by Johnnie Ray (Columbia) at number 12.

The sight of American singer Johnnie Ray at number 12 in the UK's initial hit parade was perhaps a sign of things to come, as the man who took the US by storm with his heartwrenching, emotion-charged performances had finally made his mark in Britain.

In December 1951, Johnnie Ray and The Four Lads had topped the Billboard Bestselling Pop Singles chart with 'Cry', which held the number-one spot for over two months and sold more than two million 78rpm records. The man dubbed the 'Nabob of Sob' was on his way and he would arrive with a new style of music – and some controversy.

And so it was that the double-whammy of a new commercial radio station broadcasting a wider range of entertainment programmes and a chart of the bestselling records paved the way for a new generation of teenagers, who had been born during World War II, survived German bombing raids and then endured the dismal realities of rationing – with its weekly allowance of 13 ounces of meat, two pints of milk, a single egg and two loaves of bread. These girls and boys were eager for something new to arrive in their lives, something that was exciting and, most importantly, something that was theirs and theirs alone.

But before all that would come to pass, it was time to bid farewell to the Forties – a decade that had depression written all over it – and herald the arrival of the Fifties.

The USA, in 1948, was experiencing the first signs of a new musical style as 'jive' dancing took hold in the bars, dance halls and 'juke joints' frequented by America's black community where they listened to a heady mix of blues, gospel and jazz. By 'rolling, reeling and spinning', America's black youngsters invented a dance style known as 'rock and roll'. And it was implicity linked to sex – much to displeasure of nice society, who preferred their entertainment to come from harmless big bands and accomplished ballad singers.

In the same year, the head of CBS Records' laboratories, Dr Peter Goldmark came up with a plan to expand everyone's listening pleasure: he invented the 12" microgroove long-playing record which turned at 33rpm and offered up 23 minutes of uninterrupted playing time per side. But while the British could read about these developments in the UK, they wouldn't see any of these newfangled discs for a few more years.

However, what we did have in the UK back then was a radio show on the BBC entitled *Record Roundabout* with host Jack Jackson offering a heady combination of comedy clips and the most popular music of the day, plus of course the long-established *Family Favourites* and *Housewives Choice* – both of which were first broadcast in the mid-Forties.

Interestingly it was Jackson's original broadcasting style which inspired one young man to pay particular attention to radio presenters. 'Jack Jackson was the first DJ I really noticed,' says the man who would go on to become known as 'Whispering' Bob Harris. 'He was the first, to my knowledge, to use a sound-effect, a gag or some other device played from tape to link one record to the next.'

There was also jazz, of course, and jazz clubs, particularly in London, where ambitious young players such as Humphrey Lyttelton, Ronnie Scott, Johnny Dankworth and Tony Crombie gathered to entertain the fans who favoured either the Dixieland style of 'trad jazz' or the more intricate bebop version known as 'modern jazz'.

Venues such as the Feldman Swing Club, Club 11 and the Bag O'Nails were all up-and-running before the Fifties arrived. The music on offer caused concern at the headquarters of the BBC, where the 1948 Policy Guide was being produced to ensure things did not get out of hand.

While the little booklet confirmed that it was 'The corporation's policy actively to encourage British music so long as it does not lead to a lowering of accepted musical standards', the big-wigs in Broadcasting House, perhaps with an eye to the future, were particularly concerned about any effects upon classical music. The booklet warned that: 'the jazzing by dance bands of classical tunes or the borrowing and adaptation of them is normally unacceptable.'

In the midst of this news, *Melody Maker*'s Musician's Poll for 1949 offered up 22-year-old saxophone and clarinet player Johnny Dankworth in pole position, followed by rival sax and clarinet man Ronnie Chamberlain and alto saxophonist Leslie Gilbert.

On a much more practical level, Britain's first launderettes arrived in the same year – there would be over 2000 in the country ten years later – plus the famous Kenwood Chef food mixer created a stir in the kitchen. It was invented by Kenneth Wood (whose house Kenwood, in Surrey, would be bought by John Lennon in 1964 for £20,000). The new Land Rover and Morris Minor cars were launched – despite petrol rationing still being in place.

Children were kept entertained by Enid Blyton's first *Noddy* books, by the news of the birth of a polar bear called Brumas at London Zoo, Charles Warrell's *I-Spy* books, which would attract over 500,000 youngsters by end of the decade, and trainspotting through the popular Locospotter's Club.

With the new decade there also came the good news that restrictions on the sale of soap, paper and petrol were all to be lifted (following the end of clothing rationing in the late 1940s) and 1950 also brought with it the first filter cigarettes – Player's Bachelor brand – and the launch of the *Eagle* comic which cost 3d and introduced radio's space hero Dan Dare to the printed page.

A new listening phenomenon also attracted the eyes and ears of teenagers: Bakelite portable radios. These newfangled machines heralded the start of an unhealthy but immensely popular late-night pasttime as young music fans began listening to Radio Luxembourg in their bedroom – under the bedcovers after lights-out.

And what the kids would have heard were probably some of Britain's bestselling tunes of the day which, according to a *Melody Maker* listing from June 1950, included 'My Foolish Heart', 'Dearie', 'Oh You Sweet One', 'Let's Do It Again' and 'Jealous Heart' while new releases came from the likes of Pearl Bailey, Jack Jackson, The Deep River Boys, Louis Armstrong, Mel Torme and Jo Stafford. The sheet-music charts which appeared in the music papers were the forerunners of the record hit parade and were the first indication of the most popular songs and singers of the day as music forced its way into the lives of everyday people.

As Decca launched the 12" vinyl long-playing record in Britain, so news came from America that rivals RCA Records had developed a newfangled 7" format which spun at 45rpm and carried either one or two songs per side in the form of a single, or more tracks on an Extended Play (EP) record. The list of new titles in Decca's first 'LP Supplement' included Robert Farnon, Edmundo Ros, Stanley Black and The Old Time Dance Orchestra alongside news of the revolutionary Deccalian 'record re-producers' (record players). These new record players would have been available to buy on Hire Purchase (HP) which, along with mail order catalogues, became a popular and easier way for cash-strapped families to buy goods and clothing they previously could not have afforded.

Clement Attlee returned for a second time as a Labour Prime Minister in February 1950 – he followed his 1945 victory with a win by a majority of just five seats. America signalled an end to its post-war financial aid to Britain under the Marshall Plan which had begun in 1948. Britain was now left to its own devices but with manufacturing industries and food production continuing to struggle, the country was still weighed down by the effects of World War II.

The lack of housing was a major problem for post-war Britain, particularly in big cities such as London, where a combination of the bombings of World War II and the practices of notorious slum landlords had led to a demand for out-of-town homes. In 1951 Londoners were expected to wait for up to ten years for a council house – while for the people of Dundee it could have been as long as 15 years. The solution to the problem, in the southeast at least, was to build new towns outside the capital city: in the early Fifties families moved out to places such as Stevenage, Hatfield, Harlow, Basildon, Bracknell and Crawley.

Radio producer Tony Hale was born in southeast London in 1940 and recalls growing up in the 1950s in a country which he describes as 'brown.' Just because it was a post-war period, according to Hale, did not mean that much had changed from the days before World War II. 'People returning from the war wanted what was there before they went away – men wanted big bands and women wanted crooners and they all wanted 'sitcom' radio shows with catchphrases. But the country was brown – the clothing was brown – and everybody's ceiling was brown because everybody smoked.'

Consequently, light entertainment became an important lifeline for everyday people, who looked to music, films and television for some sort of release and relaxation. The movie *Annie Get Your Gun* was a major box-office success alongside *Dance Hall,* a British film made by Ealing Studios aimed at a female audience, which told the story of four factory girls and their visits to the local dance hall. Starring Petula Clark and Diana Dors, it featured music from the big bands of Geraldo and Ted Heath and opened at London's Marble Arch cinema in June 1950.

During the summer of 1950, England's football team was finally entered in the World Cup for the first time. Having decided not play against 'Johnny Foreigner' in the first three competitions, England found themselves tipped among the favourites for the tournament in Brazil, but 1-0 defeats by Spain and then by the un-fancied underdogs from the USA brought England's chances to an abrupt and embarrassing conclusion.

While French designer Christian Dior held his first ever British fashion show at the Savoy Hotel in London in 1950, the BBC offered up on radio the *Archie Andrews Show* – with Peter Brough as a 'radio ventriloquist'. *Mr Pastry* and *Watch With Mother* arrived on television, despite the *Daily Mirror* warning the nation that 'if you let a TV set through your front door, life can never be the same.'

And around the country, music fans could go and see the likes of the Billy Cotton Band, the Edmundo Ros Band, Anne Shelton, Ivy Benson's All-Girl Orchestra, Felix Mendelssohn and His Hawaiian Serenaders or the wild-haired Dr Crock and his Crackpots, as they toured the provinces and played to packed houses.

The music news that made the headlines included the story of a new 'overnight' singing sensation called

Frankie Vaughan; the police being called to the stage door at the London Palladium to control hordes of screaming fans shouting for US star Larry Parks – who had risen to fame in the film *The Jolson Story* and the follow-up *Jolson Sings Again*; and big-band leader Harry Roy signing a deal worth £90,000 to appear at London's Lyceum ballroom for three years.

By the end of 1950, London was at the very heart of all things new as it adapted to reflect the changing moods and fashions. New jazz clubs such as the West End, the London and the Flamingo opened in Soho, where coffee bars were also beginning to take hold and draw in teenagers with a few bob in their pocket and a desire to establish their own identity.

For five months, as of May 1951, the people of United Kingdom were invited to celebrate the country's post-war progress, and its advances in science, technology and design, by attending the Festival of Britain. Labour MP Herbert Morrison said it was all about 'the people of Britain giving themselves a pat on the back' and over eight million of them made it to London and paid 5s (25p) to enjoy the Dome of Discovery and the landmark cigar-shaped steel Skylon. Things turned sour briefly when the Musician's Union complained about the use of foreign musicians at the Festival. They were eventually satisfied when British bands were finally booked to play at festival events. The gardens in Battersea Park – home to a giant fun fair – and the Royal Festival Hall are the only things that remain from those celebrations. Visits to London for the Festival were not the only trips the people of Britain enjoyed in the early Fifties as families took holidays in caravans, on campsites and at farms, or stayed at holiday camps and seaside boarding houses.

It was during the Festival of Britain that two Soviet spies, Guy Burgess and Donald MacLean, defected from the UK to the USSR. This was a time when *Woman's Hour*, *The Archers*, *What's My Line?* and the *Goon Show* were all making their debut broadcasts on the BBC. And *The Lavender Hill Mob*, *The Man In The White Suit*, *The African Queen*, *Oliver Twist* and *A Streetcar Named Desire* were all in cinemas around the UK.

Jazz gradually became the favourite genre of both the music papers and the smoky cellar clubs which attracted the 'hippest cats' of the day, while the theatres and ballrooms continued to provide safer and more popular fare. Big bands and balladeers - both male and female – still ruled the roost and all around the country there were theatres and ballrooms which offered up the real star names or a local alternative. Future *Dallas* star Larry Hagman and singer Mary Martin were starring on stage in London in the hit musical *South Pacific*. In Manchester there were the Baths and Plaza Ballrooms while Bristol offered the Victoria Room, and in Birmingham and Liverpool there were the Tower and Orrell Park ballrooms respectively.

However, in America there were signs that a new musical movement was under way as R&B-based singer/saxophonist Louis Jordan, the highly charged balladeer Johnny Ray and an 18-year-old piano player and singer calling himself Little Richard took their music to both America's black and white audiences.

Around the same time, in Memphis, Tennessee, band leader Ike Turner settled down to record a track entitled 'Rocket 88', which featured elements of swing, blues and even fuzz guitar – a precursor of things to come. Released under the name Jackie Brenston and His Delta Cats – Brenston wrote the song and played saxophone on it – 'Rocket 88' was a song about the popular Oldsmobile Rocket car. It was arguably the record that launched an everlasting musical genre called rock 'n' roll.

Certainly it was a style and a phrase which influenced a radio disc jockey named Alan Freed who made his debut on WJW radio in Cleveland, Ohio in July 1951. Billed under the name 'Moondog', Freed broadcast a new nightly show entitled *Moondog Rock 'n' Roll Party*, but both the BBC and Radio Luxembourg were still a long way from joining in with the celebrations.

Nevertheless in January 1952 the BBC made a move that would put them on nodding terms with pop music. *Hit Parade* was a new television show which featured British singers – Eve Boswell, Carole Carr, Dick James and The Stargazers accompanied by Cyril Stapleton and his Orchestra – offering the eight most popular songs of the day, as featured in a *Melody Maker* chart. The host was a Canadian named Victor Bannan and he had a style which appeared to be something altogether new for audiences and reviewers alike. *Melody Maker*'s 'Scanner' column suggested he had an 'accent and a fast extravagant way of announcing' although the writer conceded that 'television got as near as possible to copying America in the first of its new *Hit Parade* programmes' before adding, '*Hit Parade* has basically what it takes to make good television.' Not exactly a ringing endorsement; but not quite damning with faint praise either.

So even if there wasn't actually a British hit parade in the sense of a chart of bestselling records, the BBC at least acknowledged that popular music had an audience which they could not continue to ignore.

In the early 1950s Britain had four major record companies: Decca, EMI, Philips and Pye ruled the roost as far as bestselling UK artists were concerned, and they distributed records for the most important American labels such as Brunswick, Columbia, Capitol, Mercury and RCA .

Decca's roster of home-grown artists included Vera Lynn, Lita Roza, Dickie Valentine, The Stargazers (the only British vocal group to have two number ones – a record they held until The Beatles took control in 1963) and David Whitfield. EMI had Ray Martin, Max Bygraves, Josef Locke, Donald Peers, Joe Loss and Victor Sylvester. Anne Shelton, Winifred Atwell and The Beverley Sisters were all with Philips, while Pye/ Polygon had Pet Clark, Jimmy Young and Gary Miller.

Of course they also held the trump cards when it

came to the big-selling US acts, such as Rosemary Clooney, Frankie Laine, Al Martin, Eddie Fisher, Nat King Cole, Guy Mitchell, Perry Como, Jo Stafford and Johnnie Ray.

All this recording activity being centred around just a few labels could well have been a source of some confusion for record buyers. For instance, an advert on the front page of *Melody Maker* in March 1952 from music publishers Francis Day & Hunter listed five versions of the song 'Cry', which Johnnie Ray had taken to the top of the US chart two months earlier. Alongside Ray's successful release on Columbia there were versions by Vera Lynn (Decca), Paul Chapman (Brunswick), The Four Knights (Capitol) and Jimmy Young (Polygon).

This growing interest in popular music, according to *Melody Maker*, led to EMI readying themselves to launch their own LP (long-playing) records – two years after rivals Decca – as the paper reported that the company had 'completed prototypes of gramophones designed for LPs.'

At the same time newspapers were full of rumours that 'commercial TV films' were being made in west London, which was seen as a sure indication that commercial television in Britain was on its way – although the arrival of Sooty on the BBC was also seen as an historic moment. The glove puppet animal burst onto the scene – courtesy of puppeteer Harry Corbett – at the same time as Airfix launched their first model airplane kits and Lesney introduced their range of scale-model vehicles.

With Winston Churchill back in Downing Street from October 1951, as Prime Minister of a Conservative government, Britain then gained a new monarch in February 1952 when King George VI died and his daughter Princess Elizabeth acceded to the throne.

On the music front, among the new releases to catch the ear of the reviewer in 1952 were 78rpm records from Dave Brubeck, Stan Getz, Frankie Laine and Dickie Valentine – four titles which emphasized the importance of, and rivalry between, jazz and pop music. But in Britain's list of the top five Bestselling Tunes in October of the same year, it was pop which dominated proceedings, thanks to 'Homing Waltz', 'High Noon', 'Auf Weiderseh'n Sweetheart', 'Blue Tango' and 'I'm Yours'.

NME's launch of Britain's first ever Hit Parade in November coincided with EMI finally releasing its first LPs but, more importantly for the weekly music paper, it boosted circulation by 50% and gave it a foothold with Radio Luxembourg, as the new chart became the basis for a regular new show on Radio 208.

At the end of 1952, more than 2000 Londoners died after air pollution caused by industrial smoke led to 'smog' engulfing the capital city and eventually led to the introduction of the Clean Air Act. However, the tragedy failed to put off a trio of visiting American artists attending a major music show at the Royal

Albert Hall on December 27. Scat-singing bandleader Cab Calloway, gospel group The Deep River Boys and jazz pianist Mary Lou Williams topped the bill for two shows set for 3pm and 7.30pm, with tickets priced from 2s 6d. (25p). Also on the bill were the home-grown artists Eddie Calvert, Leslie 'Hutch' Hutchinson and Harry Dawson.

A new year began with EMI stealing a march on its rival record companies by launching the first 7" 45rpm singles in the UK with releases from the likes of Eddie Fisher, Humphrey Lyttelton, Judy Garland and Guy Mitchell, while *Melody Maker* took the opportunity in January 1953 to look back at the best of 1952.

They judged the Best US Vocal performances to be Peggy Lee's 'Fever', Billy Eckstein with 'Someone To Look Over Me' and 'Tenderly' by Rosemary Clooney while the Best of British prizes went to Tony Brent with 'Walkin' To Missouri', Gary Miller and 'If Someone Had To Hold Me' and 'Love Where Are You Now' by Lita Roza. And Al Martino – the man who topped the first ever British Hit Parade – was judged to have the Most Grating Voice and was dubbed 'the one-man wall of sound.'

But the success of crooners and the numerous big bands from the US or the UK meant nothing to many of the new generation – it was their parents' music. 'My dad was a professional musician who played with Edmundo Ros and Henry Hall,' explains Tony Hale, who would become Head of Music for London's

Capital Radio two decades later. 'He liked big band music and as a consequence, of course, I hated it!' Hale was no more impressed with the top singers of the day. 'I didn't like Al Martino or Dickie Valentine. In fact I was just watching, hating everything and waiting for something. You fed yourself on little scraplets from American movies and TV shows which excited you.'

Finally, to the delight of children everywhere, sweet rationing ended in February 1953 and sugar also came off the banned list before the year was out. The revolutionary range of G-Plan furniture was launched in the same year that Dylan Thomas wrote *Under Milk Wood* and Ian Fleming introduced the world to James Bond in the novel *Casino Royale*.

Not surprisingly, London was still at the heart of all things new and when Italian film star Gina Lollobrigida opened the Moka coffee bar in Frith Street, Soho, it came equipped with the country's first Gaggia coffee machine. Frothy coffee was here and it made such an impact that Frith Street quickly became known as Froth Street.

It wasn't just in swinging Soho that coffee bars were opening up. 'We had two coffee bars in southeast London where I lived,' says Hale. 'One was basically for spivs but it had a juke box so you could hear some music. And the other was an Italian coffee bar where you got 'frothy coffee' from a Gaggia machine the size of a house.'

The spring and summer months of 1953 were

enlivened by the 'Matthews Cup Final' at Wembley, when the legendary Stanley Matthews finally led Blackpool to victory; Edmund Hilary and Sherpa Tensing conquering Mount Everest; and the coronation of Queen Elizabeth II on June 2, which resulted in the sale of over 100,000 new television sets. On the back of Britain and the Empire getting a new monarch, model makers Lesney also shipped over one million of their model coronation coach, complete with horses.

In the 1950s, London's famous Palladium theatre was the 'place to play' and stars from Britain, Europe and America took their turn to top the bill. An announcement in March 1953 confirmed that, during March and April of that year, the acts booked were Max Miller (3 weeks), Johnnie Ray (2 weeks), Tennessee Ernie Ford (2 weeks) and Gracie Fields (3 weeks). The inclusion on the list of American chart-topping singer Johnnie Ray brought out his growing legion of fans and after the 'Prince of Wails' had set foot on the stage, the *NME*'s reviewer was moved to declare that he was 'the greatest showman who ever infused life into cold words and music.' He was further moved to comment that 'using a long pencil-mic and a neverending cable, he strode the stage like a caged restless lion seeking an escape from some sort of frustration of his own emotional creation.'

Johnnie Ray had arrived in Britain to be greeted by screaming girls and the controversial banning of his drummer Sonny Fede. The Musician's Union had objected to the American musician taking the place of a British player in the orchestra pit at the London Palladium, explaining that 'we will not have it assumed that foreign musicians can wander into a British orchestra freely. A British drummer would not be allowed, under similar circumstances, to play in the US.' On the back of this furore, officials from the MU and the American Federation of Musicians held their first meetings to discuss the restrictions on visiting musicians.

While an American sex symbol named Marilyn Monroe was making an impression in the film *Gentlemen Prefer Blondes* and Burt Lancaster and Deborah Kerr were shocking audiences with their seaside antics in *From Here To Eternity*, a new leather-clad anti-hero called Marlon Brando was appearing in the movie *The Wild One* and adding fuel to the youthful rebellion that was building on both sides of the Atlantic.

But still the *NME*'s 1953 Poll results focused on big bands, jazz musicians and established singers - Ted Heath was voted Top Big Band and Johnny Dankworth's Seven as Best Small Band while Lita Roza and Dickie Valentine were Top Female and Top Male Vocalists ahead of Ronnie Scott being named Outstanding Musician.

Nothing much was changing on the music front as *NME* put on their own Great Record Ball at the Royal Albert Hall in September. For 8s 6d (42½p), fans could see and hear Britain's leading singers Roza, Valentine and Dennis Lotis alongside support acts such as Eddie

Calvert, Pet Clark, Winifred Atwell, Pearl Carr and
Teddy Johnson, Dick James and Mantovani and his
Orchestra.

However, things were beginning to change in
America. On the back of Frank Sinatra – the country's
most popular singer – signing to Capitol Records,
a new group called Bill Haley and The Comets took
rock 'n' roll onto the US charts for the first time
when 'Crazy Man Crazy' made it into the Top 20 in
May 1953. A couple of months later an 18-year-old
apprentice machinist named Elvis Presley walked into
the studios of the Memphis Recording Service and
asked if he could make a private recording as a birthday
gift for his mother.

Meanwhile in Britain the BBC managed to annoy
music fans by announcing that they were banning
two versions of 'Answer Me' (by David Whitfield and
Frankie Laine) and Lee Lawrence's version of 'Crying
In The Chapel'. Apparently both songs were objected
to by various religious groups but the subsequent ban
gave the advantage to rival radio station Luxembourg,
who never stopped playing the discs and, as a result,
both versions of 'Answer Me' hit the number-one spot
in the UK in December 1953.

On the other hand the BBC's *Light Programme* won
over a host of listeners when they began broadcasting
the popular series *Journey Into Space*, which at its peak
boasted a larger audience than any of the TV shows
that were aired at the same time … something that has

never been repeated in the history of broadcasting.

While this may have signified a new shift in the power of popular radio, there were stories in the press of a group of teenagers who wore clothes inspired by the 'dandified' Edwardian era, which upmarket tailors in London's Savile Row had tried to revive as a fashion for well-off young men.

However, it was young and predominantly working-class men from south and east London who quickly adopted the style of wearing long drape jackets, tight drainpipe trousers, narrow 'slim Jim' ties and fancy embroidered waistcoats. These so-called 'Edwardian Boys' were soon dubbed Teddy Boys and they were on the lookout for their own music to go with their new identity.

If Teddy Boys were on the move in 1954, there were no signs that Britain's musical tastes were likely to change in any way to reflect any sort of rebellious youth movement. The *NME* Poll Winners were still Ted Heath (Big Band), Lita Roza (Female Vocal) and Dickie Valentine (Male Vocal) although Ronnie Scott now had the Best Small Band.

This was a time when the BBC found itself overwhelmed by all the protests that came their way whenever somebody discovered a lyric that they were the least bit uncomfortable with. Scottish singer Annie Ross was placed on the banned list because her song 'I Want You To Be My Baby' included the line 'come upstairs and have some loving'. US star Johnnie Ray was also kept off the radio because of some 'grunting' during his song 'Such A Night' which, strange as it may seem, topped the UK chart but failed in America – as did 'The Kid's Last Fight' and 'Dime And A Dollar' by US stars Frankie Laine and Guy Mitchell respectively, both of which charted in Britain.

The fact that Ray had already notched up seven UK hit singles – including five top ten entries – didn't put him above the BBC's regulations or regulators and after 'a raft of complaints' that 'Such A Night' was 'too suggestive', it was tossed to one side in May 1954 – which, oddly, was a month after the record had hit the number-one spot in Britain, thanks in the main to Radio 208.

Just as all food rationing ended in Britain, so Wagon Wheels, Sugar Puffs and Frosted Flakes arrived. In the same year, famed England footballer and cricketer Denis Compton featured in a series of adverts for Brylcreem. Even though the sporting hero was no idol for Teddy Boys, they happily daubed their hair with Brylcreem to create the all-important DA (duck's arse) style, with its gravity-defying front quiff. And to get the all-important look, it cost them from 1s 8d (8p) to 4s 6d (22½p) for a tub or just 2s 6d (12½p) for a handy tube.

Families, teenagers and Teddy Boys – if they could get in – were also able to enjoy the brand new experience of eating a round meat patty served in a bun at something called a Wimpy Bar, following J. Lyons' decision to license the name and the product from its American owners. The first British Wimpy Bar was opened in the Lyons Corner House in Soho's Coventry Street but pretty soon other Wimpy Bars began to spring up around the UK as the influence of America crept ever nearer.

The new-found rebels in Britain's society – along with a host of everyday regular but impressionable teenagers – were also savouring the return to the big screen of the rebel Marlon Brando in *On The Waterfront* alongside the newest kid on the block James Dean. The star of *East Of Eden* and *Rebel Without A Cause* became a posthumous anti-hero when he died in a car crash in September 1955, aged just 24. At the same time most families were enjoying BBC TV's *The Grove Family* - the earliest known soap opera – or spending an evening playing the newest parlour game, Scrabble.

Music and records continued their steady climb up the list of attractions and hobbies. In the months before the *NME* chart opted to list the Top 20 Best Sellers in their Hit Parade, Decca added to their range of 45rpm 7" discs on the market at a cost of 5s 6½d (27½p) – compared to EMI's at 6s 1d (30p) – and the new Regentone Handy-Gram appeared in the shops. Advertised as a 'portable electric three speed gramophone playing standard and LP records', it came in a carry case coated in 'the latest Flexi-Fibre' and was priced at 15gns (£15.75p) including tax.

Despite the arrival of new records and record

players, the headline acts touring the UK in November 1954 still didn't represent a move towards any sort of new music. Guy Mitchell was in Bradford, Johnny Dankworth in Burslem and Newcastle, Eric Delaney in Hanley and Joe Loss in Leicester and at the same time the release of jazz records was on the increase – 700 of them were issued in November 1954 compared to 270 in the whole of 1950.

In America, the *Billboard* music trade magazine reported that all the major record labels would introduce new state-of-the-art 'high fidelity' recordings before the year was out. They also forecast that America's $250 million record market would be split with 78rpm discs accounting for 52%, the newer 45rpm format registering 28% and LPs selling just 20%

Bill Haley and The Comets decided to follow 'Crazy Man Crazy' with a new song called '(We're Gonna) Rock Around The Clock' and they recorded it in New York in April 1954. However, when the disc stalled at 23 after just one week on the US chart, they opted to record a cleaned-up version of the R&B song 'Shake Rattle And Roll' which eventually found its way to number seven in America in November 1954.

In late 1954 Tony Barrow – who famously went on to become press officer for The Beatles – was working for the *Liverpool Echo* where he reviewed records and interviewed music personalities. One of the stars he spoke to that year was American singer Al Martino and Barrow recalls asking him about a new musical style. 'I asked him about rock 'n' roll and he said it was nothing new. He then explained that he had just been up to Wildwood, a beach resort in New Jersey, and heard Bill Haley perform 'Rock Around The Clock' for the first time in May (on Memorial Day) 1954.

Barrow adds that Martino – the first singer to top a British Hit Parade – said that as far as he was concerned 'Wildwood was the birth place of rock 'n' roll.'

But for Britain, rock 'n' roll was still a million miles away, as Barrow recalls. 'I was getting records for review for the newspaper and among the first singles was one from Guy Mitchell, and Jo Stafford and Johnnie Ray were the other big names back then. I got to know about this thing called rock 'n' roll but it didn't take over the world in a few minutes – it was a much slower process than history would have us believe.'

And in December of the year in which Elvis Presley signed to Sun Records and performed for the first time as one of the Blue Moon Boys – with Scotty Moore and Bill Black – Britain finally had a rock 'n' roll record in its own Top 20. 'Shake Rattle And Roll' reached number four in the chart, where Bill Haley and The Comets sat, a tad uncomfortably, alongside the likes of Doris Day, Frank Sinatra, Rosemary Clooney, Vera Lynn and Winifred Atwell.

This was a sign that the times they were a'changing. Albeit slowly.

Chapter 2

1955: Skiffle Opens The Door To Rock

Although 'Shake Rattle And Roll' remained in the British Hit Parade throughout the first three months of 1955 and Haley's recording of '(We're Gonna) Rock Around The Clock' made a surprise (and brief) two week appearance in January, peaking at number 17, this didn't signal any sort of rock 'n' roll explosion.

In fact neither of the major music papers – *Melody Maker* or *New Musical Express* – printed a single story about Haley and his successful records during this period. But the papers did observe that British popular music was heading in a new and different direction – towards a combination of American folk and country blues styles which became known as skiffle.

British equivalents of the US jug bands, skiffle groups had begun playing in jazz clubs as far back as 1953 when they were featured as stand-in entertainment during the interval. Renowned jazz trumpeter and guitarist Ken Colyer led his skiffle group as an off-shoot of his own jazz band and their appearances at the London Jazz Club near Marble Arch in the summer of 1953 were reviewed in *Jazz Journal* which observed that 'the Skiffle Group which takes over during the interval … is obviously going to be the success of the year.' They highlighted versions of 'Freight Train Blues', 'Long Gone John' and 'New York Town' plus a performance of 'John Henry' by a young musician called Lonnie Donegan.

Scottish-born guitar and banjo player Donegan joined Colyer (guitar), Chris Barber (bass) and Bill Colyer (washboard) in an early skiffle group before, after a period with Chris Barber's Jazz Band, he stepped out with his own Lonnie Donegan Skiffle Group in 1954.

So it was that skiffle grabbed the attention of music fans, musicians and aspiring players who were impressed by the fact that it didn't require expensive instruments (guitar, banjo, washboard and a bass made from a tea chest were the bare essentials) or any great musicianship to form a skiffle group. Such was its appeal that it was estimated that there were close to 50,000 skiffle groups in Britain in the mid 1950s, while sales of guitars and banjos more than doubled.

Hearing Donegan on BBC Radio on a Saturday night – when he took over in the interval spot from Chris Barber's Band – had a profound effect on Tony Hale's musical education. 'Lonnie Donegan and 'Bury My Body' was the one for me. It was straight from the chain gang. When we got the record (it was on the 1956 45rpm EP with 'Rock Island Line') we played it time after time in my mate's living room and I cried and cried. It was the first time I really understood the power of music.'

Skiffle was big but rock 'n' roll was still knocking on the door and Bill Haley's follow-up to 'Rock Around The Clock' was well received by Radio Luxembourg presenter/producer Geoffrey Everitt in his *NME* review section in January 1955. 'More wonderful beat, which is something we never seem to get in this country' was his initial observation of 'Dim Dim The Lights', before he urged, 'if you can only afford one record this week I suggest you make it this one.' His words fell on deaf ears, as the record sank without trace in Britain.

With EMI buying Capitol Records in America for $8.5 million – and gaining a roster of acts which included Frank Sinatra, Nat King Cole, Dean Martin, Peggy Lee and Jo Stafford – so pop music achieved new levels of interest. As the *NME* became the world's biggest selling music paper, with a circulation in excess of 100,000, American trade figures reported that 45rpm singles had for the first time outsold 78rpm records, while juke boxes were poised to invade the UK.

On the back of sales in the US of over 500,000 machines, hopes were high in Britain for a similar response and a host of the latest jukebox models were put on display at the Amusements Trade Exhibition held in London's New Royal Horticultural Hall in February 1955. With the arrival and spread of coffee bars, jukebox manufacturing had begun in Britain in 1953 and by 1955 more than 50 machines were being produced every month – and sold at a cost of £600. From less than 100 juke boxes in the UK in 1945, there would be 15,000 in operation by 1958.

But it wasn't just juke boxes that made an impression in 1955. The BBC launched a new television sports programme called *Sportsview* while the DIY magazine *Practical Householder* was launched. The Bounty bar, after first being tested in 1951, was re-launched as 'far and away the most exotic chocolate treat' and it arrived alongside the no-less-exotic fish fingers and Nesquik. And they could all be enjoyed by children while they watched the latest TV shows such as *Crackerjack*, *Davy Crockett* and *The Cisco Kid*.

While all this was going on Radio Luxembourg was cementing its position as the leading purveyor of pop music to Britain's growing audience of teenagers. Although it still broadcast *Dan Dare* – sponsored by Horlicks – alongside Hughie Green's *DoubleYour Money* quiz show and a talent show called *Opportunity Knocks*, it was attracting nearly nine million listeners plus the attention of the major record companies who were keen to sponsor their own shows in an effort to promote their new releases. EMI spent over £30,000 on airtime which they shared with programmes such as *Hour Of Decision* with preacher Billy Graham, Michael Miles' *Take Your Pick* quiz show and *Italy Sings*, sponsored by the Italian Tourist Office.

And as records banned by the BBC – 'Answer Me', 'Hold My Hand' and 'Such A Night' – became best sellers, so record companies focused more attention and more resources on the station which was by now broadcasting from both Luxembourg and studios in London. EMI hired Shaw Taylor and Muriel Young as presenters while Decca opted for Jack Jackson and

Pete Murray, and Philips went for Guy Standeven —
and they were all heard alongside Horace Batchelor's
legendary 'Infra-Draw Method' for winning money on
the football pools — which turned the Bristol suburb of
Keynsham (spelt K-E-Y-N-S-H-A-M) into a household
name.

Tony Hall — who first got a job at Decca in 1954 — was
another of the company's voices on Radio Luxembourg
(with his familiar sign-off line 'That's all from yours
sincerely Tony Hall') where he hosted one of their
sponsored shows while also plugging their records to
producers at the rival BBC. 'Luxembourg was bought
airtime and record companies stuffed it with their own
records but the reception was never great — if you
were stuck between two hills you couldn't always get a
signal,' he recalls.

In the spring of 1955 Britain's pop chart was
dominated by a 19-year-old Irish singer named Ruby
Murray, who scooped five places in the Top 20 including
her number one hit 'Softly Softly'. Things weren't set
to change much when it came to the year's other best
sellers. Joan Regan, Alma Cogan, Dickie Valentine,
Eddie Calvert, Malcolm Vaughan and David Whitfield
were the British acts who vied for chart success against
American artists such as Frankie Laine, Tony Bennett,
Eddie Fisher, Doris Day and Pat Boone.

Fisher was in fact one the first American stars —
quickly followed by his wife Debbie Reynolds — to
appear in the famous HMV record store in Oxford

Street which had re-opened in 1939 after a fire damaged the original shop opened in 1921. His visit in 1955 coincided with HMV deciding to sell 'records of the competition' alongside the releases from parent company EMI. And as records from Decca, Philips and Pye became available, so the HMV store stopped selling kitchen appliances and even record players and televisions. Within two years the store recorded a 21% increase in record sales; in March 1957, EMI label releases accounted for close to £17,000 worth of business while 'other marks' brought in around £7000.

Strictly Come Dancing judge Len Goodman, who was born in 1944, recalls that crooners and balladeers were 'the forerunners to rock 'n' roll' – particularly if you were 'a bit highbrow' – while he also admits that the first record he ever bought was trumpeter Eddie Calvert's 'Oh Mein Papa', which was the first UK number-one record to be made in EMI's famous Abbey Road studios. Oddly in the US it was a vocal version of the song called 'Oh My Pa Pa' by Fisher which topped the chart.

At the same time adverts were appearing for a forthcoming visit by jazz giants Oscar Peterson and Ella Fitzgerald who were set to appear at London's Royal Albert Hall on February 22 – tickets from 40s (£2) to 15s (75p) – before heading off to Newcastle, Dundee, Edinburgh and Leicester. There was also news of a merger between the Pye and Polygon record labels and a chance 'for the modern troubador' to buy a Spanish

Finger guitar for just £17.19s (£17.95p) including tax.

In April 1955 – the month when scientist Albert Einstein died and Conservative leader Anthony Eden took over as Prime Minister from Winston Churchill – US singing sensation Johnnie Ray told his British fans that the big buzz in America was for vocal groups and he picked out The Chorales, The Fontane Sisters, The Crew Cuts, The Four Lads and The Four Aces as acts to watch out for.

However for *NME* reviewer Geoffrey Everitt it was Bill Haley who continued to make the biggest impact. Writing about the single 'Mambo Rock' he declared, 'Bill Haley's brand of music is the most exciting that I've heard for years', and later in the year he would declare that 'Two Hound Dogs' (the B-side of 'Razzle Dazzle') was 'just about the most interesting and exciting disc it has been my pleasure to listen to for a very long time.'

But even as 'Mambo Rock' hit the UK Top 20, the British media continued to ignore Bill Haley. And they weren't the only ones, as he was significant by his absence from any adverts placed by Decca, the distributors of his American Brunswick label. While the *NME* reviewed his discs, neither they nor *Melody Maker* carried a single picture, let alone a feature on the new bestselling singer.

They did however carry a bizarre report that Don Roper, the captain of Arsenal, would be joining the *NME*'s advertising department while he continued to play First Division football (it seemed that *NME* boss

Maurice Kinn was an Arsenal fan) plus an advert for the new Elizabethan Tape Recorder which cost 52gns (£54.60p) and came with 'contemporary circuits and contemporary styling' plus a mike and some tape.

But the big rock 'n' roll news was that DJ Alan Freed was busy touring America with his First Anniversary Rock 'n' Roll Party. The self-styled first 'King of Rock 'n' Roll' grossed over $150,00 in one week when his tour, featuring Chuck Berry, Tony Bennett, The Nutmegs and The Cardinals, appeared in New York.

But rock 'n' roll still had its fair share of dissenters and Los Angeles-based DJ Peter Porter told his listeners that 'all rhythm and blues records are dirty and as bad for kids as dope', which prompted Freed to answer, 'There's nothing they can do to stop this new solid beat of American music from sweeping across the land in a gigantic tidal wave of happiness.' And there were signs that Porter might have been right, as a Fats Domino show in Connecticut was cancelled by the local police following 'a recent near riot' at a neighbouring rock 'n' roll dance, while reports came in from Jacksonville, Florida of a near-riot at an Elvis Presley concert when girls in the 14,000 strong crowd started tearing at his clothes.

At the same time, Chuck Berry was a new name on the US charts as 'Maybellene' hit the top five just after Bill Haley's '(We're Gonna) Rock Around The Clock' was reissued in America on the back of the song being featured over the opening credits of a new movie entitled *Blackboard Jungle*, starring Glenn Ford as a High School teacher dealing with a bunch of badly behaved students.

Haley's record raced into the US chart, occupied the number-one spot for eight weeks and became both one of the biggest-selling singles of all time and a landmark record in the history of popular music. But there was disquiet over its connection with juvenile delinquency. In contrast, all this came about at the same time as Walt Disney was opening his original all-American family theme park Disney Land in Anaheim, California.

In Britain in the summer of 1955, Decca Records gave the country's newest music craze a boost as they began recording Ken Colyer's Skiffle Group, ahead of commercial television (ITV) beginning on September 22 with a new music show called *TV Music Shop* – hosted by husband and wife team Pearl Carr and Teddy Johnson – being shown on the third day of transmission.

A month later the BBC launched a new show on their Light Programme with the first edition of *Pick Of The Pops*. Hosted by Franklin Engelman, it was billed as a choice of 'current popular gramophone records' but did not reflect the country's best sellers. The first *Pick Of The Pops* using the format of a chart run-down came two years later, and was presented by Alan Dell who took over the controls in 1956 before handing the microphone to David Jacobs.

By October 1955 the American Federation of Musicians and Britain's Musician's Union had agreed to end the ban which had existed since 1935 and stopped UK musicians playing in the US and American players coming to Britain but allowed vocalists to have exchange rights. The first bands to benefit from the new reciprocal arrangement were the Ted Heath and Stan Kenton Orchestras.

By now '(We're Gonna) Rock Around The Clock' was back in the UK charts on the back of its success in America and the eventual release of the film *Blackboard Jungle*, which had been held up by the British Board of Film Censors. The BBFC initially decided against giving the film a certification on the basis that the violence was 'quite revolting' and that the film 'filled as it is with scenes of unbridled revolting juvenile delinquency' would have 'the most damaging and harmful effect on older teenagers, who would be able to see it if it was granted an X certificate.'

Eventually, after cuts had been made, the BBFC relented and issued an over-18 certification for the film which opened in London before Christmas 1955 with one movie critic suggesting that it was 'one for those with strong stomachs.' The movie business was equally wary of the film and denounced it as 'degenerate', while a planned showing at the prestigious Venice Film Festival was cancelled.

However, by the end of November, '(We're Gonna) Rock Around The Clock' had established itself as the first rock 'n' roll record to reach number one in the British Hit Parade where it remained for five weeks during a 17-week stay on the chart. Rivals for the top spot in the final week of November were 'Love Is A Many Splendored Thing' by The Four Aces (remember Pat Boone's tip) and 'Hernando's Hideaway' by The Johnston Brothers.

British rock 'n' roll singer Marty Wilde was one of the people who went to see *Blackboard Jungle* – despite the fact that he was only 16 years old. 'I was a big tall lad and must have skipped in,' he recalls. But it was the opening music that made the biggest impression. 'I had heard a couple of rock 'n' roll tracks but they didn't really grab me, but 'Rock Around The Clock' really did and when you heard it in the cinema it was like getting four bells and pulling the jackpot on a one-armed bandit.'

Once he had seen the film and heard 'Rock Around The Clock', Wilde went and told the fellow members of his amateur skiffle group that things had to change. 'I went straight back to the band and said there will be no more skiffle, there'll only be rock 'n' roll from now on.'

Paul McCartney was even younger than Wilde – he would have been around 13 – when he bluffed his way in to see *Blackboard Jungle* in Liverpool with the even younger George Harrison by his side – and he was rewarded for his efforts. 'The first time I heard 'Rock Around The Clock', shivers went up my spine so we had to go and see the film just for the title song.' However, it seems that his future band mate John Lennon was less than taken with the music of Bill Haley, explaining that his records 'didn't do anything for me.'

Despite the success of his recordings, Haley remained a decidedly un-hip idol to many teenagers in the mid-Fifties. According to Len Goodman he was 'a strange looking geezer with a silly little kiss curl – I was never a great punter of Haley', while aspiring young musician Darrell Smith-Lyte, a guitarist and singer in the skiffle group Les Hobeaux, saw Haley as 'a podgy 35 year-old' (he was in fact 30 years of age) but he still liked what he heard. 'I loved the beat, the guitar solo. It was a unique piece of music and a milestone.'

Meanwhile up in Liverpool, a future member of a local skiffle group called The Quarry Men heard the same record. 'I remember listening to Bill Haley and thinking what a strange voice he had – the tonal quality was really quite unique,' says Rod Davis. 'But he did look like somebody's uncle who had just come off the golf course and I was always bothered by the kiss curl which I read was to take people's attention away from the fact that he only had one eye.'

Bruce Welch was up in the north east of England in 1955 when he and fellow Shadow Hank Marvin first became aware of Haley. 'We heard records on Luxembourg and occasionally on the BBC's *Forces Favourites* or *Housewive's Choice*, and then 'Rock Around The Clock' came along. The music of Haley was fantastic but not the image – he didn't really inspire you because he looked like a bank manager – but he was rock 'n' roll for us back then.'

And even fellow American musician and songwriter Neil Sedaka was less than impressed with the chart busting success of the singer from Detroit who lost the sight in his left eye as a child. 'I didn't care for Bill Haley. For me the music was mediocre and he represented rowdiness,' says the Brooklyn-born youngster who wrote his first songs in 1952, aged just 13. 'I never cared for his work but he was the first and did represent a major cultural move.'

Another dissenting voice from America was legendary songwriter Burt Bacharach who told *Sunday Telegraph* writer Mick Brown in 2013 that the new music of the 1950s was not any sort of inspiration to him. 'I didn't like Billy Haley and The Comets, I didn't like rock 'n' roll per se. It was all a little too simplistic harmony-wise, and those pure vanilla chords,' says the man who wrote his first hit record with partner Hal David in 1957 – Perry Como's 'Magic Moments'.

For one young man living near Chelmsford in Essex who was just getting into music in the mid-Fifties, 'Rock Around The Clock' was a major development. 'Rock Around The Clock was the first rock 'n' roll record I ever heard. It was just amazing and so different', recounts Micky Blowes who also has some other music-related memories. 'There used to be the Top 20 show on the radio and my sister would write them all down in order. And then there was Jack Jackson on Radio Luxembourg – but the reception used to fade in and out and you had to fiddle with the dial all the time to get a signal.'

According to Blowes, the county town of Essex had just one major record store back then. 'We used to buy our records in Daces where they asked whether you wanted 78s or 45s and they had individual listening rooms.' But as an apprentice printer, earning a weekly wage of just £1 18s 7d (£1.93p) in 1955, records were a luxury. 'I think they were about 6s (30p) each which was a lot of money. There wasn't a lot left in my wage packet if I bought a record,' says Blowes.

Despite not quite wowing everyone, Bill Haley's continuing success finally earned him a major feature (and photo) in the November 4 issue of the *NME* under the headline 'The Meteoric Rise Of The Comets'. This article confirmed that the group's four releases – 'Shake Rattle And Roll', 'Dim Dim The Lights', 'Mambo Rock' and '(We're Gonna) Rock Around The Clock' – had sold over five million copies in America, that over 8000 Bill Haley fan clubs had been set up in the US and that Haley had earned more than $500,000 from his concert appearances.

The feature concluded by saying: 'Bill Haley and his Comets are likely to last as long as R&B lasts. And as R&B, in one form or another, has been going now for approximately 30 years, we can look forward to having Bill and his riotous colleagues around for quite a while yet.'

Having said all that –and with Bill Haley at number 12 in the list of Britain's Top Selling Artists for 1955 – the

NME's Poll Winners were, once again, members of the old guard which refused to be moved by rock 'n' roll. From the US came Top Male Singer Frank Sinatra and Top Female Doris Day while Dickie Valentine continued as Top British Male Singer alongside newcomer Ruby Murray as Top British Female.

If skiffle was being heralded as Britain's newest music craze at the beginning of the year, the growing number of fans attending the newly opened London Skiffle & Blues Club in Soho's Wardour Street finally swayed Decca into issuing two skiffle records in November 1955 – Ken Colyer's 'Take This Hammer' and a version of the Lead Belly classic 'Rock Island Line' by Lonnie Donegan.

However, the arrival of skiffle didn't make any great impression in the Brixton home of young Jan Parsons. She was 13 in 1955 and while her father was playing classical music on the family gramophone, she was saving up to buy a Ruby Murray record. Surprisingly, Parsons was allowed to watch American television shows such as Perry Como's – which her dad dismissed as 'a bloody load of American rubbish' – and she recalls the arrival of skiffle. 'My dad said that was a load of rubbish as well'.

Chapter 3

1956: Preesley or Preswick or Presley – it's still Elvis

Despite being dismissed as 'rubbish' by some, skiffle did impact on a generation of young music fans and serve as an inspiration to many – thanks mainly to Lonnie Donegan, the Glasgow-born son of a professional violinist.

His recording of 'Rock Island Line' became a major top-ten hit in the UK in February 1956 – it reached the same number-eight spot in America in April – and convinced Donegan to give up the banjo in favour of the guitar and also to form his own skiffle group. It also moved Marty Wilde, despite his new-found love of rock 'n' roll. 'I only ever really liked one skiffle song and that was 'Rock Island Line' and Donegan kept a hold on the charts with his skiffle for quite a while until rock 'n' roll arrived.'

Similarly Rod Davis eventually took to skiffle in a big way. 'For some reason I was never really taken by rock 'n' roll although I was interested in music, but we didn't hear about skiffle in Liverpool until 1956 and Rock Island Line.' And for future chart topper and million-seller Bruce Welch, it was skiffle which made all the difference. 'Skiffle was the catalyst for anyone who wanted to play the guitar.'

'By 1955 I had a guitar and then along came this guy

called Lonnie Donegan who was the inspiration for most guitar players in this country,' adds The Shadows rhythm guitarist, who also recalls his initial rivalry with the man who would become his musical partner for over 50 years. 'Hank Marvin had a skiffle group called The Crescent City Skiffle Group and he was the banjo player. I was in the same school and had a skiffle group called The Railroaders but while we loved rock 'n' roll cum skiffle, Hank was more of a purist, playing Lead Belly songs.'

In a music paper article in January 1956, Donegan's 'Rock Island Line' – for which he received just a £50 session fee and no royalties – was credited with 'accidentally cashing-in on two very strong trends in the pop business.' The feature explained that the first trend was 'the narrative gimmick' while the second was 'the rock 'n' roll craze as exemplified by 'Rock Around The Clock' and 'Sixteen Tons'.'

For actor Jim Carter (*Lipstick on Your Collar* and *Downton Abbey*, among other credits) the arrival of Donegan represented a breakthrough in music. 'Anybody could get hold of a guitar and do it themselves. Three chords was all it took – that was all 'Rock Island Line' was.' Carter, who is a Donegan expert, added that 'Working class kids suddenly realised you don't have to go to music lessons on a Saturday morning … you can pick up a thing and you can thrash it.'

While Donegan was the only skiffle artist to make any sort of an impression on the charts – he followed

'Rock Island Line' with 'Lost John' and 'Dead Or Alive' in 1956 – things were happening in the area of central London known as Soho which became a magnet for young men (and a few women) with an eye on a career in pop. 'It was a lot more cosmopolitan in Soho where they had juke boxes and you could listen to music in the coffee bars,' says Wilde. 'I would go up there as often as I could but it was expensive and difficult to get there with changing trains and buses.'

Soho and Charing Cross Road also represented an Aladdin's cave of opportunity for Smith-Lyte. 'With all the record shops, music shops and coffee bars, Soho was a great scene where people became more aware of live music whether it was skiffle or rock or trad jazz. And new clubs were opening all the time for music.'

Arguably the most famous and historic coffee bar to open in the heart of Soho – an area surrounded by four of London's major thoroughfares (Oxford Street to the north, Regent Street to the west, Shaftesbury Avenue to the south and Charing Cross Road to the east) – was the 2-Is in Old Compton Street.

Originally run by three Iranian brothers – when it was, accordingly, named the 3-Is – it became the 2-Is when one of the brothers left, and that was the name retained by new Australian owners Paul Lincoln and Ray Hunter, who were former wrestlers. They re-opened it in the late spring of 1956 as a coffee bar with a basement that eventually became home to the host of emerging skiffle groups. One of the first was probably

Wally Whyton and The Vipers, who ended up playing there on July 14 1956 at the end of a day-long Soho Fair, organised by local French restaurant owners to celebrate Bastille Day.

Whyton, who went on to be a children's TV presenter and the respected host of BBC Radio 2's *Country Show* until his death in 1997, recalled that he and his band dropped into the 2-Is for a coffee and asked if they could play. 'They agreed and we went down to the basement. We started playing and it seemed that within minutes the place was busy. It seemed to work well and Paul (Lincoln) asked us to make a regular stop over.'

With a capacity of around 80 in the basement (although the lack of stringent health and safety regulations back then meant it regularly exceeded 100) and an entrance fee of 1s (5p), the 2-Is quickly became the hottest new music venue in town. It even saw off the competition from the next-door coffee bar, The Heaven And Hell, with its brightly lit upstairs 'Heaven' and dark basement 'Hell'.

Smith-Lyte and his skiffle group Les Hobeaux became regulars at the 2-Is after they won a skiffle competition run by EMI Records. 'We got an audition with the EMI producer Norman Newell and then met Paul Lincoln who booked us for the 2-Is. And then, once we had signed to EMI, he became our manager,' says Smith-Lyte. 'We were paid £30 for recording six sides for EMI – we could have had a royalty deal but £30 was a lot of money in those days so we took the money and ran.'

The arrival of skiffle meant that rock 'n' roll had competition for the ears (and the cash) of the music-crazy youngsters. While trad jazz continued as a live attraction, it made few in-roads into the charts – or as a teenage fashion statement. 'The guys with beards were the ones who liked trad jazz,' says Len Goodman who, like everybody else, was being urged to read Richard Attenborough's weekly *Record Column* in the *News of The World* where there was also news of a visit to Britain in April 1956 by Bill Haley, who was reported to be earning £7000 a week in America from his records and concerts.

Alongside music, fashion was becoming an important issue for teenagers like Jen Blowes who remembers scouting around Chelmsford for up-to-the-minute items. 'It was difficult to buy fashionable clothes in Chelmsford back then, when it was a market town. There were fluorescent socks and tight waspie belts that clipped together and I got my first pair of jeans when I was 12 from an aunt who in lived in London.' And with her 3d (1p) pocket money she would go to Woolworths and buy a 'little bottle of perfume or something along those lines.'

The fashion stakes were still being led by the young men who, a couple of years earlier, had begun to adopt an Edwardian style of dress and been tagged as 'Teddy Boys'. With the arrival of rock 'n' roll music, these adolescents had a loud, raucous sound to hang their quiffs on – and an added bonus was that the older generation hated the new rock music almost as much as they detested Teddy Boys.

Skiffle player Smith-Lyte recalls that the competition between skifflers and rockers went further than just music. 'The image for some rockers was the most important thing and there were different styles of dress and different fans.' And it wasn't just around London that Teddy Boys made an appearance on the streets, sometimes armed with bicycle chains, knuckle dusters and flick-knifes. 'There were a few around Chelmsford but they didn't cause any great trouble. They used to hang about in a place called the Long Bar which was a long narrow milk bar that opened around 1954,' recalls Mickey Blowes.

David Hughes, later to become a writer for *Disc* magazine, has similar memories of the Teddy Boys in Kent. 'They all gathered in a milk bar near the Granada cinema in Maidstone where they preened themselves. I remember the long jackets, the drainpipe trousers and the extraordinary shoes and them forever quiffing their hair – I was desperate to get a DA.'

While they took great satisfaction from being the centre of attention, Hughes reckons that they had to have a job in order to be a Teddy Boy. 'They had to be earning money to be able to afford the outfits – they weren't going to be able to buy them if they were on the dole.'

'The only people who could afford Teddy Boy outfits were the ones with jobs, who would buy it all on hire purchase,' recalls South Londoner Jan Parsons. 'I saw Teddy Boys in Brixton but they didn't mean much to me as I was only about 14 and they weren't particularly scary, although parents were very wary of them because they looked threatening,' she says.

Len Goodman was on the other side of the River Thames in East London. 'Teddy Boys were everywhere and they came from every background: they weren't just working class youngsters.' Future BBC Radio producer Tony Hale had a much closer view of them than most. 'My elder brother was a Teddy Boy with all the drapes and everything else. And he also had a bicycle chain under the lapel of his coat and the toffee hammer in his pocket – plus knuckle dusters!'

He agrees that most of the youths who became Teddy Boys were at work rather students at school or college. 'The outfits came before rock 'n' roll and they chose long drape jackets to show that in a period of austerity they could afford more cloth than others could – none of those Teddy Boy outfits were cheap.'

Nevertheless, Liverpudlian Rod Davis believes there was a social divide, and rock 'n' roll was a distinctly working-class phenomenon – one that he wasn't quite part of. 'We weren't working class, we were lower middle-class and grammar-school boys, which made us targets for the guys down the road off the council estate. Rockers came off that estate, they loved rock 'n' roll and they picked on us.'

His theory also extends as far as Teddy Boy clothing.

'There were lots of guys on the council estates around Liverpool who had left school at 15 and gone to work so they could afford the Teddy Boy gear which we couldn't, even if we had wanted to.' Bruce Welch, who remembers getting into serious trouble for having a DA ('duck's arse') haircut, agrees with Davis. 'He's probably right that the majority of Teddy Boys came off council estates as people there went to work early, as opposed to grammar-school boys, and they could afford the clothes.'

On the other hand, Tony Barrow, who was a journalist in the mid-Fifties, takes the view that what Davis says might be 'too clean a statement' and adds, 'It's not entirely true to say that Teddy Boys came from council estates and were working class. The music was being heard on jukeboxes in coffee bars and on Radio Luxembourg and had an appeal to a wide range of teenagers who came from all sorts of backgrounds.'

In Liverpool, in a rival newspaper to the one that employed Barrow as a music critic, there were the beginnings of a campaign aimed at ending the era and influence of Teddy Boys. Certainly the *Liverpool Evening Express* pulled no punches in an editorial printed in the mid-Fifties. 'The exaggerated clothes they wear proclaim their basic self-insufficiency. The shoes often have inch-thick soles and raised heels to flatter stunted height ... the Teddy suit is, in effect, a prop to sagging personalities and a sop to mentalities starved of worthwhile impulses.'

Marty Wilde was born Reginald Smith in the London borough of Greenwich in 1939. He had, by his own admission, a working-class upbringing which did lead him – albeit briefly - towards the uniform of the Teddy Boys. 'I was working in Eastcheap as a messenger and my attitude towards clothes was changing as I had some money to spend. I was a Teddy Boy for a while, although I don't really know where all the fancy clothes and stuff came from.' Reflecting on his own outfit, Wilde recalls, 'I got my Teddy Boy clothes from Burton's in Deptford where I had a suit made with a long drape jacket and drainpipe trousers with 6" bottoms.'

But his new appearance did not go down well in the Smith household. 'My father didn't like any of it. It was a threat to him and he didn't like the fact that I had a duck's arse haircut. He said that if I kept the DA then I wouldn't be able to go on holiday with the family. And that was what happened – they left me alone at home for a week.' Looking back, Wilde says it was all part of 'finding music and fashion that was for our generation and for me it all came as one big package.'

The man who would go on to manage The Rolling Stones and The Small Faces, Andrew Loog Oldham was a big fan of Teddy Boys and what they stood for. 'Teds were magnificent specimens with an attitude way above any station. They were the first teenagers to stand up, let it rip and be counted', he says. 'Teds draped and duck-arsed themselves into national outrages that make headlines. They spent their newly disposable income taking the piss.'

And it wasn't just the boys who were finding a new identity. Teddy girls, who were known as 'Judies', began to wear drape jackets, pencil skirts, rolled-up jeans, straw boaters, flat shoes or espadrilles together with long clutch bags as an accessory – and much of it was homemade. 'If you wanted a nice pair of tight jeans you just bought what you could find and then altered them on the sewing machine to make them tighter', explains Jen Blowes, while Jan Parsons had a favourite hunting ground in South London. While she didn't have any jeans back then, Parsons was a regular at Brixton market and a store called Bon Marché. 'There were no other shops to buy fashion from. We had felt skirts which were stiff because of the petticoats, which we used to stiffen with sugar. We had wide elasticated belts and a little white blouse – you only had the one outfit, which was fine as you only went out once or twice a month.'

As a teenage girl growing up with new fashions and styles all around her – Mary Quant opened her first boutique Bazaar in Chelsea's King's Road in 1955 – Parsons recalls that her father was 'mortified' by it all, even though she wore no make-up but did have permed hair.

As the demand for the latest in blue jeans swept through Britain, Bruce Welch recalls that they were just one of many new fads and fascinations arriving from across the Atlantic. 'We became teenagers in about

1956 and we copied everything from America – cars, music, clothes – there was a huge social change going on.' Not surprisingly, Welch especially remembers how music moved on. 'The change from the likes of Sinatra and Frankie Laine to Bill Haley and Elvis was enormous. Singers and orchestras never moved onstage or on television but then we saw Elvis and Haley and others who moved about. And again we got it all from America.'

Alongside the arrival of new clothes, and with an increasing selection of musical sounds to choose from, it was only a matter of time before a true teen idol would make an appearance. And so it was that Elvis Presley – who was signed by RCA Records for an impressive $40,000 – arrived. He began his assault on Britain's pop music scene at about the same time as *Around The World In 80 Days* and *Reach For The Sky* hit the cinemas, and *Hancock's Half Hour*, *Lenny The Lion* and *The Lone Ranger* first appeared on television.

In 1956 Presley's records were issued in Britain through EMI who licensed American RCA recordings for release on their HMV label, but the man in charge of HMV took some persuading to issue Presley's first disc. When Wally Ridley got a package from RCA containing six sides by Presley, it came with a note. 'It said that I probably wouldn't understand a word and wouldn't know what on earth the records were all about, but that I should release them as the singer was going to be an absolute giant,' recalled Ridley.

But when he put out 'Heartbreak Hotel' and 'I Was The One', the man who had produced both Ronnie Hilton and Malcolm Vaughan was in for an even bigger shock. 'We got the worst press we had ever got for an HMV release. They said you couldn't understand a word and that it was disgusting, and at first we got no broadcasts anywhere,' said Ridley.

Tony Barrow was writing record reviews on the *Liverpool Echo* at the time and remembers receiving a copy of 'Heartbreak Hotel'. 'I had a copy so early – and we were completely unaware of who he was – that I introduced him as Elvis Preesley –with a double 'e' in the middle. I liked rock 'n roll records, there was something new about them, but I wasn't sure how far it was going to go.'

The *NME*'s critic Geoffrey Everitt, such a fervent admirer of Bill Haley, was surprisingly unconvinced by the singer from Tupelo, Mississippi. 'If you like gimmick voices then Elvis will slay you, but if you appreciate good singing I don't suppose you'll manage to hear this disc through ... If this is singing, I give up!'

However, American singer Neil Sedaka had no doubt as to the merits of the newly discovered singer. 'I loved Elvis and once you saw him that was it – he had the whole package,' he says, while Bruce Welch recalls the impact Presley had on him as an aspiring young musician. 'You heard 'Heartbreak Hotel' and thought 'wow' and then you saw him ... no one had seen a man look like Elvis.'

Having seen a photo of Elvis Presley in the *NME* and read about 'Heartbreak Hotel', John Lennon was keen to hear the record. 'I first heard it on Radio Luxembourg ... it was the end for me. He turned out to be fantastic,' and Presley's influence went, unsurprisingly, even further for the future Beatle. 'Once I heard it and got into it, that was life, there was no other thing. I thought of nothing else but rock 'n' roll apart from sex, food and money – but that's all the same thing really.'

And Lennon's famous songwriting partner Paul McCartney was equally moved by sight and sound of the teenager from America. 'Somebody pulled out a music paper and there was an advert for 'Heartbreak Hotel'. Elvis looked so great. Then when we heard the record there was the proof.'

Having bought Bill Haley's 'See You Later Alligator', Nick Mason bought Presley's 'Don't Be Cruel' in 1956 and then the album *Rock 'N' Roll* (which was released in America under the title *Elvis*). 'This seminal album was bought by at least two other members of the Floyd', says the band's drummer. 'Not only was this fantastic new music but for a teenager it also had the additional frisson of receiving the kind of parental welcome usually reserved for a pet spider.'

Equally impressed by Presley's first album was a young would-be rock guitarist from Dartford in Kent called Keith Richards. Recalling that Elvis had a section all to himself in the notebook he kept to record details of important songs and artists, Richards said, 'The very first album I bought. 'Mystery Train', 'Money Honey', 'Blue Suede Shoes', 'I'm Left, You're Right, She's Gone'. The crème de la crème of his Sun stuff. I slowly acquired a few more but that was my baby.'

Press reports came from America describing Presley as 'a wild and turbulent rocker' while at the same time they reported that he was accounting for 50% of all RCA's pop record sales in the US. An early advert in the *NME* alerted people in the UK to Presley by quoting *Daily Mirror* writer Patrick Doncaster, who described the singer as 'The King of Western Bop' before adding, 'Take a dash of Johnnie Ray, add a sprinkling of Billy Daniels and what have you got? Elvis Presley. He is twenty, single, scorns Western kit for snazzy jazzy outfits. Will British girls fall for him? I think it's likely.'

Even though he had reached his teens in 1953, Tony Hale knew he wasn't a teenager – 'because they hadn't been invented yet' – and he still yearned for something to happen, like the rest of his generation. 'I was still just waiting but you didn't know what for.' For him and his schoolmates, Fab 208 was the one thing that offered an opportunity to hear new music. 'It was word of mouth, playground chat where somebody had heard something and they passed it on. I got into it when someone sang 'Heartbreak Hotel' as we queued for registration.'

Around the time the record topped the US charts in April 1956, 'Heartbreak Hotel' was being advertised for sale in the UK at 5s 7d (28p), including tax, for a 78rpm disc with a reminder that it was also available from HMV as a 7" 45rpm single. In May 1956 'Heartbreak Hotel' entered the *NME* chart at 15 – on the back of a front-page advert which featured a full-page photo of Presley with the tag line 'He's riding the crest of a teenage tidal wave'. And by June it had risen to number two.

Cliff Richard was still at school in Cheshunt, Hertfordshire when 'Heartbreak Hotel' came out and he has never forgotten hearing the record for the first time. 'I remember clearly hearing Elvis for the first time. My friends and I were just wandering about and there was this car – I think it was a fancy French Citroen. The guy jumped out and left the engine running and the windows were down and on the radio we heard Elvis singing 'Heartbreak Hotel'. Before we could find what it was or who it was, the guy had got back in his car and drove off.'

For apprentice printer Micky Blowes buying 'Heartbreak Hotel' with his own money brought with it a degree of disharmony in his family. 'I took it home and put in on the Dansette and my dad went absolutely crazy', he explains. 'He shouted 'Who is that' and I said 'It's Elvis Presley dad' and he then said, 'Listen to me. I will not ever have Elver Preswick played in this house'. He loved Bing Crosby so it was a big change for him.'

For Blowes' wife Jen it was a magazine article that turned her onto Presley. 'There was a picture of him and the man writing about him said that he sounded like someone who is trying to sing with a mouthful of cabbage. But he was handsome and good-looking and in those early pictures he looked a bit like Rudolf Valentino.'

The big interest in America's newest singing star continued with a newspaper story suggesting negotiations were underway to bring the 'hit disc sensation' to Britain, although a later report confirmed that it wouldn't happen until the spring of 1957. At the same time an *NME* profile told readers that Presley was 6ft 2', weighed 160lbs and was unmarried and went on to explain (a sad omen of things to come perhaps) that, 'he has a huge appetite and is reputed to eat a dozen eggs and either two steaks or a pound of bacon for breakfast.'

In fact, according to founder and owner of the *NME* Maurice Kinn, Presley's arrival changed the direction of the music paper. 'From the moment Presley started to stir an interest, we didn't stop. That was our policy: if somebody was in the charts that was our signal to give the people what they wanted.' And in that respect the *NME* differed from its main rival, according to Kinn. 'We went for stars in the hit parade, as opposed to being a poor man's *Melody Maker*, making big stories out of the fourth trombone change in Teddy Cox's Orchestra.'

If Presley's arrival on the scene influenced the biggest selling music paper in Britain, his impact also affected top selling singer Johnnie Ray, whose regular visits to the UK involved sell-out concerts. After touring here in 1956 he returned to America to be met with questions about a new sensation he had never heard of. 'I was asked 'What do you think of Elvis Presley?' I said 'Who is Elvis Presley?' Big mistake. I had been gone for two months but the damage was done. The press got onto it right away, saying it was sour grapes on my part.'

By now Presley's performances on stage and television were also making headlines with viewers to Milton Berle's US TV show and newspaper critics complaining that 'his hips swing sensuously from side to side and his entire body takes on a frantic quiver … his movements suggest, in a word, sex.' This resulted in him famously being filmed from the waist up during a later appearance on the *Ed Sullivan Show.*

Presley was the biggest news in the pop world and rock 'n' roll was now forcing its way into every household in Britain – whether they liked it or not. Speaking on BBC Radio 4's *Today* programme in 2013, Mick Jagger reflected on the impact the singer and the music had on society back then. 'Rock 'n' roll from its very inception – before we came along – was all about looking a bit odd and dressing up in extreme ways. It had been shocking in the Fifties period – Elvis was very shocking to people. It's hard to believe now, looking back, but Elvis was totally shocking – possibly even more than us.'

However, there were other things going on apart from rock 'n' roll as the first ever Eurovision Song Contest took place in Lugano, Switzerland in May 1956 (when it was won by the Swiss artist Lys Assia), while a couple of LPs – costing £2 each – made it into the new extended *NME* Top 30 bestsellers chart for the first time thanks to Frank Sinatra's *Songs For Swinging Lovers* and the soundtrack from the film *Carousel*.

And it wasn't just stories about music that made the newspapers, as a new record was set in cricket in the summer of 1956 – one that stands to this day. Surrey spin bowler Jim Laker took an unprecedented 19 wickets for England in the fourth Ashes Test match against Australia at Old Trafford, including all ten wickets in the tourist's second innings.

But it was music that continued to grab people's attention, particularly as more and more American performers made their way into the British charts. Pat Boone, Carl Perkins and Frankie Lymon – described as 'the first war baby to become a best seller' – were among the new best sellers, plus Gene Vincent, whose record 'Be-Bop-A-Lu-La' was dismissed by the *NME*'s Alex MacIntosh as a 'straightforward junior idiot chant.'

By his own description, Tony Hale was a 'good little boy' until he heard the music of an ex-US sailor from Norfolk, Virginia, named Vincent Eugene Craddock. 'Gene Vincent was the man who said 'Follow me – I am the devil, but it will be fun'. And I went for him over Elvis because everybody was going down the Elvis route. The first record I ever bought was Vincent's 'Race With The Devil' in late 1956.'

But there was other music that had an impact on the young Hale. 'I remember hearing calypso music on the

radio, on the back of the Empire Windrush arriving
from Jamaica (the ship brought over 400 people from
the Caribbean island to London in 1948 and housed
them in Clapham in southeast London). And in 1956,
in the Italian coffee bar in south east London, I heard
'When Mexico Gave Up The Rumba And Took Up
Rock And Roll', which was a sort of pre-rock 'n' roll
record.' American singer Mitchell Torok reached the
UK top ten in September 1956 with this novelty song,
which he followed with 'Red Light Green Light'.

For David Hughes, 13 year-old Frankie Lymon and
his backing group The Teenagers represented a major
shift in musical taste. 'My earliest memory is coming
back from scout camp on a bus, singing all the usual
scout songs, and then me and my mate Peanuts
suddenly bursting into 'Why Do Fools Fall in Love'.
This coincided with Hughes being able to go into his
local record shop – Murdochs in Maidstone – to listen
to records he had heard on Luxembourg. 'I listened
under the bedclothes with a huge portable radio with
a battery the size of two bricks which my granny had
given me. In the winter you were under six blankets
with the radio holding them up.'

Hughes was listening to the record company
sponsored shows on Luxembourg which ran from 7pm
– 'you only heard about a minute of each record' – but
he also recalls that music shows were broadcast on the
BBC at weekends. 'There was only one proper radio in
the house and I used to bag it to listen to Saturday and

Sunday morning music shows.'

In September 1956, with America's leading rock 'n' roll disc jockey Alan Freed broadcasting his *Jamboree* show on Luxembourg regularly every Saturday night, the first rock 'n' roll movie made its way to Britain. *Rock Around The Clock* starring Bill Haley, The Platters, Little Richard and Freddie Bell and The Bellboys. It arrived without any sort of a health warning, although reviewer Charles Govey suggested, 'Let us not kid ourselves … you may find *Rock Around The Clock* horrifying,' before conceding that it was 'a film the young fans are going to turn out in their thousands to see.'

The film showed Haley and his band in their famous tartan jackets and rolling around the stage at a Saturday night dance in the fictitious town of Strawberry Springs ('population 1470') while a local brother and sister demonstrated the jive. Described as the 'first rock n roll exploitative movie', *Rock Around The Clock* also introduced British teenagers to a whole new language as the American kids used phrases such as 'gone man', 'crazy man', 'dig it' and 'daddy-o'.

When the film – summed-up in the *Times* newspaper as a movie that 'cannot profitably be described in the terms of normal criticism' – went out on general release to the picture houses it brought an unexpected reaction to the streets of Britain. Crowds were reported to be 'singing and jiving' both inside and outside the cinemas, in addition to smashing windows and generally upsetting the local constabulary.

After the arrest of nine youths following the movie being shown at the Trocadero in London's Elephant & Castle district, the *Times* carried a letter from one of its readers calling for the film to be banned. The writer claimed that 'the hypnotic rhythm and the wild gestures have a maddening effect on a rhythm-loving age-group and the result of its impact is the relaxing of all self-control.'

With disturbances reported in Manchester, Burnley and Bootle plus the London areas of Woolwich, Croydon, Dagenham, West Ham and Peckham, the authorities in Birmingham, Blackburn and Preston took the decision to ban the film altogether. In Birmingham – Britain's second largest city – officials issued a statement saying the film was banned because 'if exhibited the film would be likely to lead to disorder.'

The important Rank cinema chain banned all Sunday night showings of *Rock Around The Clock* as apparently Sunday – God's chosen day of rest – was the favourite night for gangs of Teddy Boys to go out in search of a bit of trouble. At the other end of the scale, in a commendable effort to keep up-to-date with goings on, Queen Elizabeth II asked for a special viewing of the film during her summer break at Balmoral Castle in Scotland. She chose it over *The Caine Mutiny* and presumably had no trouble getting it past the local council watch committee.

While Jan Parsons heard about the riots, they had little or no impact on her as a 14-year-old girl in South

London, but Bruce Welch, who was a 15-year-old boy
in the north east of England at the time, has a different
memory. 'All my contemporaries were there, tearing
all the seats out in the Regal cinema in Newcastle – it
had that effect on people,' he says, before suggesting
that the press had a hand in it all. 'There was trouble
but it was all a bit exaggerated by the newspapers.
Donald Zec wrote in the *Daily Mirror* that he gave this
new music six months.'

Ex-journalist Tony Barrow remembers that there
were fights in Liverpool before rock 'n' roll came
along. 'Affrays did happen at jazz dances and there were
regular fights at venues in the north west. In fact an
integral part of the budget for any dance in those days
was the cost of the police on the door and you could
actually hire different ranks at different prices.'

Acknowledging that fights did move from clubs to
cinemas with the arrival of rock 'n' roll films, Barrow
also suggests that there was a hint of one-upmanship
about it all which meant that when a fight was reported
in one town, 'The next town where the film was
showing would want to go one better.'

There was also trouble at the Palace cinema in
Maidstone, where David Hughes recalls reading the
story in his local paper. 'There was a story about local
Teddy Boys ripping up the seats and there was a bit
of 'if they can do it somewhere else, then so can we'
about it all. I think all they wanted to do was dance in
the aisles but there was an overreaction by the people

in charge and then it all got out of hand.'

John Lennon was one young man who went to see *Rock Around The Clock* in Liverpool and his fellow Quarryman Rod Davis recalls his reaction to the showing. 'Apparently John said afterwards that he was disappointed that there was no seat-slashing or fighting.' Ringo Starr was taken to see it by his grandparents while he was recuperating from a stay in hospital. 'The film was sensational because the audience ripped up the cinema which was great to watch,' explained The Beatles' drummer before he added, 'I didn't join in because I was a sickly child; I was just so excited that they were doing it for me.'

Meanwhile, in Chelmsford, local cinema owner George Watkins prepared himself as the impact of *Rock Around The Clock* spread across Britain and as far as Norway, where police used batons to disperse 600 youngsters who had gathered in a park after watching the movie.

The local newspaper in the county town of Essex ran a front page story in September 1956 under the headline 'Riot squad is ready' in which they reported that Watkins had hired 'a six-man rock 'n' roll riot squad' to deal with any trouble during the showing of *Rock Around The Clock* at his Select cinema.

The story described the movie as 'the film that has set teenagers all over the country rioting, leaving a trail of wrecked cinemas' and explained that local boxer and ex-Coldstream Guardsman Owen Manning would be among the minders. 'I like this kind of music but I'm not a Teddy Boy. If there are any troublemakers we'll deal with them outside the cinema,' he told readers, who were seemingly unconcerned about the idea of vigilantes taking to the streets in an effort to keep the peace.

While the cinema's owner said he was expecting about 4000 people to watch the film during its seven-day stay in Chelmsford – enhanced by the fact that it was banned in other nearby towns – he added, 'If there are any naughty boys, we would be glad of Mr Manning's assistance.' Watkins also warned that trouble at *Rock Around The Clock* would deter other similar types of films from being shown in his cinema and perhaps in the county.

In the end everything apparently went off smoothly with no punch-ups or disturbances as Jen Blowes, who was in the audience, confirms. 'There was a packed cinema for *Rock Around The Clock* when I went to see it in Chelmsford and people were dancing in the aisles but they didn't cause any trouble. I sat up against the wall in a corner and just watched them,' she says.

Meanwhile at the Pavilion cinema in London's Piccadilly Circus, Tony Hale was experiencing what he calls his 'first rock 'n' roll event' and it involved watching *Rock Around The Clock* right around the clock – for a whole day. 'Me and my school mates went to see *Rock Around The Clock* and when we got hungry we sent somebody out to get some food and bunked him back in through the bog window. We were there from 11am to 11pm – 12 hours of *Rock Around The Clock*!'

And while he and his mates behaved themselves throughout their day-long experience, Hale recalls that there was some rowdy behaviour. 'Youths and Teddy Boys did slash the seats because they were easy to rip out and cut up and if there was an authoritarian commissioner in the cinema telling them to behave, then they'd ignore him and do the opposite.'

Bill Haley's reaction to all the violence and the headlines was to tell the British press and its readers, 'I'm not worried by the riots that you've had in Britain,' before suggesting that the whole thing might even have been some sort of bizarre PR stunt. 'It was a gimmick that backfired and I got burned,' he said before turning his attention to plans for his UK tour.

Throughout 1956 Bill Haley continued to release hit records and cause a degree of pandemonium at concerts across the United States, with police being called to break up fights. One man who had a close-up view of Haley's on-stage antics was British band leader Vic Lewis who joined Haley, Clyde McPhatter, Chuck Berry and Frankie Lymon for a US concert in 1956, and Tony Barrow recalls Lewis telling him of his first experience on a US rock 'n' roll show. 'I remember Vic saying that his band went down badly with the hostile American teenagers as he didn't realize what rock 'n' roll involved. He was told by other band leaders to learn the 'rock 'n' roll beat', which was absolutely alien to him and his musicians. What chance had 16 white bandsmen from Britain, now that rock 'n' roll had burst on to the scene?' The band leader also observed that Haley had 'eccentric choreography, with a ridiculous kiss curl hanging down and mature men lying on the floor to play their instruments.'

With *Rock Around The Clock* at the movies and rock 'n' roll records making up about a third of the UK Top 30 chart - thanks to the likes of Haley, Presley, Vincent, Lymon and new arrivals Fats Domino and Little Richard – it was only a matter of time before the club scene changed. During the summer of 1956, what *Melody Maker* called 'The Rock-And-Roll Craze' was spreading across the land. 'Although music critics and the press continue to blast rock-and-roll, the craze is gaining ground with rock-and-roll clubs opening throughout the country and records sales soaring,' reported the music paper.

As the famous London jazz club Studio 51 closed down in August (only to re-open in September as a rock 'n' roll venue featuring Rory Blackwell's Rock 'n' Rollers), so celebrated jazz drummer Tony Crombie took the decision to form Britain's first full-time rock 'n' roll band and take them out on the road for a nationwide tour of one-night stands featuring, as an added bonus, dance demonstrations for the fans. Before the end of the year, Crombie and His Rockets earned a record deal with EMI's Columbia label and reached number 25 in the UK charts with 'Teach You To Rock', which was heralded as the first British-made rock 'n' roll hit.

Meanwhile up in Newcastle, Bruce Welch and Hank Marvin were busy with their own skiffle group The Railroaders. 'We would play in pubs and village halls and then we turned to rock 'n' roll and played on some local talent shows called 'Go As You Please', where you got £2 if you won,' recalls Welch. 'We were only 15 but we booked all our own gigs and got quite famous locally.'

While Welch and his band mates had their focus firmly fixed on rock 'n' roll, it was a skiffle player who set them on the right road. 'When I was about 15 we met Chas McDevitt who had played at the Newcastle Empire. We told him we wanted to get into the business of making music. He was very kind and said to us 'you'll never do it from here' and then we knew we had to go to London. That was the best advice we ever got.'

If Welch and his pal Marvin – or Bruce Cripps and Brian Rankin as they were known to their families – were yearning to get to London, one young man was already there and busily holding down two jobs. 'I started playing guitar when I was about 15 – I was taught by an undertaker who lived down our road,' recalls Terry Slater, 'and was working in the strip clubs in Soho and at Billingsgate fish market.'

Slater, who would go on to a career as a musician and a publishing and record company executive, started work as a fishmonger at 4am, slept most of the day and then went to work as a guitarist and singer in some of Soho's more exotic clubs which, in those days, were owned by Maltese businessmen. 'I'd go down to the clubs in the evening, play and sing and get a free meal and about £2 a night. It was kind of cool.' Eventually he worked out that music was a more lucrative living than fish. 'Then, when I realised that I was earning more money from playing than I was from being a fishmonger, I quit.'

But even the growing popularity of rock 'n' roll didn't make it any more palatable to a generation of parents. 'My parents disapproved of rock 'n' roll and they couldn't understand the records I was listening to and then buying,' says David Hughes who recalls finding an unlikely ally in the household. 'I was in bed, ill with something, and our cleaning lady took pity on me and brought her gramophone and some 78s to the house. She played them loud enough for me to hear them upstairs and she was mad keen on Johnnie Ray and Frankie Laine and she brought the first ever Everly Brothers record ('Bye Bye Love') with her.'

With Presley reported to have sold 10 million records in America in a year, to have been paid £35,000 for his appearance in the film *Love Me Tender* and become the first artist to receive a gold disc for a record before it was released – 'Love Me Tender' chalked up advance sales of over one million – it was apparently time for some serious analysis of the new musical phenomenon.

Although he had a preference for Gene Vincent,

Hale understood the success and appeal of Presley. 'He was a composite of the black music he heard in church and the country music he absorbed from radio. He was a creation of the things that were around him but was more than the sum of the parts because he had the sneer, he was staggeringly good looking and he frightened your mum and dad … and that was the best thing.'

Elvis Presley's 'Don't Be Cruel' – the flip side of his UK number two hit 'Hound Dog' – marked a milestone moment in Jan Parsons' listening journey. 'His 78rpm record was the first one I bought with my own pocket money'. But not everyone was immediately bowled over. Rod Davis still had serious reservations about the young singer from Tupelo. 'When Elvis first appeared I didn't like his little twitch, he was totally in love with himself and I thought he was a complete pillock, but all the other guys thought he was great.'

American psychologist Dr Ben Walstein was at the time invited to analyse rock 'n' roll and he started by listening to 'Blue Suede Shoes' which had become a major hit for both Presley and the song's composer Carl Perkins. 'Well the first impression I get from it has to do with this business of 'don't step on my blue suede shoes' … 'don't hurt' … 'allow me to have a sense of independence'. The interesting thing about this has, I think, to do with the adolescent's desire for some degree of privacy.'

The learned doctor went on to suggest, 'I think that

there is some sexual component in this in that one may say that blue suede shoes represent something that has not been tried yet by the adolescent.'

Perhaps inspired by this report, the *NME* published a major four-page rock 'n' roll supplement in late 1956 when they put the spotlight on the following top ten 'Rock 'n' Roll Stars': Bill Haley, Elvis Presley, Carl Perkins, The Platters, Clyde McPhatter, Pat Boone, Ruth Brown, Gene Vincent, The Teen-Agers and Dinah Washington.

The special insert also carried a photo of Presley with two young ladies and a caption which read, 'Elvis Presley is reported to be entirely fancy-free as far as the opposite sex is concerned', plus adverts for a record shop in Blackpool called Starpics which claimed to carry the 'finest display of rock 'n' roll records in the north'; a singer named Alan Stewart ('a few dates still available'); and one for Players cigarettes which bragged, 'Whatever the pleasure, Players complete it.'

1956 was the year during which, on the one hand, actresses Grace Kelly and Marilyn Monroe married Prince Rainier III of Monaco and playwright Arthur Miller respectively while, at the other end of the scale, the Soviet army of the USSR took to the streets of Budapest to quell an uprising by the people of Hungary. It also saw the Suez Crisis erupt when Egypt seized control of the Suez Canal and Britain and France joined forces to launch a blockade. The result was that petrol rationing was re-introduced in Britain six years after it had ended following World War II and all advertising of petrol on the newly launched ITV channel was banned.

The people's protest in Hungary and the Soviet regime putting tanks on the streets of Budapest had a major impact on Hale and his band of budding musicians, who chose it as a cause they should support. 'The first time my school group ever played in public was at the school in 1956 as a benefit to raise money for the people of Hungary. But the headmaster got it into his head that we were going to play rock 'n' roll', recalls the musician, producer and radio broadcaster.

'He was about to pull the plug when we had to go to his office and swear that we wouldn't play rock 'n' roll. We had three guitars and a tea-chest bass but no drums and no bass guitar and we did half an hour and raised £16 for Hungary.' And from there Hale and his band moved steadily onwards and upwards. 'We were playing school halls, village halls, youth clubs and then pubs where you looked old enough to get in.'

By October, with Decca boss Edward Lewis confirming that total sales in Britain of Bill Haley's 'Rock Around The Clock' had reached 643,000, an up-and-coming British singer was busy making his first recordings for the same Decca label. Bermondsey-born Tommy Hicks was singing at the 2-Is coffee bar when he was spotted by PR man and photographer John Kennedy who, with the backing of impresario Larry Parnes, took over management of the 20-year-old merchant sailor and named him Tommy Steele.

As a seaman, Hicks had spent time in America and in 1955 he found himself in Norfolk, Virginia where he took a seat to watch something called the *Grand Ol' Opry Traveling Show* where he recalled watching, 'All manner of men and women dressed in different costumes playing different instruments, but they had one thing in common: country music.'

But it was the arrival on the stage of a young man in horn-rimmed spectacles which made the evening memorable for Steele. 'He played an electric Gibson guitar and like everybody else that night he played country. He played three songs ... but in the middle of the third he did something that to my ears was remarkable. He changed the rhythm. For the first time in my life I was listening to rock'n'roll and it was being played by a fella called Buddy Holly.'

On the back of that experience Steele, when he arrived in New York, rushed to a record shop and bought a copy of Carl Perkins' original version of his song 'Blue Suede Shoes'. And on the way back to Britain, the youngster learned how to play the song, which then became part of his earliest shows at the 2-1s.

Out of the navy and determined to pursue a career in music, Steele – having being turned down by Parlophone manager George Martin – signed with Decca and they fixed him up with a song called 'Rock With The Cavemen' written by Lionel Bart and Mike Pratt. After making his TV debut on BBC's *Off The Record*, Steele's first single peaked at number 13 on the eve of his opening show as top of the bill at Sunderland's Empire Theatre where, on his arrival, he saw a huge poster declaring 'The Dynamic Tommy Steele – Britain's Teenage Idol – With The Steelmen.'

Steele topped a bill made up of acts such as Mike and Bernie Winters ('TV's Crazy Funsters'), Josephine Anne ('The Crazy Gang's Girlfriend'), Thunderclap Jones ('Wild Welshman Of The Keyboard) and Reg 'Unknown To Millions' Thompson. The rock star's performance, wearing what were described in the local press review as 'drain-pipe trousers and a checked shirt,' drew the following comment: 'The tousle-haired teenager hip-swivelled around the microphone, strumming his electric guitar to the accompaniment of a rock 'n' roll quartet billed as the Steelmen.'

When *Melody Maker* celebrated their 50th anniversary in April 1976, they featured a major retrospective about every decade from the 1920s onwards. In their review of 1950s Chris Welch wrote that 'The roots of the Sixties rock revolution are to be found in the skiffle boom of 1956' and added that Steele's debut release 'was the first successful British attempt at producing a rock and roll record.'

With 'Rock With The Cavemen' selling over 25,000 copies in just three days and sharing a place in the charts with Bill Haley (who had five titles in the Top 30), Elvis Presley and Gene Vincent, Steele's rise to fame prompted *NME* to note, 'Nothing is more fantastic than the speed with which Britain has produced its answer to

Elvis Presley.' All this success prompted rival EMI boss Sir Joseph Lockwood to admit years later that he was 'very mad when I found out that he had got engaged by Decca – he was almost the first pop star that appeared on our UK scene.'

Perhaps not surprisingly the *NME* Poll for 1956 showed Bill Haley as the World's Outstanding Musician – he had packed in seven UK top 30 hit singles and his debut album *Rock n' Roll Stage Show* had reached number 30 – ahead of Elvis Presley, who also had seven chart hits and finished at number three in the Best US Male category – behind winner Frank Sinatra and Haley.

Best UK Male was once again Dickie Valentine while Tommy Steele, after just one hit, made a showing at number 12. Steele's second hit 'Singing The Blues' made its debut appearance on the chart in December 1956 and prompted music critic and future TV host Keith Fordyce to suggest that 'for the first time Tommy really justifies his rapid entry in to the hit parade with a strikingly individual performance.'

As rock 'n' roll grew, so the desire to dance grew along with it and new clubs were springing up all over the UK where local bands played music while youngsters danced away to their heart's content. In Birmingham there were the Grand Casino and Tony's Ballroom plus Stella's Bar while the City Hall in Hull, Leeds' Starlight Roof, the Palais in Stockton and the Rialto York were all packing in people keen to enjoy the new hit tunes.

While Tony Crombie was busy offering fans dance

demonstrations during his UK rock 'n' roll tour, the Locarno Ballroom in Leeds came up with the idea of lunch-time rock 'n' roll sessions when teenagers, for an entry fee of 3d (1¼p), could dance to Lew Stone's Orchestra or the Larry Cassidy Quartet.

And the dance they were all doing was, of course the jive, which is described in the Concise Oxford Dictionary as 'a style of lively dance popular in the 1940s and 1950s, performed to swing music or rock and roll.' With its origins in 1930s Afro-American society, the jive developed from the jitterbug and was popular during the swing era of big bands such as Glenn Miller, Benny Goodman and Stan Kenton before it became the favourite dance of a new breed of rockers 'n' rollers.

Jan Parsons was a jiver who was never actually taught to jive. 'I just picked it up,' she says. 'I went to a dance club near Lambeth Palace where they did waltzes and things like that but we went there for the rest in the middle, between the proper dancing, when they played records and you could jive.' And down near Chelmsford, in her home village of Writtle, Jen Blowes and her friends went through the same process of self-education.

'I went to the local club and we just did it. We worked out how to jive between ourselves although there was one boy who was brilliant so we all watched him and took it up from there. One minute we were all dancing to skiffle and then we were jiving to rock 'n' roll records – it all seemed to happen very quickly.'

For professional dancer Len Goodman, jiving represented the start of a life-long love affair with dancing. 'I was a jiver – that was how I started dancing,' explains the man who didn't take up ballroom dancing until he was 21. 'I was always out at dance halls jiving. They had bands and played records and then juke boxes arrived in coffee bars but I was never taught to jive. I just picked up jiving because at that age the main objective was looking for girls and the place to go to do that was dance halls.' And the music he was dancing to was special – 'rock 'n' roll was probably the first teenage music, it was something we could own.'

But while Len and Jan and Jen were jiving away to rock 'n' roll, the *Daily Mail* was busy telling anyone who would listen that this new popular entertainment was not only over here ... but was also 'deplorable, tribal – and from America.' These were precisely the things that made it attractive to the youth of Britain.

Chapter 4

1957: Haley's Comet Hits Britain

Events during January 1957 served only to add
to the confusion went it came to music, as the
'establishment' and a new generation of young fans
continued to clash in a head-to-head conflict over the
merits of rock 'n' roll.

While the headmaster of a school in Nottingham
banned his students from attending twice-weekly
lunchtime rock 'n' roll dance sessions in a nearby
village hall – 'we used to have a lunch time ballroom
dancing session at the school and now it's flopped
completely', he told parents – the first homegrown
rock sensation Tommy Steele hit number one with
'Singing The Blues'.

Uniquely Steele shared the top spot for one week in
February 1957 with the American singer whose original
recording of the same song also topped the US chart.
Guy Mitchell, who had two other UK chart toppers in
1953, was a major attraction who made regular visits to
Britain throughout the 1950s. One man who saw him
in concert back then was Reg Dwight – long before he
became better known as Elton John.

He was among the crowd at London's leading
theatre. 'I remember going to see Guy Mitchell at the
London Palladium. They used to have Saturday night
shows at the Palladium and Guy Mitchell was starring

in this one show and at the end of his set, he took his sock off and whirled it around his head. I thought 'what a funny guy'.'

With Steele at the top of the chart – and with his record selling over 100,000 copies in a single week – his management team saw it as the right time to branch out and 'go for the West End' as they put it. But when they mentioned performing at one of London's most up-market cabaret venues, the Café De Paris, Steele was unconvinced. 'You want me to work in a caff?' was his immediate reaction.

Slowly he was convinced that some time spent at what his people termed 'The epitome of London night life' would not be a complete waste, but even so Steele astounded the audience – plus 'every top theatre critic in town' who gathered in the Piccadilly nightspot – by appearing in blue suede shoes, blue jeans and matching yellow scarf and socks.

However, it wasn't just rock 'n' roll which attracted criticism. Skiffle also had its knockers and, even as the prestigious Royal Festival Hall was busy holding skiffle sessions featuring Ken Colyer, The Vipers and the Bob Cort Group, Swansea council refused to allow Lonnie Donegan perform at Brangwyn Hall as they felt, 'This type of music was a type of music that would attract an exuberant crowd of youngsters.'

But there was no confusion over the rock 'n' roll acts who were attracting the most interest. While Presley had four records in the charts during the first month of the new year – 'Hound Dog', 'Love Me Tender', 'Blue Moon' and 'Don't Be Cruel' – Bill Haley's forthcoming tour of the UK was setting new records. According to *NME*, 'never in the history of British entertainment has there been such colossal interest and fantastic ticket demand.'

The man who was starring in the new movie called *Don't Knock The Knock* – 'if you enjoyed *Rock Around The Clock* you should like this even more' said the critics – was also being hailed as the first artist to sell a million records in the UK when '(We're Gonna) Rock Around The Clock' passed that magic sales mark.

Despite Donegan and a few others sticking to their skiffle principles, there was a change afoot in British music and some of the players saw what was coming. 'The skiffle bubble burst when rock 'n' roll arrived,' admits Smith-Lyte, 'and a lot of skiffle guys couldn't actually play guitar that well, so that was a bit of a handicap.'

Having been inspired to play guitar by Donegan while he also learnt the banjo, Rod Davis found himself invited to join The Quarry Men in 1957 alongside Eric Griffith, Pete Shotton, Bill Smith and John Lennon. 'We were 100% skiffle at that time but there was a tide of rock 'n' roll music and it was difficult to play rock with a skiffle line-up – you had to have a lead guitar and that meant having an electric guitar and an amplifier.'

Lennon's growing fascination with rock 'n' roll meant that the other members of his group also became interested in rock 'n' roll – all except for Rod Davis. 'I was a banjo player and you couldn't join a rock 'n' roll group as a banjo player. John was mad keen on it although he liked some skiffle and I've still got his copy of 'Rock Island Line'.

'The Quarry Men's repertoire was rapidly becoming rock 'n' roll but if you played the wrong music in front of the wrong audience then the animosity was palpable,' explains Davis. 'There was a huge difference between rock 'n' roll fans and jazz or skiffle fans – jazz music was for intellectuals and what those fans hated was rock 'n' roll. I remember arguing on stage with John when he wanted to play some rock 'n' roll and saying to him 'don't get everybody annoyed' but he went ahead anyway.'

Skiffle's number-one man Lonnie Donegan also represented something very important to George Harrison. 'He was a big hero of mine," he recalled. 'He had a much bigger influence on British rock bands than he was ever given credit for. In the late Fifties he was virtually the only guitar player that you could see.'

The new year started with a brand new pop show on commercial television when Associated-Rediffusion launched *Cool For Cats* with host Kent Walton playing records and discussing them during the weekly 15-minute broadcast, which occasionally boasted The Dougie Squires Dancers for a touch of added glamour.

Six weeks later the BBC responded with their own new pop show titled *Six-Five Special* which was trailed as the BBC's 'all-out drive to capture teenagers.' They chose to broadcast the show during the 'extra hour' which was the gap between 6pm and 7pm, after children's television had finished and before the start of adult programming.

The first show, which according to the BBC was intended 'For the young at heart', went out on Saturday February 16 1957 with host Pete Murray announcing: 'Welcome aboard the Six-Five Special. We've got almost a hundred cats jumping here, some real characters to give us the gas, so just get on with it and have a ball.'

Murray, who had cut his teeth on Radio Luxembourg, was joined by co-host Josephine Douglas, guests Tommy Steele and Lonnie Donegan, plus resident acts Don Lang and his Frantic Five and singer Wee Willie Harris with his Teddy Boy outfit and a shock of pink (and occasionally green) hair.

For all the excitement within the BBC, some viewers had grave reservations about *Six-Five Special*. Even though future Slade singer Noddy Holder remembers that it was 'the first time you'd seen pop stars, rock 'n' roll stars appearing on TV', he was less impressed with the fact that it featured jazz musicians playing rock n' roll on a live TV show and some odd interruptions. 'Trouble was they used to put in little bits of public service announcements teaching you to how to cross the road or how to stay healthy – it wasn't very hip.'

Tony Hale goes further. '*Six-Five Special* was shite!

These were not rock 'n' roll people. It was a dreadful show that could have been made by Lord Reith in 1927, and they had public information notices during the show – very rock 'n' roll!' On the other hand, for David Hughes, it was a 'crucial' show. As his family didn't own a television, Hughes went to his granny's on a Saturday night to watch it and while he found that Lang playing the trombone was 'a bit weird', he reckoned Wee Willie Harris was 'alright.'

The impact of rock 'n' roll was also felt in many foreign lands, and it was responded to with varying degrees of severity. Iraq banned 'Rock Around The Clock' as being 'dangerous to teenagers'; Egypt announced that all rock 'n' roll music was 'against public morals'; Iran decided that rock 'n' roll dancing was 'harmful to health'; while Cuba banned all rock 'n' roll television programmes for being 'immoral and profane' - although that only lasted for two days.

Bill Haley arrived in the UK fresh from a sell-out tour of Australia, where he played to over 300,000 people. He arrived at Southampton Docks on the liner Queen Elizabeth on February 5 1957 to be met by around 4,000 fans. A further 2,000 were waiting for him when he got to Waterloo Station where he was held up by the crowd for over 20 minutes despite a 50-strong police cordon.

While, according to *Melody Maker*, Haley's arrival was 'the biggest musical bombshell to hit Britain since the war exploded' there was some concern in the House of Lords about Haley's forthcoming UK appearances. In answer to Lord Lucas' question as to whether statute allowed for the removal of seats in cinema to allow dancing during Haley's concerts, Lord Mancroft suggested, 'I don't think the statute has got round to rock and rolling yet.'

Despite his less than popular appearance in America a year earlier, The Vic Lewis Orchestra were booked as support to Haley and The Comets alongside balladeer Malcolm Vaughan (who also appeared with his comedy partner Kenneth Earle as Earle & Vaughan) and penny whistler Desmond Lane. The 18-date tour of the UK kicked off at the Dominion Theatre in London on February 6 with tickets costing between 5s 6d (27½p) and 21s (£1.5p) at all venues.

The opening show of his British tour brought the 32 year-old Haley a round of complimentary reviews with *Melody Maker* suggesting that 'if noise is the measure of success then Bill Haley and The Comets are a sensation', while rivals *NME* reckoned the opening night was an 'overwhelming triumph.' Even the reviewer from the rather more staid *Daily Telegraph* was moved to note, 'I enjoyed the fun of the Haley type of entertainment' before adding somewhat desperately, 'let no cat call me square.'

Decca employee and part-time disc jockey Tony Hall not only worked on Haley's releases but also went to his opening night. 'I was absolutely horrified,' he says. 'There were these old men – an old bass player lying on his back; it was so corny and looked dreadful.' Watching Haley and six-piece band cavorting on stage all dressed in bow ties and tartan tuxedos, served as a warning to Hall. 'I knew that his sales would be dead the moment people actually saw Haley and his band. And his sales just died after he toured. Everybody flocked to the Dominion but nobody went back.'

Equally unimpressed was Andrew Loog Oldham, who was even less flattering about the man he went to see at the Dominion Theatre. 'Haley was a nightmare,' commented the man credited with opening one the UK's first independent record labels – Immediate – in 1965. 'A paltry thirty-five minutes from this fat, kiss-curled housewife from the middle of America, the uncle you never wanted. Confronted by the mediocrity that was Haley, I thought for moment rock 'n 'roll was over'.

However, one 17 year-old schoolboy who saw Haley at Edmonton Regal was moved in a good way by the experience even though he had to pay a high price. Harry Webb, who not long after would become Cliff Richard, and his mates bunked off school to be sure of seeing Haley. 'We got the tickets and decided not to go back to school, but someone snitched on us and we lost our prefect badges,' he recalls. 'But I needed to be there. It was my first rock concert and it was unbelievably exciting.'

Richard Sarstedt had arrived in England from India in 1954 and been sent to boarding school in Croydon where, as an impressionable 16 year-old, he discovered both the guitar and Bill Haley. Three years after landing in Britain, Sarstedt was among the crowd at a cinema in West Croydon watching his hero on stage. 'Going to see Bill Haley was a big moment in my life even though they were chucking chairs about. But that one song – 'Rock Around The Clock' – changed the world,' says the man, who a few years later would top the chart as Eden Kane.

When the Haley caravan hit Manchester on February 13, two 15-year-old schoolboys who had already been initiated into rock music by the records of Elvis Presley, Gene Vincent, Fats Domino and Jerry Lee Lewis were about to blown away again by another American hero. Future stars of The Hollies, Graham Nash and Allan Clarke were just 15 and 14 years old when they went to the Odeon Theatre to see Bill Haley and according to Nash the evening left an 'indelible mark on my soul.'

As he and his future Sixties popstar mate hung over the balcony, the curtains opened. In the words of Nash: 'There he was – Bill Haley, in the flesh. He wasn't pretty to look at, he wasn't Elvis, wasn't sexy, but, man, could that cat put on a show.' The future member of the supergroup Crosby Stills Nash & Young reckoned that that night, 'Manchester had been launched into the rock 'n' roll era.'

During the tour, Haley took time out to speak to the British press and he explained that he wanted to come to our shores to prove that 'the kids who like rock 'n' roll weren't all bad' and that by listening to rock 'n' roll youngsters 'are going to be stimulated into taking greater interest in all forms of music.' But this wasn't what rebellious teenager rock fans wanted to hear from the man who had been dubbed the second William the Conqueror.

And he went further by adding that 'there is nothing harmful about rock 'n' roll and I'm very glad to have been able to prove that point.' Whether it was these remarks, or simply the idea of a tubby, balding man in his 30s leading a youthful rebellion, we may never know, but either way Haley's journey to the stars was about to begin its burn-up.

As far as Bruce Welch was concerned, the bubble began to deflate when Haley set foot in England. 'When he got off the boat he was wearing a trilby hat and an overcoat. He looked old while Elvis looked like nobody had looked before.' And it wasn't long before the *NME* described Haley as 'a homespun fellow' while the *MM* suggested he looked like 'a genial butcher.'

After a run of 12 UK hit singles, which started in December 1954, Haley's last British hit came in the month he toured Britain when 'Don't Knock The Rock' reached number seven in the chart. In just over two years he had notched up one number one single – '(We're Gonna) Rock Around The Clock' – plus one chart album ... and nine of the titles included the word 'rock'.

As Bill Haley's domination of rock 'n' roll music

came to an end, it was Elvis Presley's turn to dominate proceedings. 1957 saw the newly crowned 'King' achieve a grand total of 12 British hit singles in a single year including his first UK number one – 'All Shook Up'. And with his income increasing with every hit, Presley opted to spend $100,000 of his hard-earned cash on a 23-room mansion called Graceland, which was set in 13.8 acres of Memphis.

The interest in music in general and rock 'n' roll in particular resulted in increased record sales and the arrival of a host of new electrical equipment. Dansette were at the top of the tree in terms of popular sound equipment, thanks to their GEM portable transistor radio at 11½ guineas (£11.55p); their 'light elegant compact' Consort tape recorder for 22 gns (£23.10p); and their Bermuda record player – complete with 'BSR 4-speed changer, genuine diamond needle and sockets for stereo' – which cost 16½ gns (£17.32p), with legs offered as an optional extra for another 2 gns (£2.10p).

After the success – and troubles – of the film *Rock Around The Clock* and its follow-up *Don't Knock The Rock*, music movies began to grab the public's attention. As Tommy Steele starred in *The Tommy Steele Story*, with Humphrey Lyttelton and Chas McDevitt's skiffle group, plans were underway for a British rock 'n' roll film called *Rock You Sinners* which featured home-grown rockers such as Tony Crombie, Rory Blackwell and Dickie Bennett.

But it was a new movie from America which had the

biggest impact. *The Girl Can't Help It* starred actress and sex-symbol Jayne Mansfield alongside singing stars Little Richard, Eddie Cochran, Gene Vincent, The Platters, Fats Domino, Julie London, Eddie Fontaine and Ray Anthony ... and it was in colour. And as far as Paul McCartney is concerned it is 'still *the* great music film', and it inspired him to buy Gene Vincent's Be-Bop-A-Lu-La – 'the first record I ever bought.'

The former Beatle has been joined by a host of other music fans who watched bewitched as Jayne Mansfield's swirling walk down the street to Little Richard's raucous rendition of the title track led to ice blocks melting and milk bottles exploding. "It was wonderful', says Len Goodman. 'It had Jayne Mansfield and numbers from Eddie Cochran and Little Richard and it was an introduction to those American acts.'

For Ian Dury, Gene Vincent represented the epitome of his own ambitions. '(He) got to me more than anybody else; he was in a special little category because he was what I wanted to be as a singer,' said the future frontman of The Blockheads. 'I didn't know he was crippled at the time, so that didn't have anything to do with it.'

It was Vincent's appearance in *The Girl Can't Help It* which made the biggest impression on Dury who, in 1977, wrote his tribute song 'Sweet Gene Vincent'. 'That was before he was Mr Leather. It was when he was wearin' plaid and had pale blue hair. It was his thinness, his wastedness, Gene Vincent. His face, his music and his singing.'

Having the chance to see these American rock stars in *The Girl Can't Help It* was equally significant to Tony Barrow. 'It was important in terms of rock music as we were ignorant of the visual aspect of these acts – we had no idea what these American artists looked like,' he recounts, while Tony Hale has another particular memory from the film. 'What I remember musically is The Treniers – there were hundreds of them (there were just seven in fact), they ran around, they had sax players who did steps while they played and a drummer who was shaped like a hill – he was fat (he wasn't) and had a huge smile (he did).'

And all that meant one thing to the future radio executive and producer. 'It was extraordinary because it was more than music – it was music hall, the musicals of the 1920s and 1930s, but to me it was magical,' Hale explains. 'And Little Richard was the same – the wildness of the delivery was the thing that made it for me.' American singing star Neil Sedaka admits to 'remembering it well – Little Richard standing at the piano and his wonderful scream.'

Two young men who, in 1957, were on the verge of finding stardom in the British music business were Marty Wilde and Bruce Welch and they both saw – and vividly remember – *The Girl Can't Help It*. 'It was subtle and funny and it was the first chance we had to see these artists in colour', says Wilde. 'We knew so little about them it was like they came from another planet.'

For Welch the film was '*The* rock 'n' roll movie and you didn't have riots at that movie because it was just so good.'

Future Hollies member Graham Nash was another teenager who watched the film in awe. He had gone to the Borough cinema in Manchester's Ordsall Park district to see *The Girl Can't Help It* and recalled that it was a life changing experience. 'Mind blowing! All my favourite rock 'n' rollers were in the movie. And the scene where Jayne Mansfield first appears was unbelievable to a 15-year-old kid.'

Hot on the heels of Haley's tour came teenager Frankie Lymon and his backing group The Teenagers, and after taking the title of Britain's youngest chart topper – aged just 13 – with 'Why Do Fools Fall In Love', he then became – at 14 years of age – the youngest act to top the bill at the London Palladium in March 1957.

During their tour they also played at the Brixton Empress theatre where Jan Parsons remembers seeing them and she remembers what she wore. 'When I went to see Frankie Lymon with my friend I wore a felt skirt, a blouse, little black velvet shoes and fluorescent socks – and my dad was appalled that I was going out like that.'

While Lonnie Donegan – fresh from playing in America as the Musician's Union's nominated exchange act for Bill Haley's visit to the UK – topped the British charts with 'Cumberland Gap' and The Vipers ('Rock

Me Daddy-O'), Chas McDevitt with Nancy Whiskey ('Freight Train') and Johnny Duncan ('Last Train To San Fernando') all kept the skiffle flag flying for a little while longer, the place that helped launch their style of music was changing with the times.

On the back of Tommy Steele's discovery and success, the 2-Is in London's Soho was fast becoming the Mecca for the country's aspiring young rock 'n' roll acts. Wee Willie Harris emerged from the basement club before arriving on Six-Five Special – and even name-checked the coffee bar in his debut release 'Rockin' At The 2-Is' – while a packer in the HMV record shop named Terrence Williams was discovered (and renamed as Terry Dene) by owner Paul Lincoln, who also managed Darrell Smith-Lyte and his group Les Hobeaux.

Signed to 2-Is Promotions – they even wore cream coloured jackets emblazoned with the name – Smith-Lyte and his fellow band members saw the changes in the coffee bar-cum-club at first hand. 'People like Haley and Presley had a huge impact and lots of people in the 2-Is took to looking like Presley. The place was crowded in those days with up to 200 in the cellar downstairs. There was no booze in those days but there were drugs – mainly benzadrine. I wasn't interested,' he says.

And while Les Hobeaux continued to play the skiffle circuit, they also found themselves booked on tour with the likes of Harris and Dene, courtesy of the 2-Is management. 'We were the closing first-half act on some dates on the Moss Empires circuit when Wee Willie and Dene were headlining. Harris made a nice sound and knew what he was doing but Dene was a lot less talented.'

According to Smith-Lyte, rock 'n' roll was the music of a new generation and while 'a lot of people were intolerant of it', he and his group gradually got to know and understand rock 'n' roll and what was expected of them as working musicians. 'We had to make our own way on the tours which involved travelling on the bus to places like Cardiff and getting reimbursed afterwards.'

When he eventually got a car, Smith-Lyte found himself befriended by the group's bass player in order to avoid having to take his large string bass on public transport. And on a couple of trips they found themselves joined by an up-and-coming bass guitarist named Jet Harris, but even with a car it was still a mighty slog. 'We'd do six days on the road and then a Sunday show in somewhere like Weston Super Mare – we were very naive and taken advantage of. And the places we'd stayed at with landladies were pretty grim as they never heated the rooms and the food was horrible.'

Sarstedt was another youngster who was inspired to form a group by skiffle and try his hand at making music. 'We had a skiffle group called The Fabulous Five and we were the most out-of-tune outfit you've ever heard,' he says. Also in the band at the outset was brother Peter Sarstedt, who played the tea-chest bass - 'which was an exacting trade in those days' says

Richard – and a second brother Clive who stepped into the line-up a little later.

The fact that none of them drove or owned a car meant, according to Richard, that somebody who was both a musician and driver had to be recruited. 'Our early drummer was the one with the car, which was an essential in those days as you couldn't take all the stuff on the bus.'

But it wasn't all music and movies in 1957. Singer Beniamino Gigli, conductor Arturo Toscanini and composer Jean Sibelius died, as well as actor Humphrey Bogart. While America began the year with the same man in charge after Dwight Eisenhower was elected President for a second term, Britain had a brand new leader as Harold Macmillan succeeded Anthony Eden as Prime Minster – and famously told the nation 'most of our people have never had it so good.'

Britain exploded its first H-bomb in May and awarded the first £5000 Premium Bond prize in July at the same time as parking meters made their appearance on the streets of London, while the USSR launched a dog named Laika into space.

Back on stage, Tommy Steele was sharing the bill with American act Freddie Bell and The Bellboys, who toured Britain on the back of their hit 'Giddy-Up-A Ding Dong'. 'Honesty compels me to admit that the indescribable din let loose by these two turns caused – to put it mildly – something of a furore around me,' a reviewer for the *Daily Telegraph* reported.

At the same time, singer Pat Boone, who hit the charts with rock songs such as 'Ain't That A Shame' and 'Tutti Frutti', risked the ire of his rival rock 'n' roll singers by saying, 'I don't think anything excuses the suggestive gyrations that some go in for.'

Ironically Boone found himself well placed in *NME*'s survey of the UK's bestselling discs for the first six months of 1957. Using a system of awarding points for positions in the Top 30 chart – number one was worth 30 – Guy Mitchell led the pack with Boon at number two and the rest as follows: 3) Johnnie Ray; 4) Lonnie Donegan; 5) Tab Hunter; 6) Little Richard; 7) Elvis Presley; 8) Frankie Vaughan; 9) Bing Crosby & Grace Kelly; and 10) Tommy Steele.

The growing interest in new artists and their hit records persuaded the record companies to increase the price of 'pop' 78rpm records from 5s 7d (28p) to 6s (30p) and from 6s (30p) to 6s 7½d (33p) for what was called a 'second wave of releases', while 12" LPs cost 37s 6½d (£1.88p).

The good news was that it still cost the same just to hear these records, as a radio-only licence remained at £1 (it was increased in 1946 from the original licence fee of 10s (50p) introduced in 1922), but if you wanted to watch and listen, the Government increased the cost of a dual TV/radio licence to £4, up from the 1954 rate of £3.

Newly signed to Decca and fresh from his tour with Les Hobeaux, Terry Dene hit the charts for the first time in June 1957 with 'A White Sports Coat (And A Pink Carnation)', which peaked at number 18 behind a rival version by The King Brothers, which reached number six. Although it wasn't a hit in the UK, the original version by singer Marty Robbins was a best seller in the US and a popular song on radio and juke boxes in the UK, which is where Tony Hale heard it and spotted a major difference.

'Listen to two versions of something as anodyne as 'A White Sport Coat' and the American version has some guts to it while our versions were utterly without life,' he says. But US/UK versions weren't the only records that upset him. 'You got dreadful cover versions here – like the Embassy records which we always called 'chocolate records' because they were about as much use as a chocolate record.'

And as a skiffle player who recognised that things were changing, Hale recalls a moment when the change hit home. 'We were moving towards rock 'n' roll when we heard 'Whole Lotta Shakin' by Jerry Lee Lewis which had that boogie piano style that I had hated when my dad played Fats Waller records years earlier. And now it was part of rock 'n' roll.'

On July 6 1957 in Liverpool, The Quarry Men got together to play at St Peter's Church fete in advance of their performance on the Carroll Levis TV Star Search talent show. In the crowd to watch the group led by John Lennon was Paul McCartney, who was later introduced to the group's leader and impressed him with his musical knowledge and ability.

'I did 'Twenty Flight Rock' and knew all the words. The Quarry Men were so knocked out that I actually knew and could sing 'Twenty Flight Rock',' recalls McCartney. 'That's what got me into The Beatles.' But for Rod Davis the writing was on the wall as far as The Quarry Men was concerned and by the end of his fifth year at school he called it quits. 'The band was becoming more and more rock 'n' roll and on July 29 1957 we went on a family camping trip to France and I never played with them again.'

While jiving had become the latest dance craze to sweep the nation, another altogether weirder movement was becoming the latest fad in the dark, dingy and overcrowded clubs of London. The huge number of people who crowded in to see singers and groups perform in tiny cellars and basements – with no great regard for health or safety – meant that jiving was almost impossible and as a result something called the 'hand-jive' arrived.

During his early days as a freelance photographer, controversial film-maker Ken Russell captured teenagers dancing with their hands in The Cat's Whiskers coffee bar in Kingly Street, just behind Hamleys toy store in central London, where he claimed the 'hand jive' was invented in the mid-Fifties.

After his photos had appeared in *Picture Post*, he went on the record to say, 'Everyone was jiving there with their hands because there was precious little room to do it with their feet.' While the idea of making hand movements in time to the music originated in America with the people who danced to R&B records, it was music fans in The Cat's Whiskers – the largest seller of Coca-Cola in Britain at the time – who brought it to the attention of Britain's rockers 'n' rollers.

And it seems that change was also afoot in the world of fashion, as Teddy Boys and Teddy Girls began moving away from brothel creepers and espadrilles as a revolutionary style of shoe became the new best seller. Called the winklepicker, these shoes with sharp pointed toes took their name from the pins or sharp objects people used to eat winkles.

By August, Elvis Presley's popularity in Britain was such that the first official UK fan club was formed by Jeanne and Doug Saward and in the same month, up in Liverpool, The Quarry Men made their debut appearance at a new club called the Cavern which had opened as a jazz venue eight months earlier. According to Tony Barrow, the owners of the new Liverpool club instructed all up and coming groups they booked to play skiffle as it went with trad jazz. But, says Barrow, 'gradually the bands began to play what they wanted which included rock 'n' roll.'

While skiffle was acceptable as an attraction during the interval – when the jazzers took their regular and sometime lengthy drinks break in nearby pubs – rock 'n' roll was definitely off the playlist at the Cavern, but it didn't deter John Lennon who decided to sing

'Hound Dog' and 'Blue Suede Shoes'. His efforts were greeted with a short note from club owner Alan Synter telling him to 'cut out the bloody rock.'

The *NME*'s 1957 poll – the music paper's sixth annual event – had Presley as number one World Singer and World Music Personality, but not Top US Singer (which went to Pat Boone) with Doris Day as Top US Female. On the UK front, Dickie Valentine chalked up another win as Top Male, just ahead of Tommy Steele, while Alma Cogan was Top Female and Lonnie Donegan led the Best Small Skiffle Group section.

With rock 'n' roll firmly established as the number -one music of choice for the youngsters of Britain, American author Jack Kerouac's book *On The Road* opened up the route into the new 'Beat Generation' of poets, authors and playwrights, which included Colin Wilson, John Braine and the original 'angry young man' John Osborne, whose play *Look Back In Anger* had opened a year earlier. And pretty soon it was the 'beatniks' who took over and spilled out of London's trendiest coffee bars and jazz clubs.

The more the popular press sniped at this new 'beat culture', the more attractive it became to a generation of students and aspiring artists, actors and designers who craved creativity and the unconventional – and a uniform all their own. The new beatnik style was built around sloppy jumpers or polo-necked sweaters (in black), sandals and duffel coats, with the men opting for beards and women opting for white make-up and black eyeliner.

This new fashion proved to be something of a dilemma for one young student at Liverpool College of Art. As an enthusiastic Teddy Boy who was now an art student, John Lennon found himself torn between dress codes. 'I became a bit artier … but I still dressed as a Ted in black with tight drainies. I imitated Teddy Boys but was always torn between being a Teddy Boy and an art student. One week I'd go to art school with my art school scarf and my hair down and the next week I'd go for the leather jacket and tight jeans.'

At the same time as beatniks arrived, so two new very young British singers appeared. Thirteen year-old Laurie London signed a deal with EMI Records, while 16 year-old Harry Webb quit his own Quintones vocal group to join the Dick Teague Skiffle Group and tour the pubs and clubs of Hertfordshire. And *Six-Five Special* producer Jack Good, in the search for new home-grown talent, found spots for Terry Dene and Jim Dale, and promoted as 'hopefuls' both The John Barry Seven and a new singer named Reg Smith, who had been snapped up by leading impresario Larry Parnes.

Following on the heels of Tommy Steele – 'soft' forename and 'hard' surname – Parnes renamed Smith as Marty Wilde, signed him to a recording deal with Phillips Records and, despite Good's enthusiasm, arranged his debut TV appearance on the rival BBC show *Off The Record* where he sang his unsuccessful debut single 'Honeycomb'.

While Wilde was taking his first steps on the rocky road to fame, a teenage girl in Liverpool was also seeking some excitement on a different level. Joyce Baker lived on a council estate in Huyton and knew two girls who worked at the pools company Vernons that were members of the company choir which sang in old people's home around Liverpool.

'I had a job in the Liver Building in Liverpool when I got in touch with the Vernons Girls' chaperone Miss Finnegan and asked if I could audition to be a reserve singer – you didn't have to work at Vernons to be a Vernons Girl,' recalls Baker.

Although the Vernons Girls provided homely entertainment for some of Liverpool's more senior citizens, Baker had her ear cocked for the latest sounds. 'I was a big fan of rock 'n' roll, which had a huge impact on all the young girls. We were a bit like little Teddy Girls I suppose, with tight skirts, a little scarf around the neck and a short hairdo which we used to make into a kind of DA at the back. '

While her parents were less than impressed with her outfit – which was finished off with flat shoes and ankle socks – Baker was careful to keep out of trouble. 'I didn't get involved, but people I knew used to get hauled into the police station because they had bicycle chains and had been in fights. It was part of what was happening – there was a lot going on.'

Finally, in October 1957, McCartney teamed up with The Quarry Men to make his debut appearance at the New Clubmoor Conservative Club in Liverpool, where he played a (reportedly not very good) guitar solo during a version of 'Guitar Boogie', which was written by Arthur Smith and later cited as a precursor to rock 'n' roll. This was also the month when Elvis Presley's new film *Jailhouse Rock* opened in Memphis at Loewe's State Theater where the singer-turned-film star had worked five years earlier.

While Queen Elizabeth had requested a private screening of *Rock Around The Clock* a year earlier, it was now the turn of her sister Princess Margaret to get involved in the new music scene. The November issue of *Dance Teacher* – the official magazine of the Midland Dance Teacher's Association – carried a damnation of the Princess for endorsing rock 'n' roll and 'hastening the demise of ballroom dancing.'

'From 1938 until last year rock (or jitterbug) was not respectable. Nice people did not do it,' *Dance Teacher* explained, and finished by avowing that the young Princess would 'get no bouquets' from the ballroom dance teachers of Britain for her actions.

What 'nice people' did for enjoyment and relaxation in 1957 probably involved *Woman* magazine, which since 1938 had consistently increased its appeal to the women of Britain. By 1952 the weekly publication was selling over 2.5 million copies and this went up to a massive 3.5 million by 1957, which meant that *Woman* was read by one out of every two women aged between 16 and 44 in the UK.

At the Royal Variety Show held in London in November, the Queen watched Britain's leading rock star Tommy Steele and, according to reports, 'clapped along' to his hit 'Singing The Blues'. However, within a month, Steele lost some of his rock 'n' roll credibility by signing up to appear in pantomime.

Perhaps in an effort to keep the rock 'n' roll flag flying for the Hicks family, Tommy Steele's brother Colin Hicks – also signed by Parnes but never given a new name – went on the road in a ten-week variety tour with Marty Wilde. One of the bands that backed Hicks as he tried to make a name for himself on the rock circuit was Les Hobeaux, the skiffle outfit that Darrell Smith-Lyte watched turn into a rock 'n' roll group – and, as he recalls, things occasionally got out of hand.

'When we were backing Colin Hicks, he tried to flirt with a couple of girls in the audience but the boyfriend of one of them began a verbal punch-up with Hicks in the theatre which brought a few boos,' says Smith-Lyte. Later, with Hicks nowhere to be seen, Smith-Lyte left by the stage door where he made a casual remark to a few of the girls who were hanging about. 'Then these three guys who were in the theatre rowing with Hicks appeared and my guitar went one way and I went the other, but fortunately the police were there to sort things out.'

In the months following US music magazine *Billboard*'s prediction that 'good music' was making a comeback although 'rock 'n' roll discs continue to dominate the pop market', a host of new stars appeared from America. Fats Domino charted with both 'Ain't That A Shame' and 'Blueberry Hill' ahead of Chuck Berry and 'Another School Day'.

They were followed in July by The Everly Brothers and 'Bye Bye Love' – a record they were paid $30 to record under the guidance of family friend and musician Chet Atkins – and then came Paul Anka with his number-one hit 'Diana'. Just ahead of Larry Williams' bizarrely titled 'Short Fat Fanny' and 'Reet Petite' by Jackie Wilson, came Jerry Lee Lewis' debut for Sun Records, 'Whole Lotta Shakin' Goin' On' which was immediately banned by most of America's radio stations on the grounds that it's not-so-subtle sexual innuendo was 'vulgar.' Even so the record reached number three in the US and introduced Lewis to the UK chart for the first time in late 1957.

Also debuting on the charts – and reaching number one – were The Crickets with 'That'll Be The Day', a song co-written by the group's singer Buddy Holly who also hit the charts as a solo artist in 1957 with 'Peggy Sue'. Texan Holly had signed two recording contracts – one with Brunswick Records as a member of The Crickets (with Jerry Allison, Niki Sullivan and Joe Maudlin) and one for a solo career with Coral Records.

While these acts were finally breaking through in Britain, they were established among the very best sellers in America, where a 16-year-old student was making his debut with his high school vocal group. 'I was in The Tokens at first,' says Neil Sedaka, who soon after went on to write songs for doo-wop groups such as The Penguins, The Channels and The Cookies while listening to the best in US music. 'I loved Fats Domino and Chuck Berry, whose marriage of words and music was magical, and Elvis and also Eddie Cochran who I thought wrote very good songs.'

As far as John Lennon was concerned, Chuck Berry 'really wrote stuff' even though his songs didn't always make sense to a teenager in Liverpool. 'Chuck Berry is one of the all-time great poets, a rock poet. The lyrics were fantastic, even though we didn't know what he was saying half the time,' said Lennon.

Tony Barrow, who worked with Lennon and his fellow Beatles in the Sixties, was also on hand to see the effect people like Berry and Holly had on the aspiring young songwriters. 'I think John and Paul were inspired to write their own songs while every other band around Liverpool were just playing Berry and Little Richard songs. They were very much inspired by those rock 'n' roll acts and it was their way of being different.'

Another musician who was overwhelmed by the music coming out of America was guitarist Joe Brown, who remembered the day his band's washboard player invited him to his house. 'He said I should go round to his house as he's got a record to play me. He had hired a gramophone from a company called Radio Rentals.'

The record was Little Richard's 'Long Tall Sally', his first UK top three hit, and Brown recalled the impact the song had on him the very first time he heard the opening chorus. 'Little Richard – rock 'n' roll. It just hit skiffle a knockout blow on the jaw.'

The arrival of all these new stars just about completed Len Goodman's musical wish-list as well. 'You didn't want to listen to what your parents liked and along came all my heroes – Little Richard, Jerry Lee, Buddy Holly and The Everlys ... that became my music then.'

For Tony Hall, the arrival of Buddy Holly gave him new opportunities at both Decca and Radio Luxembourg. 'On the Decca show I was told what to play by my bosses but I got round playing the records I hated by inventing something called America's Top Ten and playing records out of the *Billboard* chart,' says the man who went on to manage The Real Thing, Loose Ends and Lynden David Hall. 'I thought most of the British versions were inferior so I played the originals – Buddy Holly and hit R&B records from Atlantic.'

Reflecting on the state of rock 'n' roll on Britain's main radio broadcaster in the Fifties, Hall remembers that the BBC not only played very little rock 'n' roll but also had some strict rules. 'You couldn't use the word dedication because of the religious connotation and you had to submit a script to the BBC for approval at least ten days ahead of a show.'

Six-Five Special ventured out of their BBC studio to broadcast a rare live show from the 2-Is coffee bar with The King Brothers, Chas McDevitt, Wee Willie Harris and Don Lang, while ABC TV launched their rival offering Top Number, with Alma Cogan, Ronnie Hilton and Glen Mason on the first show.

Alongside the news that Elvis Presley was being lined up to play Hank Williams in an MGM bio-pic of the country and western star, a school headmaster in Bridgewater, Somerset was bemoaning the political knowledge of his 14 year-old students, compared to their awareness of rock 'n' roll. He calculated that out of a class of 30, only four knew of Pandit Nehru, the Prime Minister of India; just seven had heard of Nikita Khrushchev, leader of the USSR; 12 children were aware of American President Dwight Eisenhower. But, he claimed, 'Everyone was on Christian names terms with a Mr. Presley.'

The students would also no doubt have been aware of Little Richard who, in November 1957 and under the headline 'Little Richard Packs It Up', announced his retirement from show business in order to 'devote his life to evangelism and make only spiritual recordings.' The singer from in Georgia, USA had racked up eight UK top 30 hits in just over a year and on the eve of his 'retirement', recorded eight songs before entering theological college in Alabama.

The *NME*'s Top 30 chart for December 13 1957 featured Harry Belafonte at number one with 'Mary's Boy Child' but he was followed by a host of rock 'n' roll records from the likes of Elvis Presley ('Santa Bring

My Baby Back' and 'Let's Have A Party'), Paul Anka ('Diana'), The Crickets ('That'll Be The Day'), Little Richard ('Keep A Knockin'), Buddy Holly ('Peggy Sue') and the home-grown talent of Tommy Steele ('Handful of Songs').

Also in the mix at number two were Don and Phil Everly with a record which, despite being banned in America, still managed to top the US chart. 'Wake Up Little Suzie' seemingly upset both its producer and US radio stations with its implied suggestion that Suzie had not just 'slept over' but maybe had been with her boyfriend.

Surprisingly even the BBC didn't see this particular nuance and it seemed that the great British public were equally untroubled by Suzie's sleeping habits as they forked out to buy this and another 80 million records during 1957. The breakdown showed that 64 million of these discs were jazz and pop titles, with a third (26 million) being LPs, EPs and 45rpm records against 52 million 'old fashioned' 78s.

Chapter 5
1958: Marty. Cliff and Billy Fly The Flag

By early 1958, the programme that the BBC had devised for the 'young at heart' had made such an major impression on the youth, the new teenagers and the so-called young adults that *Six-Five Special* reported viewing figures in excess of six million. And it wasn't the only the television show that was setting new records as Britain displayed a growing enthusiasm for all things rock 'n' roll. Decca's plan to release Elvis Presley's latest record 'Jailhouse Rock' in the second week of January had to be shelved when their record factory was unable to meet the demand for advance orders which stood at over 250,000. When RCA's new UK agents finally managed to ship the record, it became the first single to enter the *NME* chart at number one and sold over 750,000 copies in three weeks.

Such was the interest in rock music and rock 'n' roll stars that a Manchester vicar persuaded the BBC's Home Service to include records by Presley, Lonnie Donegan, Frankie Vaughan and Tommy Steele in the religious programme *Lift Up Your Hearts*. 'Religion should be sold,' the minister argued. 'Teenagers need religion and if it is presented in their language then it can be sold to them.' In contrast Little Richard, who was about to enter the Seventh Day Adventist college in America, warned, 'I'd like to tell my fans that rock 'n' roll glorifies Satan.'

All this followed Alan Freed's Christmas Show at the Paramount Theatre in New York – featuring a star-studded bill with Buddy Holly and The Crickets, Fats Domino, The Everly Brothers, Jerry Lee Lewis and Danny and The Juniors – which broke all box-office records and resulted in Fats Domino taking home $28,000 for his week's work.

In competition with the rising number of American music makers releasing records in the UK, some of Britain's newest stars were busy taking their first steps on the ladder to success. While Adam Faith gave up his role as singer with skiffle group The Worried Men to sign a solo deal with EMI's HMV label and Harry Webb and The Drifters took part in an audition for the BBC's *Saturday Skiffle Club* programme, Marty Wilde's 'Afraid Of Love' – a track on his debut EP – was described by *Melody Maker* as being 'delivered with the appropriate touch of maudlin sentiment … this should register with adolescent romantics.'

Wilde recalls that he got into music through the efforts of impresario Larry Parnes. 'Larry's father was very wealthy and had several fashion shops in the west end of London and from there Larry got into showbiz.' After Wilde had been seen appearing at the Condor Club, by the up-and-coming song writer Lionel Bart, he and his family played hosts to Parnes, who quickly became known in the business as 'Mr Parnes, Shillings and Pence.'

'One Sunday Larry Parnes came down to our flat in Greenwich High Road and signed me up when I was 17,' says Wilde. 'I went in on a deal giving me 60% and him 40% but it was a chance to break the mould of where I lived and what I was doing. I knew it was what I wanted from the moment I saw *Rock Around The Clock* and heard Elvis' first album.'

A stable-mate of Wilde's in the Parnes' roster of artists found himself on the receiving end of both good and bad news in 1958. During his appearance at Liverpool's Royal Court Theatre in the pantomime *Goldilocks* in early 1958, Tommy Steele was heckled by students who, in turn, were pelted with ice cream cartons and orange peel by the singer's fans.

But if this episode had any lasting effect on Steele, it was probably forgotten when he was offered £2000 a week to star in a show at the prestigious London Palladium. He turned it down with his agent, explaining: 'The money doesn't matter. Tommy is earning plenty, nor does he *have* to play the Palladium.'

At the same time, rival singer Terry Dene made the headlines for all the wrong reasons following his arrest in Gloucester for causing damage to cars, shop windows and a telephone box. Fined £155, his actions were depicted in the media as the perfect illustration of 'everything that is wrong with rock 'n' roll.'

Despite the six-million-plus viewing figures for *Six-Five Special*, producer Jack Good decided to leave the BBC show in February 1958, a year after it was launched, but kept his future plans under wraps while *Melody Maker* confirmed rock's growing status in the UK with the headline: 'The Rock Sets In' above a story about sell-out UK tours by Buddy Holly and Paul Anka which concluded, 'The beat, like it or not, is here.'

On the eve of his first visit to Britain, Holly picked out his favourites for the same music paper. 'I like the Everlys as well as any of the artists. And Elvis is still one of my favourites, he helped us all plenty by paving the way. Eddie Cochran is another good artist.' In direct contrast to all these rebellious American best sellers, British orchestra leader Mantovani found himself lauded and applauded in the US when London Records gave him a special gold disc to recognise eight of his albums each selling 250,000. And he was given the award by Franklin D. Roosevelt, son of the late President Roosevelt, who was general counsel and a director of London.

Buddy Holly and The Crickets opened their UK tour with a show at the Trocadero Theatre in London's Elephant And Castle district on March 1 and in the audience that night was Len Goodman. 'I was still at school when I went to see him, but he was great and rock 'n' roll meant everything to me back then,' says the dancer and TV judge, before reflecting on another schoolboy memory. 'I was a milk monitor and I remember going round all the classrooms singing The Everlys' 'Bird Dog'.'

Supported by Gary Miller, The Tanner Sisters and The Montanas, with Des O'Connor as host, the opening night of Holly's 25-date tour was given a mixed review by *Melody Maker*'s man in the Trocadero. 'Excellent show but disappointed that Buddy Holly and the Crickets were on stage for little more than 20 minutes. With tickets up to 10s 6d (52½p), short weight is hardly forgiveable.'

For Radio Luxembourg disc jockey and Decca man Tony Hall, Holly's opening show holds a very particular and highly personal memory. 'On the night he was playing at the Trocadero one of his front teeth fell out and I had to get some chewing gum so he could stick the tooth back in and do that night's show.'

The Holly show moved on to the Midlands with two shows in Birmingham Town Hall on the evening of March 10 – one of which garnered the following observations from a local journalist. 'Buddy Holly, leader of the group, is a studious-looking young man who totes his electric guitar like a sawn-off shotgun and carries around a giant-sized amplifier which even made the Town Hall organ pipes flinch. He plays and sings with a brash exuberance and adds a few Presley-like wiggles which had the teenage audience squealing with delight.'

Seemingly happy enough with Holly's contribution – which was classed as '70 per cent of the act' – the reviewer seemed less enthusiastic about Crickets Joe B. Maudlin and drummer Jerry Allison. 'The rest of the group consists of a bass player whose ability was lost in the noise and a drummer who plays with sledge-hammer precision.'

On March 21 Jan Parsons travelled from Brixton in south London as far as the Walthamstow Granada in east London with her boyfriend to see the Buddy Holly show. 'It could have been a birthday present,' says the Jan, who was born on March 25. 'Nobody moved at all – everybody just sat in their seats. It was all very basic but he was fantastic. He just stood there on stage in front of a big curtain and they all wore suits and looked very smart.'

By the time he arrived in Britain, Holly had racked up three top ten hits in the UK and his 1957 US debut album *The Chirping Crickets* – with sleeve notes which included the unfortunate lines, 'Listen now, as four young Crickets give out with the most delightful 'chirping' you have ever heard' – was issued to tie-in with the tour. As there was no official British album chart, sales were impossible to judge but there was no doubt about the impact the album had on all young, aspiring guitar players ... in part because of the front cover photograph.

'As soon as we saw a picture of Buddy Holly with his Fender Stratocaster that was like a blow with a sledge hammer to us as skifflers, but it inspired John Lennon – particularly as he wore glasses,' recalls Rod Davis. On the eve of leaving the northeast of England to travel to London, Bruce Welch also saw the same album cover and was equally moved. 'We saw the Stratocaster on the cover and thought 'Wow, it looks like a space rocket!'.' He also recalled the effect Holly's picture had on his best mate. 'Buddy Holly gave anybody with glasses hope – as with Hank Marvin and John Lennon. Hank got his horn-rimmed glasses because of Buddy Holly.'

Lennon later recounted the impact Holly had on him. 'Buddy Holly was great and he wore glasses, which I liked although I didn't wear them in public for years and years. But (he) was the first one that we were really aware of in England who could play and sing at the same time – not just strum but actually play licks.' But for Paul McCartney it was another side of Holly's career that made an impression. 'John and I started writing because of Buddy Holly. It was like 'Wow. He writes and is a musician'.'

In fact McCartney was so impressed with Holly's writing that in 1976 he reportedly paid close to $10 million to acquire the rights to the songs written by Holly, plus those co-written with fellow Cricket Jerry Allison and producer Norman Petty.

The guitar pictured with Holly – the Fender Stratocaster – had been invented by Californian Leo Fender in 1956 as the follow-up to his original 1948 mass-produced Broadcaster model which was transformed into the better known Telecaster in 1951. It cost around $250 dollars to buy but was unavailable in this country because of Board of Trade regulations

which would ban the import of American goods –
including cars and guitars – into Britain until 1960,
leading to British guitarists being forced to settle for
German Hofner, Czech-made Resonet or Japanese
Antoria models.

'The least bad ones were Hofner,' says Davis, 'and
then there was a trickle of decent guitars which
transformed the music scene.' But while other guitars,
including the Gibson Les Paul 'gold top' model and
the newly invented Gibson Flying V, were available in
America and envied by ambitious young musicians in
this country, it was Fender's 'Strat' that created the
biggest stir.

Despite having bought the Crickets debut album –
with the photo of Holly and his guitar – Eric Clapton
was finally persuaded by the American quartet's
appearance on *Sunday Night At The London Palladium* on
March 2 1958. 'They had Buddy Holly on the show and
I thought I'd died and gone to heaven; that was when
I saw my first Fender guitar,' recalls the man known
internationally as 'Slowhand', who was on the verge
of becoming a teenager back then. 'It was like seeing
an instrument from outer space and I said to myself
'That's the future – that's what I want'.'

Having started out like so many groups as a skiffle
outfit, Richard Sarstedt's band changed players and
moved into rock 'n' roll but retained the name the
Fabulous Five. And they were also alerted to a young
man who made replica guitars. 'We went along to see

this kid who was making replica Fenders in his basement and it turned out to be Jeff Beck,' recounts Sarstedt, who then recruited him to join his band – although the future guitar hero's appearances were few and far between. 'He played when he bothered to turn up but he was pretty unreliable back then. But if he showed up everyone in the group was particularly happy as we never really expected him.'

While he didn't buy a Jeff Beck-made replica, Sarstedt did buy a guitar on hire purchase for £16. 'It was a huge amount money for me in those days and I had to pay it off over two years, but the guitar stayed in the family and in fact my brother Peter wrote his best seller 'Where Do You Got To My Lovely' on it years later.' (Peter Sarstedt hit number one in February 1969 and held the top spot for four weeks).

Eventually The Fabulous Five – both with and without Beck – were reduced to playing a few gigs at weekends as the various members got proper jobs. 'I had a job in the City and did the whole commuter thing on the bus and train for a couple of years' says Sarstedt. Their set included what Sarstedt described as 'The usual American stuff like 'Twenty Flight Rock' but we did attempt 'What'd I Say' because by then we had a piano player who knew how to play it.'

Despite his connections with Lennon and McCartney, Rod Davis remained stoically unmoved by what was happening all around him. 'Haley, Presley, Little Richard and Holly were the new heroes but I wasn't interested. It didn't have the impact on me that it had on other people. I knew that rock 'n' roll was there but I was into folk or bluegrass and I never watched any of the rock shows that were on TV.'

But it wasn't just rock shows that were on TV in the UK in 1958. The Saturday sports programme *Grandstand* started up, while the comedy series *The Larkins* and game show *Beat The Clock* were part of the light entertainment package. And new chocolate bars Picnic and Galaxy hit the shops alongside the cereal Puffed Wheat, which came with the added bonus of a free Lone Ranger mask with every packet.

Tragically, eight members of the Manchester United football team – plus a further 13 passengers – were killed in a plane crash at Munich airport in West Germany in February, and composer Vaughan Williams and Pope Pius XII also died in the year.

Life Peerages were introduced and the tradition of presenting of debutantes at court was abandoned after over 250 years. 'Debs' – girls or young ladies from aristocratic or upper class families – had been presented to the Sovereign since 1786 but in 1958 Queen Elizabeth II decided the practice had long outlived its useful purpose, although 'debs' continued to have 'coming-out' dances.

At the other end of the scale Jan Parsons recalls her visits to the West End (Central London) as a young teenager. 'On Saturday mornings I went with my mother to Selfridges. We'd go through the double doors and touch the ladies who wore fur coats – it was a different world.'

Part of the enjoyment for Parsons was seeing the range of clothing that was not available in areas of London such as Brixton. 'We looked at things that you couldn't get where we lived and then, when the shops shut at noon, we got back on the bus to come home.' While Parsons recalls one shop 'near the Astoria that started having fashion items', it was mainly the local market stalls that provided her with the latest items. 'There were a couple of places in the market that sold pointed shoes for girls but we never bought trousers – it was always skirts.'

However, alongside the West End stores, local shops and market stalls, mail order catalogues - which offered weekly or monthly payments – proved popular with the nation's shoppers. The latest man-made fibres were also becoming all the rage with Polyester, Crimplene and Courtelle which offered the benefits of permanent pleats, drip-dry and 'minimum iron.' Bikinis were also on offer for brave young things to wear at the beach or the swimming pool, while a new wide range of American make-up was introduced by Max Factor.

As more and more records poured into Britain from American singers such as Ricky Nelson, Duane Eddy and Conway Twitty, plus groups like The Poni-Tails, The Chordettes, The Champs, The Kalin Twins, The Fleetwoods and The Teddy Bears, the music papers' reviewers posted some interesting observations.

Melody Maker reckoned that Jackie Wilson was a sort of 'American Wee Willie Harris', while the *NME* decided that Connie Francis was best described as 'pert and provocative' and also took to referring to Little Richard as 'Wee Dick.'

But rock 'n' roll was still a long way from taking over the world as Tommy Steele found out when he was banned from appearing in Pretoria, South Africa because it was decided that he was 'prejudicial to public morals' following a riot by 300 youths at an earlier show in Cape Town. The same fate befell Terry Dene when his tour of South Africa was cancelled as he was considered to be 'a bad example to South African teenagers.'

Meanwhile, as newsagents W.H. Smith entered the music business with the opening of their first record department in the Kingsway branch in London, Bruce Welch and his mate Hank Marvin finally arrived in the capital in pursuit of their rock 'n' roll dream. They came down with the group The Railroaders and headed straight to the Granada theatre in Edmonton to take part in a talent show. 'We rehearsed in the afternoon and Brian Bennett (later to join The Shadows) was the drummer in one of the other bands – so we met Brian on our very first day in London,' recalls Welch.

'We lost the contest and two of the guys went back home but Hank and I decided to stay – we had left school but had no money,' says Welch who, not surprisingly, made his way straight to Soho and the famous 2-Is. 'It was the place to be because it had been in the paper as the heart of the coffee-bar scene. It was heaving, it was exciting – and we were sixteen. There were Teddy Boys there to see Rory Blackwell and Tony Crombie.'

Despite being paid only one pound, Welch and Marvin agreed to play at the 2-Is – where they met the likes of The Vipers, Jet Harris, Tony Meehan, Vince Taylor and Terry Dene – before teaming up with Paul Chester – the son of top comedian Charlie Chester – in The Five Chesternuts. Together they made a record and scored their first TV appearance. 'We made 'Teenage Love' in July 1958, and then were on *Six-Five Special*, which we had never seen until we appeared on it.'

Unsure of what lay ahead, Welch did have an idea of who they wanted to be. 'We did start out with the idea of being singers – Hank and I thought we were Don and Phil (Everly) until we heard ourselves on tape and then we needed a Plan B.' And that involved them becoming, in Welch's words, yet another 'tribute band' playing the music they heard coming out of America. 'We all had the same heroes so we would all cover the same songs.'

By May 1958 the *MM* had decided that skiffle had little or no future as – under the headline 'Skiffle On The Skids' – they broke the news that Bob Cort and Dickie Bishop (and his Sidekicks) were retiring, while The Vipers no longer billed themselves as a skiffle group. Another nail was banged into skiffle's coffin by the news that Jack Good had plans for a new TV rock

BILL HALEY'S COMETS

Personal Direction
JAMES H. FERGUSON
801 Barclay St.
Chester, Penna.

JOE GLASER, President
NEW YORK, CHICAGO, HOLLYWOOD

Bill Haley & His Comets topped the charts in the US and UK with 'Rock Around the Clock'

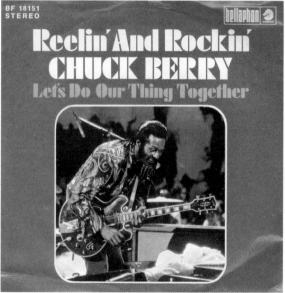

Elvis Presley and Chuck Berry – two rock 'n' roll greats whose records inspired a new generation of acts

A couple energetically twisting the night away at the Cavern in Liverpool

*The Beatles – Paul McCartney, John Lennon, Pete Best and George Harrison -
and a 'flyer' from 1963 when it cost 47p to see them at the Cavern*

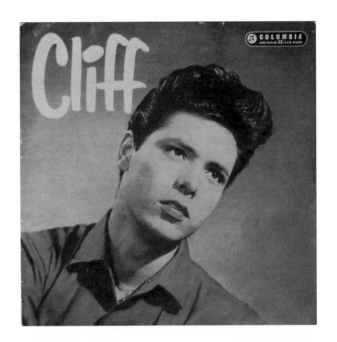

Cliff Richard and The Shadows, who charted together and separately throughout the Fifties and Sixties

 GERRY AND THE PACEMAKERS
COLUMBIA RECORDS

Gerry Marsden pictured without his Pacemakers

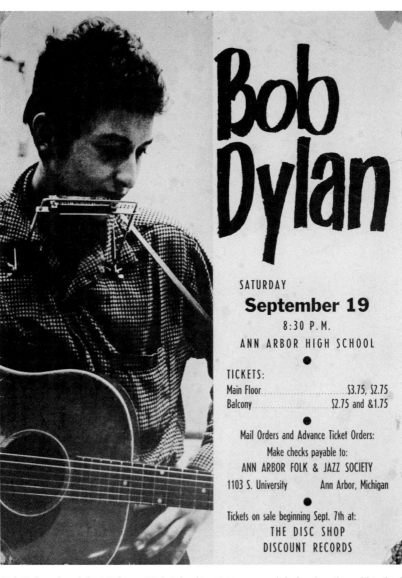

SATURDAY
September 19
8:30 P.M.
ANN ARBOR HIGH SCHOOL

●

TICKETS:
Main Floor.............................$3.75, $2.75
Balcony.........................$2.75 and &1.75

●

Mail Orders and Advance Ticket Orders:
Make checks payable to:
ANN ARBOR FOLK & JAZZ SOCIETY
1103 S. University   Ann Arbor, Michigan

●

Tickets on sale beginning Sept. 7th at:
THE DISC SHOP
DISCOUNT RECORDS

Bob Dylan played the Michigan High School in 1964 - a month before he released his third album Another Side Of Bob Dylan

Two of Manchester's finest … Peter Noone gets up close with his fans while The Hollies' front three - Tony Hicks, Allan Clarke and Graham Nash – do the business on stage

A queue to get into the Cavern, which was the hottest club in Liverpool for over 15 years

THE ROLLING STONES

The Rolling Stones line up of (l to r) Mick Jagger, Keith Richards, Brian Jones, Charlie Watts and Bill Wyman made their debut in January 1963

The Beatles with 'new' drummer Ringo Starr (third from left), who replaced Pete Best, part of an unused photo-shoot for a Liverpool jeans manufacturer in 1963

&

1/-

FEBRUARY, 1965   VOL. 1. No. 5.

BRITAIN'S LEADING
Rhythm & Blues
MAGAZINE

Featuring the Life Stories of:

SLIM HARPO and ELMORE JAMES

Photo-Features on:

THE COASTERS, JOHNNY OTIS, etc.

◀ *Jimmy Reed*

▼ *Rod Stuart*

RHYTHM & BLUES
IN BRITAIN

A Special Survey Including:

ROD STUART
ALEXIS KORNER
GRAHAM BOND
SPENCER DAVIES

A 1965 copy of R&B Scene magazine featuring Britain's best R&B acts, including a certain Rod Stuart ... or should that be Stewart?

Jimi Hendrix (left) and Cat Stevens relax backstage during their 1967 tour with Engelbert Humperdinck and The Walker Brothers; and The Monkees - (left to right) Mickey Dolenz, Davy Jones, Mike Nesmith and Peter Tork - who had six UK hits in 1967

The first record played on BBC Radio One in September 1967 was The Move's Flowers In the Rain

The Supremes - Diana Ross, Mary Wilson and Florence Ballard – were the first Motown act to top the UK singles chart

ALREADY A SMASH IN ENGLAND*
and
NOW AVAILABLE IN AMERICA ON DECCA° RECORDS

MY GENERATION
by
THE WHO
31877

* #4 ON THE ENGLISH CHARTS IN JUST 10 DAYS

Produced by Shel Talmy

The Who made it to number two in the UK with 'My Generation' but peaked at #74 with their US release

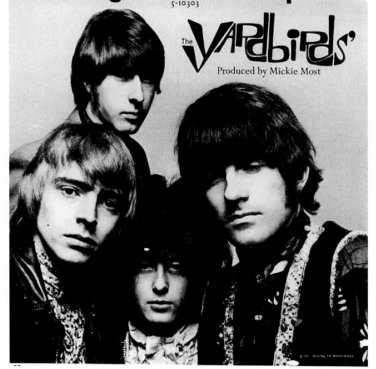

The Girls Stay
in the
Spotlight at

EPIC

from
"Jennifer Juniper"
to
"Jennifer Eccles"
Now it's

"Goodnight Sweet Josephine"
5-10303

The **YAYdbiYds**

Produced by Mickie Most

The last single release by the Yardbirds featuring (left to right) Keith Relf, Chris Dreja, Jim McCarty and (bottom) Jimmy Page

Radio Caroline's pirate station first broadcast in 1964, launched by Irish musician manager and businessman Ronan O'Rahilly, the station named after US president John F Kennedy's daughter

show which he announced, in a thinly disguised dig at his earlier BBC show *Six-Five Special*, would show 'the stars undisturbed and uninterrupted by amateur skiffle groups, coffee-bar cowboys and arty ballet dancers.'

In preparation, Good looked for an all-girl group to feature in his new show and one of the candidates was Joyce Baker, who had caught the rock 'n' roll bug and even been to see a young man called Marty Wilde in Liverpool a year earlier. 'I saw him at the Liverpool Empire when I was just one of thousands of screaming girls and I just wanted to meet him.' Part of the process towards meeting Wilde involved Baker singing at an audition in front of the people from Good's new show. 'I sang 'Stupid Cupid' and then they asked how my parents would react to me joining the Vernons Girls and going to London.'

Following the audition, Baker and three of her fellow hopefuls got into a taxi with their minder Miss Finnegan. 'She told me I had got through and then we went down to London where we stayed at the Collonade Hotel with just the one chaperone.'

At the same time Harry Webb had already decided that his future lay in music … but perhaps under a different name. While playing at the 2-Is, Webb met songwriter Ian Samwell who joined his backing band The Drifters and then spent an evening in a Soho pub with Webb, manager John Foster and fellow band member Norman Mitcham. They talked about a new name for the band's frontman. 'We were competing with names like Jerry Lee Lewis, Buddy Holly and Elvis Presley ... and Harry Webb didn't come close,' Webb confides.

The process involved suggestions such as Russ and Clifford which resulted in Russ Clifford, which then became Cliff Russard before it got to Cliff Richards and finally the S was dropped and Cliff Richard was born. 'Two Christian names – Cliff and Richard was unusual,' the singer later observed. 'And it could also be a tribute to Little Richard.'

But before Cliff could get his new name in lights, a star from America arrived in Britain in the full glare of publicity – and for all the wrong reasons. Jerry Lee Lewis brought his new bride to the UK – his 13-year-old second cousin Myra who he married in December 1957 while he was still married to his previous wife. Despite finally divorcing Jane Mitcham in April 1958, Lewis' marriage was condemned by American religious leaders, while the British media and the public launched an even bigger protest which resulted in 34 of his scheduled 37 shows being cancelled.

Melody Maker's American correspondent had told UK readers that Britain could judge Lewis for themselves, but warned 'for better or worse, they will find that he is truly the wildest of all on the current scene.' The same paper's review of his opening night commented on the sensation Lewis had caused, 'not through his frantic work on stage but the rather frantic state of his marital affairs'. It added that 'the 100,000 or so fans who might have seen him have missed very little.' The *Daily Sketch* suggested that Lewis was 'an unappetizing fellow.'

Among those who went to the Kilburn State theatre in north London to see Lewis on May 25 1958 were Welch, Marvin and Cliff Richard, although the three of them didn't know each other and didn't meet that night. 'Jerry Lee was sensational, outrageous and nobody else was like him at all,' says Welch, while producer and broadcaster Tony Hale recalls, 'The thing about Jerry Lee was that he was the 'Killer' and he would trash the local authority piano worth around £10,000 on stage and then say 'I've beaten up better pianos than this'. He just kicked the shit out of it.'

The final show on the ill-fated tour – which opened at Edmonton on May 24 – was in South London at Tooting Granada on May 26 where previously loyal and devoted fans of Lewis turned on the star and shouted 'we hate Jerry' and 'cradle robber.' With Lewis on his way out, promoters Lew and Leslie Grade brought in Chas McDevitt's Skiffle Band and singer Terry Wayne as replacements acts alongside American group The Treniers and Britain's Hedley Ward Trio to take the tour through to its conclusion in Guildford on June 29.

While Lewis' response to the hysteria he had created was to say, 'They come down on us pretty hard' before adding, 'The newspapers did all they could to destroy us,' his manager Oscar Davis was intent on getting something out of the abandoned tour. After Lewis, his wife and the rest of his entourage returned to the US – following announcements that the tour had been cancelled for what were described as 'unfavourable audience reactions and for other reasons' – Davis explained that he was going to try and collect some fees for his star turn. 'I will stay behind until this arrangement has been made. I think I shall keep Jerry back home in the States for some time.'

However, when he was 'back home' in America, Jerry Lee Lewis was forced to react to the negative reporting of his marriage and his shows being cancelled by taking out a five-page advertisement in the music trade magazines to explain himself. He said, 'I confess my life has been stormy. I confess further that since I became a public figure, I sincerely wanted to be worthy of the decent admiration of all the people who liked what talent – if any – I have.'

Despite this public pronouncement, Sun Records still pulled back the promotion of Lewis' records as US radio refused to give him airtime, while Britain's Minister of Labour Iain MacLeod faced questions from Norfolk Central MP Sir Frank Medlicott who asked, 'Is my right honourable friend aware that great offence was caused to many people by the arrival of this man (Jerry Lee Lewis) with his thirteen year-old bride. Will he remember also that we have enough rock 'n' roll entertainers of our own without importing them from overseas.'

In reply, Macleod explained that Lewis was issued

with a permit to tour the UK under the Variety & Entertainment quota agreement but admitted that 'this was a thoroughly unpleasant case.'

Around this time Hale was also busy with his own skiffle band which, like so many others, was on the turn towards a different kind of music. 'We played the 2-I's as a skiffle band and never got paid our 15s (75p) so we never went back. Then we got a residency in a pub called the Montague Arms in Peckham, which was home to some south London gangsters, and there we played rock 'n' roll.'

And Hale also recalls the excitement caused by the car driven by the gangsters' associate who booked their gigs in Peckham. 'He had a pink Vauxhall Cresta – how exciting was that! Elvis had a pink Cadillac and a pink jacket. This was before there were any girly connections to pink – it was because they could afford to have something as stupid and as flash as that.'

All this was going on while around 6000 people were walking from Trafalgar Square to the atomic research site in Aldermaston, Berkshire on the first Campaign For Nuclear Disarmament (CND) protest march, and The Beverly Sisters (twins Babs and Teddy plus sister Joy) were being banned from singing 'Long Black Nylons' on Dutch TV because the words 'might cause offence.'

With Presley firmly entrenched in the US Army (after finally being called up in March following a 60 day reprieve to finish filming), Little Richard taking religious studies and Jerry Lee Lewis embroiled in a very messy marriage, Neil Sedaka reckoned he was 'in the right place at the right time' to offer his non-controversial brand of pop songs. 'I was into more clean-cut pop which was beginning to make an impression,' he says.

Jack Good's new TV show *Oh Boy* was finally launched with two pilot episodes in June, which brought an immediate positive reaction. Aiming to pack 17 'beat numbers' into 35 minutes, Good featured Marty Wilde, The Dallas Boys, Cherry Wainer and Lord Rockingham's XI in a show which, according to presenter Tony Hall, remains, 'The most exciting TV pop rock show I have ever seen.'

Hall was recruited by Good to host *Oh Boy* – alongside fellow radio disc jockey Jimmy Henney – as a result of his visits to a jazz club. 'Jack (Good) used to come to the Flamingo so he knew my style and although he knew I liked jazz he respected me as a professional presenter. He thought my fast delivery would be good for *Oh Boy*.'

Making the pilot shows in black and white and filming them live at the Hackney Empire theatre gave *Oh Boy* an all-important edge, according to Hall. 'The show moved like the clappers but the lighting was the secret and Rita Gillespie was in charge of that. She was the secret weapon of *Oh Boy* and when it went to colour the show lost some of its magic.'

While Good was perfecting his new TV show, the recently formed Cliff Richard and The Drifters were taking part in a talent contest at the Shepherd's Bush Gaumont where they impressed an agent who passed word to Columbia recording boss Norrie Paramor, who subsequently invited the group to an audition in his office. 'We literally went to his office at EMI in Great Castle Street and we just plugged a little Selmer amplifier into the wall and strummed 'Move It',' says Richard.

And, according to the singer, 'Move It' had been written by Samwell on the bus ride over to the audition in Paramor's office which earned them the opportunity to record in a studio for the first time. It was on July 24 that Cliff and The Drifters – Ernie Shears, Frank Clarke, Terry Smart and Ian Samwell – stepped into Abbey Road's Studio 2 to make their first record. 'We went in to the studio, did a practice run and the next thing I knew we were recording,' said Richard.

And during that session, Richard recalled that he performed with a guitar slung around his neck. 'The strange thing was that I couldn't sing without the guitar even though I never played it very well. I started the session without the guitar and it wasn't working out too well and Norrie just suggested I put the guitar on. I just held it and it all happened.'

Oddly, Richard and his band weren't actually signed to EMI's Columbia division when they made their recording debut in Abbey Road – performing 'Move It' and 'Schoolboy Crush' – but that was put right on August 9 when a deal was finally done on the eve of the group travelling to Clacton-on-Sea in Essex for a four-week residency at the local Butlins Holiday Camp.

Also out on the road in Britain in those days was Terry Slater and his group The Flintstones, which had a larger line-up than most, with guitar, bass, drums, keyboards, baritone sax and two tenor saxes. 'It was quite expensive and I was responsible for it all because it was my band,' recalls Slater. And even though he was only around 16 years old, Slater was in charge of getting his band to the gigs and also for sorting out the group's finances. 'We all travelled in an old Commer van and I remember saying to everybody that they could either take a share of what we earned on the night or have a weekly salary.'

With his seven-piece group going out for between £30 and £40 a night, the teenage bandleader was relieved when, as he explained, his musicians turned down a share of the night's takings. 'They all took the salary which was better for me because if we did seven nights we were really earning and then I got to keep what was left after I paid the salaries.' But The Flintstones got even better money when they played the American Forces bases which were dotted around Britain in the 1950s. 'We earned really good money there and if you played Christmas and New Year's gigs they would pay up to £100. If it wasn't for the British groups, those US servicemen would have had no entertainment at all.'

With The Everly Brothers holding the number-one spot in the UK with 'All I Have To Do Is Dream',

Laurie London became the first UK act to earn a gold disc from the RIAA (Recording Industry Association of America) for US sales of 'He's Got The Whole World In His Hands'. At the same time the first ever US gold album award went to the musical *Oklahoma*, while in Britain the Board of Trade issued figures which showed that UK record sales in April 1958 had passed the one million mark, an increase of 22% compared to April 1957.

Two of Britain's emerging rock singers were in the news for different reasons during the summer of 1958. Marty Wilde – who was yet to have a hit record – was on the road playing a series of one-night stands around the country, and somewhere along the line the *NME* caught his act and suggested that his live performance had 'improved measurably' and added that on record he showed, 'A degree of confidence quite remarkable for a performer so youthful.'

On the other hand, Terry Dene received his call-up papers for National Service in the Kings Royal Rifle Corps, based at Winchester Barracks. But less than a year later, he was declared unfit to serve and dismissed from the army at around the same time as Wilde was rejected for National Service for being medically unfit – reports suggested he had 'defective feet'. Interestingly the likes of Cliff Richard, Bruce Welch, Hank Marvin and Billy Fury avoided being called up into the Armed Forces because they were born after 1940, the cut-off point for new conscripts set by the Government in 1957.

Meanwhile the news from America was that Alan Freed's famous package tour would definitely not be coming to the UK after all the speculation, as negotiations finally broke down over demands for a guaranteed $13,000 against 50% of the gross takings – up to $50,000 – from the shows. But what was definitely on its way was Presley's new film *King Creole* – described in the advertising blurb as 'a story pulsating with the very heartbeat of today's youth' – and the soundtrack album. To go with these, you could also buy an Elvis Presley Guitar from Selcol for 79gns (£82.19s) complete with a full-colour picture of Elvis on the head.

And at the British premier of the film at the Odeon cinema in London's Marble Arch, hearts were sent fluttering when Elvis was reportedly spotted in the building. In fact it turned out to be a stunt organised by the Presley fan club with 18-year-old clerk Deke Everett appearing as a lookalike, complete with 'pre-Army sideburns.'

But as the original rock 'n' roller Bill Haley racked up 18 long months out of the British charts since his 1957 sell-out tour, a new star arrived. Ricky Nelson had half a dozen US hits under his belt when he finally hit number one in America and the top five in the UK with 'Poor Little Fool', which was the first record to top the newly launched Billboard Hot 100 chart. But it wasn't just Nelson's performance which caught people's attention as Bruce Welch recounts. 'His record said Ricky Nelson with instrumental accompaniment – and that was James Burton on guitar, but we didn't know who he was back then.'

For Terry Slater, who moved to America in the Sixties and worked regularly with The Everly Brothers, American guitarists were the stuff of heroes. 'Scotty Moore (who played guitar behind Elvis Presley alongside bass player Bill Black) and James Burton were people you heard on record,' he says.

'As young musicians, you picked out bits of a record and then tried to play like that and you had to find out who was playing behind the singer because they weren't credited.' Years later, when he sat in on his first recording session for The Everly Brothers, Slater recalls the people he sat next to in the studio. 'I was playing bass and was seated between James Burton and Glen Campbell, who was also one of the finest session guitarists in those days.'

Pete Townshend, the man who co-founded The Who in the early 1960s, was equally impressed by these sidemen. 'I did like James Burton who played with Rick Nelson – he was a big influence', he commented in 1980. Future Rolling Stone Keith Richards was also moved. 'I never bought a Ricky Nelson record. I bought a James Burton record. It was the bands behind them that impressed me as much as the front men.' And he applied the same thinking to Presley's musicians. 'I was even more impressed by Scotty Moore and the band.'

But while Nelson's guitarist, who would later go on

to play with Presley, was making an impression on an assortment of ambitious young musicians, the quartet known as The Quarry Men were indulging themselves in a hometown recording session where they paid to play tribute to one of their heroes.

For the princely sum of 17s 6d (87½p), Lennon, McCartney, Harrison, Colin Hanton and John Lowe – who each put in 3s 6d (17½p) – went into a backroom demo-studio in Kensington, Liverpool in August 1958 to cut a shellac disc. They chose Buddy Holly's chart topper 'That'll Be The Day' as one track and a McCartney original called 'In Spite Of All The Danger' – 'a little song influenced by Elvis', according to the composer – as the B-side. They then agreed to keep the only copy of the record for a week each, although it seems Lowe kept it for 23 years before McCartney bought it back for what he described as 'a very inflated price.'

On September 13 1958 MM's Laurie Henshaw included the debut release from Cliff Richard and The Drifters in his run-down of the new singles and described the original A-side, 'Schoolboy Crush', as a 'promising disc debut', although he thought it followed the 'tortured vocal pattern that seems to be the vogue these days.' Flipping the disc, he announced that 'Move It' was 'in the Presley idiom but lives up to its title.'

On the same day, Richard and his band made their debut on Good's new show *Oh Boy* and the singer was determined to make an impression. 'I was going to be a bit outrageous and I bought myself a pink jacket, black shirt, luminous pink socks and grey suede shows ... grey because Elvis had sung about blue suede shoes and I didn't want to follow him.'

While Richard appeared without a guitar and minus his sideburns – 'Jack Good said it would make me look more original' – it was his antics in front of the cameras which made the headlines. The *NME* declared his performance 'vulgar' and suggested that 'his violent hip swinging was revolting – hardly the kind of performance any parent could wish their children to see.' Richard defended himself. 'My gyrations are conducive to the type of songs I sing. They express the rhythm and drive of the beat number.' And on the question of him being sexy he answered, 'I'm not consciously trying to be.' Meanwhile Tommy Steele was an unlikely beneficiary from the outburst against Richard as *NME* took the view that the man who made 'Singing The Blues' was altogether more acceptable and said so in print. 'Tommy Steele became Britain's teenage idol without resorting to this form of indecent, short-sighted vulgarity.'

Whether 'vulgar' or 'sexy' (or neither), Richard's debut single was soon flipped with 'Move It' being promoted as the A-side, and in October it reached number two in the UK chart and even earned a plaudit from John Lennon. 'I think the first English record that was anywhere near anything was 'Move It' ... before that there had been nothing.'

However, the first star of *Oh Boy* was Marty Wilde, who made his debut on the chart in August with a version of the American song 'Endless Sleep'. 'It was easier to do cover versions of American hits although you were always trying to get guys here to play like American musicians but it was impossible,' he suggests.

And if his plan did work it was, in Wilde's opinion, more by luck than judgement. 'If you did manage it, it was just a fluke. 'Move It', sound-wise, was a semi-fluke and 'Endless Sleep' was a semi-fluke,' says Wilde, recalling who he hired to play guitar on the track. 'Bert Weedon played guitar and I tried to get him to play like Duane Eddy and he got it and I know it helped him in his career.' In fact the Eddy-style of playing had come to the fore with the American guitar star's arrival on the scene with what the media called a 'twangy guitar' sound.

Having appeared on *Six-Five Special* before switching to *Oh Boy*, Wilde is able to compare the two shows. '*Six Five Special* was like a Sunday school tea party but I did it because it was popular. When we did *Oh Boy* we became very aware that this was it!' And how the new young British stars appeared on the small screen was all down to the show's innovative producer, according to Wilde.

'Jack Good would spend two or three days on one song. He would go over and over it until it was right – it would drive me round the bend.' One of Good's tricks involved drawing squares on a map of the stage as a guide. 'He would say how he would shoot from one angle to get darkness in my eyes and then shoot from somewhere else and I would have to look in a particular direction – but never at the camera.'

Told to think like a 'method actor' during the TV show, Wilde recalls, 'When I did look at the camera it was all arranged and never accidental. Looking down, looking up, clutch yourself … Jack had come of age by the time he got to *Oh Boy*.' And, according to Wilde all this was 'part of the game and the criticism about our movements and poses meant nothing at all.' The result was that *Oh Boy* quickly became Britain's favourite rock show – 'we'd be playing to the whole nation with 2000 kids outside the theatre shouting and screaming,' adds Wilde.

For Joyce Baker, *Oh Boy* was a 'magical mix', with Neville Taylor and The Cutters and Lord Rockingham's XI as regulars on the show alongside '16 Vernon Girls in shorts or flared skirts up on three steps on a ramp as a back drop.' But as far as Baker was concerned, *Oh Boy* was all about one man.

'Jack was the star and he was a genius who was held in great reverence by everyone and the lovely part of it all was it being live … the minute it went on air the crowd just went crazy,' she says. And she also remembers that Good had a special knack for spotting a TV moment. 'One time he picked out three of the Vernon Girls and one was wearing an eye patch because she had done something to her eye. She thought she wouldn't be allowed to appear but Jack thought it added something to the show – and it did.'

As co-host of *Oh Boy*, Tony Hall has a particular memory of the show – the one occasion when he was lost for words. 'It went out live and it was the only time I ever blanked on TV or radio. There was no autocue and I dried up during one intro – and it seemed like the longest time imaginable.'

Hall was also impressed with the efforts of the show's producer. 'Jack Good used to get down on his knees and work the audience up during the warm-ups – he was absolutely amazing. All the looks and stances and camera angles came from Jack.'

And even though jazz remained his music of choice, Hall looks back on *Oh Boy* with fond memories. 'It was against my musical tastes but I was very proud to be involved with *Oh Boy* because I thought it was ground-breaking and exciting.'

Journalist and publicist Tony Barrow was equally impressed by what he was seeing on television in 1958. 'Those shows were very exciting and followed on from the cinema success that Haley had had a few years earlier. Jack Good saw that if you could do that with a black and white film on a big screen, how much more excitement could you generate with people gyrating around the studio,' he says. 'And it brought in a younger audience.'

While all this excitement was happening on British TV, the number one star of rock 'n' roll was busy being a soldier in Germany and, as *NME* observed that Presley was now 'a mere hop from the stage of Britain', the man himself was telling the media, 'Sure I'd like to see England and if I can manage to get a three-day pass I hope to get over there from Germany.'

After failing with their debut release, 'Teenage Love', Welch and Marvin were forced to return to the 2-I's coffee bar where they appeared as The Geordie Boys while also operating the orange juice and cola machines, until Richard's manager spotted Marvin playing with The Vipers and invited him to join The Drifters.

Marvin agreed but only on the condition that his mate Welch came too and in October a new Drifters line-up of Marvin, Welch, Samwell and Smart went on the road as part of a tour featuring The Kalin Twins (Americans Herb and Hal), The Vipers, trumpeter Eddie Calvert and The Most Brothers who were Mickie Most (later to become the producer of The Animals, Donovan and Kim Wilde) and Alex Wharton (producer of The Moody Blues hit 'Go Now'), plus compere Des O'Connor.

For some, shows like these – which featured rock and pop groups alongside a trumpeter and a comedian – were only one step up from the package tours which featured novelty acts, comedians and a dance orchestra and still played in Britain's theatres. 'Some rock 'n' roll bills were dreadful because the package tour business was still run by people who made their money in the music hall of 1930s and 1940s and they didn't understand,' says Tony Hale. 'So you got a rock act and a comic and a tin whistler and some dancers all on the same bill.'

And according to Cliff Richard this was all part of the learning process. 'When I began, singers were encouraged to be all-round entertainers, to do pantomime and variety and films and so we worked with people like Des O'Connor, Joan Regan and jugglers and vaudeville people.'

While Welch recalls the running order on his first tour – 'The Kalin Twins were top of the bill and Eddie Calvert closed the first half, while we opened the second half' – he also recollects that the rock 'n' roll antics of Cliff and The Drifters caused a few problems. 'The Kalin Twins had an issue with all the screaming for Cliff who was doing his thing and I was on my back playing guitar. We did rock 'n' roll – 'Move It' and some American tracks – and eventually they moved us to close the first half with Calvert opening the second half. But it wasn't a rock 'n' roll show – it was variety.'

Even at this early stage of their careers Cliff and The Drifters resisted the temptation to look like rockers. 'We never wore drapes and we never appeared on stage as Teddy Boys. We tried to look smart and to follow the teenage fashion,' says Welch before adding, 'But looking back at the photos, we all looked like Bill Gates compared to Elvis or Marlon Brando or James Dean.'

Clothes were also important to Wilde and even though he was a rising star, he still had trouble finding the gear he needed to look the part. 'Getting American jeans was almost impossible and it was the cargo boats coming into the docks in Liverpool and London with clothes and records that made things change,' he reflects. 'But even as rock stars we struggled to get the right kind of clothes that we wanted to wear.'

Jen Blowes faced the same problem in Essex as she looked around Chelmsford for up-to-the-minute fashions. 'There was a shop called Stones where you could buy Levi jeans but they were for men so you had to alter them to fit,' she recalls. And even when she found a local shop selling authentic jeans, they still weren't accepted at most dance halls and clubs. 'Boys couldn't get into places without a suit and tie and they wore a suit to go everywhere,' she says, while recalling one particular item of casual clothing that made a lasting impression. 'Boys wore big mohair jumpers that their mums made for them.'

Mrs. Blowes also remembers that a variation on the new arrangement called hire purchase extended to local clothes shops. 'You had an account where you would pick out a dress and ask them to keep it until you had enough money to pay for it. You didn't take it away and wear it until you had paid for it.'

If looking the part was important, then sounding good was equally important but not always easy says Welch. 'We didn't have any PA on the early tours. There were sound systems in the cinemas which were usually two speakers built into the columns either side of the screen. And a microphone or maybe two mikes if you were lucky – that was it.' Undaunted, The Drifters turned up with an amplifier and guitars but minus a mixing desk and monitors and, according to Welch, 'We just played as loud as we could with just the house lights which were set across the front of the stage.'

With the arrival of *Oh Boy*, a common bond was created between rival rock stars – including Wilde and Richard, according to Welch. 'There was a camaraderie between us all back then and at that time Marty was bigger than Cliff. But we all loved rock 'n' roll and there were maybe ten artists whose records you bought - people like Jerry Lee, Little Richard, Elvis, Buddy, The Everlys and Fats Domino who were all different but all rock 'n' roll.'

And if Wilde tried to get his guitarists to play like Americans, Welch was also in awe of the sounds that emerged from the records that came from across the Atlantic. 'American recording techniques were so far ahead of ours and that was down to the equipment and the people. Our tracks were mono on one track while they had two track or even four track back then.'

And as he listened to Buddy Holly's song 'Words Of Love', Welch was left confused. 'I could never figure out how he sang with himself – it was impossible for us to do that here. The sound of American records was always superior to what we got and we didn't have the people who could do that. Here we recorded a singer and an orchestra and a choir all at once with no multi-tracking.' *Oh Boy* host Hall was another big fan of the records which were made in America – 'the musicianship and production was superior to ours.'

Wilde also reflected on the state of British songwriting at the time. 'My early records were all covers of American hits because there were no writers here who could create rock 'n' roll songs. Ian Samwell was one of the first but then I started writing my own songs.' And while most of the musicians playing on the recording sessions were jazz players – 'they were trying to play this new music' says Wilde – the situation with producers was far from perfect. 'They were from another school and a lot older than us new singers – mine was Johnny Franz but there was also Norman Newell, Norrie Paramor and Wally Ridley. They had all started out making records in the 1940s – a decade before rock 'n' roll.'

The *NME* Poll for 1958 reflected some of the changes that had taken place in popular music in just a couple of years. Elvis Presley was the World's Outstanding Singer, Top Musical Personality and Top US Male, while Connie Francis was judged Top US Female Singer and The Everly Brothers emerged as the World's Top Group. However, Britain's Top Male Singer was Frankie Vaughan, with Alma Cogan voted Top Female Singer and The Mudlarks as Top Group, but there was some comfort to be drawn from the fact that Cliff Richard and Marty Wilde were numbers one and two in the Best British Newcomer category.

Another new name was about to arrive on the scene in late 1958, when Liverpool deckhand Ronald Wycherley talked his way into Wilde's dressing room during Larry Parnes' Rock Extravaganza tour of the UK. As a budding singer, guitarist and songwriter, Wycherley – a former schoolmate of Richard Starkey before he became Ringo Starr – gave Parnes an impromptu demo which resulted in him being invited to go on stage that night and sing to his hometown audience. Within hours Wycherley was signed by Parnes and within days he was re-named Billy Fury. Within weeks he had signed a recording deal with Decca Records.

With *Oh Boy* going from strength to strength as TV's hottest show, Joyce Baker returned home to Liverpool to find that nothing much had changed. 'My family and friends were all very happy for me and nobody really changed their attitude towards me,' she says. And while there, The Vernons Girls returned to the Pools company's offices to rehearse and take dance lessons in preparation for the next show. But it wasn't all glamour and riches for the girls from Liverpool who had been transported to national acclaim. 'It was just another job,' adds Baker, 'and we earned around £12 a week.'

Another act from *Oh Boy* shot to stardom in November when Lord Rockingham's XI hit the top of the UK charts with a ditty called 'Hoots Mon' which, according to one reviewer, came 'complete with snatches of exaggerated Scottish doggerel', while Neil Sedaka was the latest tip for the top from America where the all-girl group The Teddy Bears hit number one with 'To Know Him Is To Love Him', written and produced by a young man named Phil Spector.

In the meantime, the first name in rock 'n' roll was refusing to go quietly, as Bill Haley's sold-out tour of Europe was marred by riots in Paris and Berlin with chairs smashed and members of the audience and the local constabulary injured in brawls outside the theatres. Violence was also on the agenda at Cliff Richard's show at the Elephant and Castle's Trocadero theatre where the star had to be smuggled to safety in a police car. And, according to Ricky Nelson, anyone who spoke up against rock 'n' roll 'doesn't understand it, or is prejudiced against it, or is just plain square.'

Six years after the *NME* launched the first British singles chart, rival paper *Melody Maker* announced the first Top Ten listing for LPs and proclaimed 'Sales of LPs are booming in Britain and the States. So keep in touch with Top Tastes.' Number one in the debut album chart from August 8 1958 was the soundtrack from *South Pacific* followed by: 2) *Come Fly With Me* - Frank Sinatra; 3) *Elvis' Golden Records* – Elvis Presley; 4) *King Creole* – Elvis Presley; 5) *My Fair Lady*; 6) *Warm* – Johnny Mathis; 7) *The King & I*; 8) *Dear Perry* – Perry Como; 9) *Oklahoma*; and 10) *Songs By Tom Lehrer* – Tom Lehrer.

According to the Board of Trade, during the period from January to October 1958, the British public spent over £10 million on these and many other records, a drop of 2% on the 1957 figure, which was put down to the fall in the sale of 78rpm discs. In the same ten months, sales of the new popular 45rpm records went up from 10 million to 20 million, while LP sales rose from 11 million to 12.4 million.

Before the end of the year – during which Alaska was named as America's 49th state, race riots took place in London's Notting Hill district and General Charles de Gaulle was elected as Prime Minister of France – yet another new singing star emerged. The oddly named Conway Twitty hit the top of the charts in both the UK and the US with 'It's Only Make Believe', a song he claimed he wrote in the dressing room of the Flamingo Lounge in Ontario, Canada. False rumours then spread that Twitty – who was named Harold Lloyd Jenkins in tribute to the silent film star and who took his stage name from the towns of Conway in Arkansas and Twitty in Texas – was in fact Elvis Presley.

Meanwhile, the real Presley talked to *Melody Maker* from his army home in Germany and once again tempted his legion of fans in the UK by saying that he would like to perform there. 'There's nothing to stop me coming to Britain', he said. 'But it would cost an awful lot of money and trouble. I would want to bring over my orchestra and The Jordanaires and Colonel Parker and his staff would have to come too.' The King was so near yet still so far away!

Chapter 6

1959: 'Rock is here for all time'

With Britain's new wave of rock singers vying with their American idols, the pop scene at the start of 1959 consisted of a confused collection of US originals and UK cover versions, which led up-and-coming guitar player and singer George Harrison to ponder what was going on.

'The scene was mixed,' he concluded. 'There were the big stars and then artists that you had heard records by but never really saw much of. Then there were the British artists such as Tommy Steele and later Cliff Richard. And the Larry Parnes lot; Billy Fury and Marty Wilde and others.'

Either way it was a good time to be around, according to the future Beatle. 'It was exciting because it was the first time you ever saw a pink jacket or a black shirt or a Fender Stratocaster or any electric guitar,' said Harrison, as national daily newspapers the *Sketch*, *Mirror* and *Express* picked up on the *NME*'s singles chart which also began to appear in magazines and local papers around the UK.

And while Fidel Castro was proclaiming himself head of Cuba and UK Prime Minister Harold Macmillan was preparing to become the first British premier to visit the USSR, there came news that *Six-Five Special* had been pulled by the BBC. Originally planned for a six -week run, the show held on for 20 months before it was realised that *Oh Boy* was winning the ratings war. The replacement BBC show, called *Dig This*, aired for just four months.

In fact *Oh Boy* was so successful that a touring show was sent out on the road featuring Marty Wilde, Vince Taylor and The Vernon Girls, while Cliff Richard and The Drifters — now including Jet Harris and Tony Meehan — headlined a tour with Wee Willie Harris plus Tony Crombie and The Rockets. The news of Richard's tour came along with the announcement that he and his group had signed a deal with impresarios Lew and Leslie Grade to play 30 weeks of shows in the UK during the year. The contract, said to be worth £15,000, was described as 'The highest amount paid to any British artists within six months of entering show business.'

At the same time, The Everly Brothers made a flying visit to the UK to appear on the TV show *Cool For Cats* where they received their *NME* award as World's Best Group, while Neil Sedaka was tipped in an *NME* 'predictions for the future' article as someone who 'could well develop as an outstanding name in any one of three different fields — songwriter, concert pianist or singer.' Other new names included in the feature were Billy Fury, whose debut disc 'Maybe Tomorrow' had just been released, and Vince Taylor, who had issued 'Right Behind You Baby'.

One of the people Don and Phil Everly met during their lightning trip to Britain was guitarist Terry Slater — 'we were all just hanging about in the same clubs in those days' – and, although he would later join the duo and write a number of songs for them, including the hit 'Bowling Green', he was busy back then with his group The Flinstones.

'We toured all over the place and the only real road in those days was the A1. If your agent said you were playing Birmingham, you had to leave at 10 in the morning to get to there in time to play in the evening. It took a long time and it was really hard,' says Slater who also went on tour supporting the likes of Wee Willie Harris, Dickie Pride, Gary Mills, Vince Eager, Shane Fenton and Vince Taylor. 'We played all over the place but mainly it was the Mecca and Top Rank ballrooms, although you had to have an audition to get on their shows in those days.'

Having seen off his main competition in *Six-Five Special*, Jack Good reckoned that, on the back of making stars of Wilde and Richard through his *Oh Boy* show, he was on the verge of creating a third new star. 'I think that someone will be Bill Forbes. He has appeared on the programme four or five times and is definitely catching on,' said Good, of the singer who would end up having just one top 30 hit with 'Too Young'.

Meanwhile news filtered in from America of 29 year-old songwriter/producer Berry Gordy Jnr. putting up $800 he had borrowed from his family to launch a new record label called Tamla. Based in Detroit, Gordy – who wrote 'Reet Petite' for Jackie Wilson – issued Marv Johnson's 'Come To Me' as his label's debut single in March 1959.

A month before Tamla's important first release, rock 'n' roll suffered its first and one of its greatest losses when Buddy Holly, together with the Big Bopper (J.P. Richardson) and Richie Valens, died in a plane crash in Iowa on February 3 1959, which was later identified by Don McLean in his song 'American Pie' as 'the day the music died.'

Tommy Steele said at the time, 'All teenagers have a reason to feel that they have lost something' while Irving Feld, manager of Paul Anka and promoter of the fateful tour, let it be known that he had been in talks with promoter Lew Grade to bring the ill-fated Winter Party tour to the UK with Holly, Valens and the Big Bopper.

Two months after his death Holly topped the UK charts with 'It Doesn't Matter Anymore', while Valens' song 'Donna' also charted but had to compete with a cover version by Wilde, which peaked at number three while the original American release stalled at 29. Later in the year, Wilde won another battle when his version of 'A Teenager In Love' hit number two in the chart ahead of a rival UK cover by Craig Douglas and the US original by Dion and The Belmonts.

At the same time as husband and wife duo Pearl Carr and Teddy Johnson were chosen as Britain's entries for the 1959 Eurovision Song Contest – they finished runners-up to Holland with their rendition of 'Sing Little Birdie' – a collection of tours was on the move around the UK. Wee Willie Harris and The Vipers were in Chester; Tommy Steele and Yana could be seen at the

Coliseum in London; while David Whitfield and The Tanner Sisters were playing Newcastle. And on the bill at the London Palladium were Charlie Drake, Bernard Bresslaw and Edmund Hockridge.

After ditching *Six-Five Special* and the replacement show *Dig It*, the BBC came up with something called *Drumbeat*, which aired on April 4 with Adam Faith, Vince Eager and Roy Young among the first stars. One act not on the show or on the radio was US group The Coasters whose hit single 'Charlie Brown' had been banned by the BBC because of the word 'spitball.' The ban lasted all of two weeks and the record went on to become The Coasters' only UK top ten hit.

While American stars Frankie Avalon and Fabian – best pals from Philadelphia – indulged in a spot of friendly rivalry in the charts, Britain's two top rockers were in competition for the same job – as the lead in a new film called *Expresso Bongo*. Producer Val Guest considered both Cliff Richard and Marty Wilde for the part of rock singer Bongo Herbert before choosing Richard. 'I saw him as the most likely of the two to fit the part,' explained Guest. Not to be outdone, Wilde went off to star in the movie *Paradise For Baby*.

According to Bruce Welch, rock 'n' roll had first taken a serious hold on proceedings in the UK back in 1957 when coffee bars with jukeboxes sprang up, not just in London, but in towns the length and breadth of the country. And then there were other important developments. 'In 1959 Hank, Cliff and me shared a flat

in Marylebone High Street in London's West End and a
Wimpy Bar opened up fifty yards away, which was great.
We all had scooters to get around on in those days and
hung about in the 2-I's and other coffee bars.'

March 1959 was a busy time in lots of ways as Hawaii
became the 50th state of America, just as the Dalai Lama
fled Tibet to seek refuge in India and a pair of monkeys
returned safely to earth aboard a US space rocket.
It was also when author Raymond Chandler died just
ahead of American architect Frank Lloyd Wright, while
Kingsway introduced their new, fancy and longer king-
size cigarette.

Britain's traditional April Budget brought some relief
for record buyers in 1959 as a 10% drop in purchase tax
to 50% saw 45rpm discs cut by 3½d (1p) to 6s (30p),
while EPs fell by around 5d (2p) and top price LPs were
reduced to 35s 9½d (£1.78½p) from a previous high of
37s 6½d (£1.87½p). In line with these cuts, Richard's
first album *Cliff Sings* appeared on the market and one
reviewer was moved to comment bizarrely that, 'Cliff
attacks each song with the power of a rugby full-back.'

As part of an on-going series of interviews with record
company executives, *NME* interviewed HMV boss Wally
Ridley – the man who had been so shocked when he first
heard Presley's 'Heartbreak Hotel' a few years earlier.
After he had talked about his signings Alma Cogan,
Malcolm Vaughan and Ronnie Hilton, Ridley was asked
about the lack of British rock 'n' roll on his label. 'At the
height of the rock craze we were releasing Elvis Presley',

he explained. 'And who could possibly compete with him?'

A month later, Parlophone's George Martin was in the same hot seat and he spoke glowingly about new hopefuls Lorne Leslie and Jerry Angelo plus a new *Oh Boy* discovery Dean Webb and shrewdly observed, 'It's obvious that the rock influence is here for all time.'

While the BBC considered how best to treat rock and pop music on television, Radio Luxembourg continued to dominate the airways, even though the Beeb's Light Programme opted to drop the word skiffle from *Saturday Skiffle Club* and re-schedule the show, presented by Brian Matthews, to a regular two-hour spot between 10am and midday every Saturday.

By comparison, Luxembourg were broadcasting pop and rock music for 48 of the 56 hours they were on air each week and for the first time they extended Sunday broadcasting past midnight. But this was no consolation to five youths in East Germany who were each jailed for five years after being caught listening to non-approved radio, including Radio Luxembourg.

Cast as a delinquent who wanted to be a rock 'n' roll singer, Cliff Richard's film debut in *Serious Charge*, co-starring Anthony Quayle, hit the cinemas in May 1959 just as he began filming *Expresso Bongo*. At the same time, America launched the first Grammy Awards for recorded music and decided – despite million-selling titles by the likes of Presley, Holly, Nelson and Twitty – that 'Volare' by Domenico Modugno was the Record of the Year and

Peter Gunn by Henry Mancini was Album of the Year.

On May 30, *Oh Boy* finally reached the end of the road as Jack Good pulled the plug on his show after a run of 38 weeks. The final show featured Wilde, Richard, Fury, The Drifters and Pride plus The Vernon Girls and Lord Rockingham's XI, while Good kept his plans for his next music show under wraps. By an extraordinary coincidence, the BBC launched their new music show the very next day – when something called *Juke Box Jury* hit the screens.

Under the watchful eye of host David Jacobs, a panel of guests offered comments and criticism of the latest pop releases. The 'jury' on show number one featured singers Alma Cogan and Gary Miller, plus DJ Pete Murray while Susan Stranks (who would later host children's TV show *Magpie*) completed the line-up as a 'typical teenager.'

Jacobs was another of the radio and TV presenters who impressed the man who became famous in the 1970s as the host of *The Old Grey Whistle Test*. Not only did Jacobs, who died in 2013, present the all-important *Pick Of The Pops* radio show, he also dedicated a record – 'There's A Moon Out Tonight' by The Capris – to Bob Harris on his 15th birthday, after his mum had written in with a request.

Even though it had disappeared from the country's TV screens, *Oh Boy* was resurrected for a ten-minute segment during the Royal Variety Show in Manchester in June when Richard, Wilde, Wainer and The Vernon Girls once again strutted their stuff, but this time it was in front of the Queen Mother.

Having ended the previous year by declaring he would like to perform in the UK – if the money was right of course – Elvis Presley took to his sick bed in Germany and it was left to the *NME* to call up his dad Vernon and find out details of his throat infection and high temperature. 'His grandmother and I are looking after him ... but I am afraid he may have to go into an army hospital tonight,' was what Presley Senior told the music paper. And sure enough, the singer spent the next week in the Frankfurt Military Hospital.

With the popularity of skiffle continuing on a downward path, Lonnie Donegan found himself a part-time job as a musical adviser to Pye Records specializing in jazz and, appropriately, skiffle acts including Ian Menzies and The Stompers, who he had recommended to the label. But it was still rock music that the youth of Britain were clamouring for and while Johnny Kidd and The Pirates broke into the chart with 'Please Don't Touch', despite not appearing on a single TV show, Cliff Richard was hitting new heights with 'Living Doll', which he performed in the film *Serious Charge*.

According to *NME* reviewer Keith Fordyce it was 'a quiet and easy paced song' and Richard's performance persuaded Fordyce to add, 'Here and now let me say that his voice is a delight to listen to and this style of presentation is brimful of appeal.' Before the end of the year, 'Living Doll' became both Richard's first US hit and the first rock record by a British artist to enter the American chart, while UK sales passed the 500,000 mark in just seven weeks. But the man who wrote Richard's first-ever chart topper had a major admission to make.

Lionel Bart, who also co-wrote Tommy Steele's debut hit 'Rock With The Caveman', recalled that earlier in the year he had spent time at Richard's home rehearsing in the front room with the singer and his group. Slightly embarrassed, he added that when they asked him if they had any future in showbiz, he told them to give up. Richard chose to ignore Bart's advice and soon after re-named his instrumental backing group The Shadows in order to avoid any confusion with the five black singers from America called The Drifters.

In addition to writing hits for Steele and Richard, Bart was also involved with Parnes' stable of acts producing songs for the likes of Fury, Wilde and Vince Power before moving on to create stage musicals such as *Fings Ain't What They Used To Be*, *Lock Up Your Daughters* and, most famously, *Oliver* in 1960. 'I used to have something in the Top 10 of the *NME* charts every week for about four years' said the one-time regular at the 2-Is coffee bar. 'I could see the market in those days. I could suss out who needed what song.'

Even though British rock stars were busy taking a leaf out of Presley's book and appearing in relatively low budget movies – Steele had been in *The Duke Wore Jeans* and Dene in *The Golden Disc*, while Richard was in *Expresso Bongo* and Wilde in *Paradise For Baby* – the bestselling Hollywood blockbusters were films such as *Ben Hur* with Charlton Heston, *Gigi* starring Audrey Hepburn and *Some Like It Hot* featuring Marilyn Monroe.

In the realms of television, *Oh Boy* had been successfully sold to US broadcasters and had its first ever airing in homes across America – but the response was less than flattering. TV critics panned the show, with the reviewer from the *New York Daily News* suggesting, 'George III gets his revenge – Britain sends r-and-r.' As if to prove that America was still the leader when it came to rock 'n' roll records, Presley's 'Hunk O' Love' single became his 14th consecutive million-seller in July 1959, and seven of those passed the two-million sales mark.

The up-market and influential magazine *Queen* focused on the country's finances and asked its readers, 'When did you last hear the word austerity?'. Claiming that more money than ever was swilling about in Britain, the magazine declared that everyone – 14 years after the end of World War II – was living in 'a new world … the age of BOOM!'

Even though, as they claimed, a whopping 'two thousand million pounds' was being spent in the UK, the big move in motoring was towards a revolutionary smaller car. It was designer Alec Issigonis who came up with the idea for an eye-catching car called the Mini which was launched by Morris in August 1959. Even though it was two feet shorter than standard cars such as the Morris Minor – also designed by Issigonis – the new Mini could still hold four adults and came off the production line costing £469. It was hailed as a break-through combination of convenience, economy and style.

With new cars being developed, Britain's road system also required an upgrade and the first section of a major new motorway called the M1 – linking London with the north west of England – was opened in late 1959, a year after the country's first-ever section of motorway was introduced as a bypass round Preston in Lancashire.

All this happened at a time when the average UK wage was estimated to be £11.2s.6d (£11.12½p) compared with £6.8s (£6.40p) in 1950, while the standard rate of income tax was 7s.9d (39½p), down from 9s.6d (47½p) in 1951. At the same time British teenagers were reckoned to be spending an average of £8 a week on clothes, records, cigarettes and make-up.

While jazz was never a huge seller in Britain in the 1950s – despite trad jazz showing some signs of popularity alongside skiffle – the death of singer Billie Holiday aged just 44 in July 1959 was still a major loss to music. A month later, trumpeter Miles Davis, along with sax players John Coltrane and Cannonball Adderley, released the hugely influential jazz album *A Kind Of Blue*, which attracted a wider audience.

In a year in which Americans Lloyd Price, Freddy Cannon and Neil Sedaka, plus the late Richie Valens and Big Bopper, all debuted on the UK charts, the likes of Billy Fury, Craig Douglas, Adam Faith and Emile Ford continued to fly the flag for Britain. But for many they were still second-best. 'The British rockers were pretty poor imitations of the American stars,' says Len Goodman, 'but one of my favourites was Billy Fury – he was great.'

And Tony Hale was no more impressed with the efforts of 'our' artists. 'The British singers were white boys who wanted to be musical hall stars. Marty Wilde was top man for a while out of our singers but they were all poor copies,' says the man who worked for both the BBC and Capital Radio 'Chuck Berry meant that you got a genuine rock 'n' roll record and a song but with lyrics that actually told a story and that was great, and The Coasters too had songs that had stories.'

Jen Blowes was somebody else who was a fan of Fury and being an usherette at the Odeon cinema in Chelmsford in the late 1950s gave her a unique opportunity to get close to her hero. 'I used to love Billy Fury and spent quite a lot of time with him when he came to Chelmsford. He came here two or three times and the acts never left for ages after the show because of all the fans at the stage door so we used to hang around and chat with them. He was a really nice man.' She also remembers that among the acts on the bill with the likes of Fury and Cliff Richard back then were Cherry Wainer and Dorita Y Pepe, a husband and wife act who played acoustic guitars while singing Spanish songs but were in fact Peter and Dorothy Sensier from south London.

On September 1, just a few miles down the road from Chelmsford, in Southend-on-Sea, Larry Parnes' Big Beat Show package tour opened with all the usual suspects on parade: Wilde, Fury, Dene and Pride plus Johnny Gentle and Duffy Power and an up-and-coming young guitarist called Joe Brown, who backed the singers throughout the tour. Also in the audience was TV producer Jack Good who was just over a week away from launching his new TV show.

Boy Meets Girls was the successor to *Oh Boy* and this time it featured Marty Wilde – as the boy – and a trio of Vernon Girls – as the girls. 'Marty was a huge star at the time and Jack Good pushed him ahead of Cliff Richard and put him and Joyce [Baker] in *Boy Meets Girls*,' recalls Tony Hall, who gave up his job as the show's host to Wilde. 'It was in colour and it had no great tension but it was still the show that everybody wanted to be on.'

During the 18 months since they first met on *Oh Boy*, Baker had become Wilde's girlfriend, despite all the girls being kept under strict surveillance. 'From the days of being chaperoned I went straight to going out with Marty,' recalls Baker, who explains that their minder used to go round all their hotel rooms each night to check that there were no boys in the rooms.

'The other girls used to smuggle Marty in and hide him in the bath and cover him with underwear and towels,' she says. Even half a century ago their rock star meets backing singer relationship caught the attention of the media – 'we used to get chased by the press who wanted pictures of us together,' explains Baker, adding that she and Wilde got engaged after he proposed to her during rehearsals for *Boy Meets Girls*.

While Jack Good's own group The Firing Squad appeared regularly on the show, the producer also invited some unknown rock stars from Europe including Johnny Hallyday from France and Little Tony and His Brothers from Italy, although the TV producer sensed that change was in the air. 'Rock 'n' roll isn't the same as it used to be,' warned Good. 'There is a greater demand for ballads and light beat numbers and we mustn't forget that country and western is growing.'

American singer Brenda Lee was another guest on *Boy Meets Girls* even though the 15-year-old from Georgia had not had a single UK hit record at the time. But Baker still remembers the girl dubbed 'Little Miss Dynamite'. 'There was this amazing voice coming out of this tiny thing. She came in holding her manager's hand and they stood her on an orange box – then all our mouths dropped open when she sang.'

Despite meeting all these visiting stars, Baker and her colleagues were under strict instructions about how to behave. 'The one thing we were told never to do was to ask for any autographs because the chaperone said it would have been very unprofessional. I remember meeting Johnnie Ray once and I just fell apart, even though Marty was with me.'

In the face of Good's new show the BBC decided to drop *Drumbeat* and move *Juke Box Jury* to the prime time slot of 6.50pm on a Saturday evening, while a new record from American singer Bobby Darin was judged to be inappropriate by broadcasters in both America and Britain. The man who held the UK top spot for four weeks in July with 'Dream Lover' fell foul of the radio and TV stations with his version of 'Mack The Knife', a tune from the *Threepenny Opera*.

In fact both Darin's release and a version by Louis Armstrong were sidelined because the lyrics about violence, which were deemed appropriate in the original opera, were reckoned to be too dangerous for general daytime radio and television and were even blamed for incidents of teenage violence. Banned or not, 'Mack The Knife' gave Darin a number-one hit in both the UK and the US where he also received Grammy awards for Record of the Year and as Best Newcomer.

At the same time as Billy Fury was being criticised in the press for his sexy stage antics, Cliff Richard, the original bad boy of *Oh Boy*, opted to appear in the pantomime *Babes In The Wood* at the Globe Theatre, Stockton, over the Christmas period. However, it was stressed that Richard had no actual part in the panto and would simply be a 'guest attraction' during the show's two-week run.

The 1959 *NME* Poll once again had Presley, Francis and The Everly Brothers as Top Male, Top Female and Top Group, while Richard was finally named Top British Male Singer with Shirley Bassey voted Top Female. Top British Newcomer was Craig Douglas ahead of Anthony Newley and Billy Fury. While Presley once again got the nod as World's Outstanding Musical Personality, the artist filling the runner-up spot was a relatively new name to British music fans.Guitarist Duane Eddy had racked up six British hits since September 1958 and put it all down to a Gretsch guitar he had bought in 1957. 'I had no idea how I was going to make the payments on it but I needn't have worried as it turned out to be real lucky,' he says of the guitar he used on nine hit singles, three EPs and two chart albums.' In fact, in answer to a fan's Q&A session in the *NME*, Eddy admitted to owning four guitars – all made by Gretsch – and also having a taste for steak and Mexican food but a hatred of 'eggs, toast and salads.'

Another emerging star from America, Eddie Cochran – who had hit the UK charts with 'Summertime Blues', 'C'Mon Everybody' and 'Somethin' Else' – declared that it was his 'fondest wish' to visit Britain and planned to make the trip early in 1960 when a spot on *Boy Meets Girls* was already pencilled in. However rock 'n' roll was still causing problems in other parts of the world as 15 Presley fans in East Germany were sent to prison for marching through the streets of Leipzig chanting 'Long live Elvis Presley' and for criticizing both the leader of East Germany and the local music.

Over the border in West Germany, an executive from a leading US tobacco company had flown into the country with a cheque for $25,000 to get Elvis Presley to endorse his brand of cigarettes. The non-smoking King of Rock 'n' Roll politely turned down his offer.

In amongst the rock 'n' roll, pop ballads, instrumentals (including 'Red River Rock' by Johnny and The

Hurricanes, 'Side Saddle' by Russ Conway and 'Piano Party' by Winifred Atwell) and a selection of odd-ball singles ('Little Donkey' by The Beverley Sisters, 'Seven Little Girls Sitting In The Back Seat' by both The Avons and Paul Evans, plus Tommy Steele's 'Little White Bull'), there was one comedy record which made an impact in the album chart in late 1959.

Peter Sellers, a long-time member of The Goons, released *Songs For Swinging Sellers* after six months in the studio with producer George Martin. Considered by *NME* to be a 'delicious blend of biting wit and shrewd reflections on life today', the album reached number three in the chart despite Martin seeming to downplay the end product by explaining, 'You can say it's an amusing record or a witty record, but it isn't blatantly funny.'

On the back of Cliff Richard's second number one in 1959 – 'Travellin' Light' followed 'Living Doll' to the top – two new British acts brought to an end a successful year for home-grown artists, who were responsible for a record ten chart toppers out of a total of 29. Adam Faith and Emile Ford and The Checkmates joined the list which featured Richard's two hits, plus the likes of Michael Holliday, Lord Rockingham's XI, Shirley Bassey, Russ Conway (twice) and Craig Douglas.

Adam Faith was on his fourth record deal as he moved from skiffle to rock and eventually appeared on *Drumbeat* where he was spotted and signed to make 'What Do You Want', with the influential backing of The John Barry Seven. Sales of over 50,000 a day took it to number one

– the first ever for the Parlophone label.

Ford, who was born in St Lucia in the West Indies, played in London's coffee bars and clubs before winning a Soho talent contest and a recording deal with Pye Records. This led to him making an up-to-date version of the 1916 Vaudeville song 'What Do You Want To Make Those Eyes At Me For?' and ending the year with Britain's final number one of the 1950s.

In the first week of December in the last year of the decade, Marty Wilde and Joyce Baker married in the same Greenwich church where his mum and dad had wed – and over 50 years later Baker still wonders if it was the right thing to have done while Wilde was at his peak. 'Larry Parnes decided to announce our wedding at a press conference and, with the benefit of hindsight, I think getting married might have harmed Marty's career,' she admits. 'To be honest I was happy not to get married at the time and Parnes even suggested that I was Marty's mistress, but he wasn't having any of that – he was a bit Victorian in that way.'

Acknowledging that there was a 'bit of backlash', Baker also recalls that the wedding took place around the same time as Parnes and Jack Good had a disagreement. 'It was all about airtime for Marty and Cliff, and Larry took Marty away from the show (*Boy Meets Girls*) which wasn't my fault at all.'

One man who watched all this activity with particular interest was Bruce Welch who had married, aged 17, at around the time he came to London with Hank

Marvin, who also got married back then. 'Hank and I got married at 17 but nobody knew about it and we weren't particularly famous', says Welch. 'But Marty brought about his downfall because he got married to Joyce when he was at the height of his career and then he took the press to Las Vegas on their honeymoon. In those days kids didn't want their heroes to be married. It would have affected Cliff if he had got married.'

Within a few days of marrying it seems that Wilde was back on stage as part of the Big Beat Show package tour as it hit Tooting Granada in south London – and he had a special guest on the bill alongside Fury, Dene and Vince Eager. Despite not having a UK hit record since 1956, Gene Vincent remained one of the most exciting rock 'n' roll artists around and his debut UK show got a rave review from the critics, with one of them calling it a 'sensational performance that put him way above the rest of the artists in stagecraft and showmanship.' The man from the *NME* went on to say, 'Vincent performed miracles with the mike stand … adding a peculiar half crouching stance, and his act was as exciting to watch as it was to hear.'

And Vincent ended the year with a guest spot on *Boy Meets Girls* where, according to Tony Hall, he stood out from the crowd. 'You could get an idea of the impact rock 'n' roll had on people by what they listened to and how they dressed. Most of the stars wore suits and ties on TV – except for Gene Vincent of course who was dressed in black leather even in those days.'

Chapter 7

1960: Rock With A Bit Of A Twist

Despite his earlier prediction that 'ballads and light beat' would become the new order of the day, Jack Good began the new decade sticking to his rock 'n' roll six-guns and booking another American rocker to join Gene Vincent on the first editions of *Boy Meets Girls* in January 1960.

Eddie Cochran had a trio of UK hit singles to his credit by the time he arrived in Britain on January 9 to join Vincent, Fury, Joe Brown and Georgie Fame on the latest Larry Parnes package tour, which kicked off on January 24 at Ipswich's Gaumont Theatre. And on the day before he left the USA, Cochran had recorded a new version of the song 'Three Steps To Heaven'.

In between his arrival and starting the ten-week tour, Cochran spoke to the music press about his big break – appearing in the film *The Girl Can't Help It*. 'I wasn't even a singer before I made that movie and hadn't any vocal discs at all,' he said, before explaining that it was thanks to 'multi-recording techniques' that he was able to sing and play drums, guitar and bass on the first of his UK hits.

While he also suggested that the weather in England was not entirely to his liking – it was raining and chilly – he picked up on Good's theory that music was changing. 'I think rock is cooling down … it's not as

wild these days. But it occurs to me that British fans
still go for the wild stuff in a big way.'

On January 16, Cochran made his debut on Good's
TV show alongside Vincent and regular host Marty
Wilde. 'I worked with Gene and Eddie a lot and they
loved England', recalls Wilde. 'They didn't have a lot of
experience of countries outside America but when they
came here there was a great warmth for them from the
British people – and we were very loyal to them.' And
the American duo also passed on some useful tips to
the English singer.

'They taught me everything – their style of singing
and the use of echo chambers,' explains Wilde. 'Eddie
strung his Gretsch guitar in a different way with two
first strings which meant he didn't have to try and bend
the second and third strings to get a blues sound. He
had light-gauge strings and he showed us how to re-
string our guitars – they were both happy to share all
this stuff with us.'

Cochran's appearances on *Boy Meets Girls* – there
would be three more during the tour – had the desired
effect on Andrew Loog Oldham, although he confused
the show with its predecessor *Oh Boy*. Describing the
TV show as the 'perfect showcase for the sublime Eddie
Cochran,' the pop entrepreneur was convinced that the
TV spots 'made him a legend.'

Oldham was equally convinced of the talent of home-
grown star Billy Fury as he went out on tour with the
Americans. Claiming that his debut single 'Maybe

Tomorrow' 'raised the stakes among British rock boys,' Oldham was just as sure that Liverpool-born Fury was 'the only British solo star who was comfortable sharing a stage with Eddie.'

Also watching Cochran on the telly in January 1960 was Paul McCartney and – while he also thought it might have been on *Oh Boy* – his memories are all about the performance. 'Most of the other guys like Cliff Richard and Marty Wilde were good singers, but Eddie was suddenly the first one who played guitars. He was playing 'Milk Cow Blues' and had a Gretsch guitar with a Bigsby tremelo arm and it looked very glamorous.'

On a night after Cochran and Vincent appeared on Good's Saturday evening show, Cliff Richard and the Shadows topped the bill on *Sunday Night At the London Palladium* when they were watched by over 19 million people in around 6.8 million homes in the UK. This record-breaking performance came about just ahead of the singer and his group departing for America to play their first US dates alongside the likes of Frankie Avalon, Freddy Cannon and Bobby Rydell.

Wilde was another rock 'n' roll artist who noticed a change in the look and sound of pop music. 'Tracks like 'Why' came out and people like Anthony Newley came in and that kind of rawness and energy got lost,' says the man who reached number seven in the UK chart in January 1960 with his own song 'Bad Boy'. But while he wasn't completely disenchanted – 'now and again a track would come out that was sort of rough and ready'– Wilde was determined to stick to his principles. 'Most of the managers wanted their acts to move on and be all-round entertainers and Larry Parnes had the same view with me. But I wasn't happy with that – I wanted to be left alone to do rock 'n' roll.'

The final points for positions chart listing by *NME* for 1959 also showed that things were changing as the table was topped by pianist Russ Conway with Cliff in second place and Lonnie Donegan, Marty Wilde and Elvis Presley filling the next three spots. But still the influence of American music and musicians would not to be denied and when a January edition of *Juke Box Jury* featured only records from US artists it was branded 'disgraceful' and 'a great injustice' by the *NME*.

In America in February 1960, Presley was busy receiving his first ever certified gold album for one million sales in the US of *Elvis* which had been released four years earlier. Meanwhile Cochran and Vincent continued their jaunt around the UK, including a date at the De Montfort Hall in Leicester on February 18 1960. One reviewer observed that on stage that night was 'a young man wearing black leather trousers, black leather motorcycling jacket and black leather gloves. The audience went frantic. The girls jumped up as if they had sat on a hot iron and the boys clapped and whistled. This was Mr. Gene Vincent.'

The same critic went on to comment on the other visiting artist. "When Eddie Cochran, dressed smartly in grey skin-tight leather trousers, a pink shirt and silver lamé waistcoat contorted himself in various positions, the girls went even wilder.' He finished off his critique with the words, 'I cannot believe that this is true entertainment. A clown making funny faces would have got the same results from small children. Then why do these idiotic teenagers behave in such a ridiculous fashion?'

On the other hand Jack Good in his regular column in the music paper *Disc* explained, 'Cochran is the toughest, ruggedest exponent of rock. He makes that music swing. He punches it over like a singing Rocky Marciano and the whole audience was knocked out.' Good also went on the record to answer media criticism of Billy Fury's stage antics and, perhaps surprisingly, he agreed that some of his so-called 'erotic gyrations' were a bit excessive. 'Frankly there are one or two things that he does that I would rather he didn't ... but he does tend to get carried away by his performance.'

On their return from America, The Shadows made a special journey to Manchester to catch a date on the Cochran/Vincent tour. 'We were in awe of meeting these people and we didn't have conversations,' recounts Bruce Welch. 'Just to be in the same building as somebody from America was incredible. The cars, the colour movies, the music – it was awe-inspiring!'

Sadly, however, the meeting with one of the American stars wasn't an altogether happy experience. 'Gene Vincent wasn't a very nice man,' says the Shadows guitarist. 'But he sang 'Be Bop A Lu La' – it was great vocal experience – and he had a great band called The Blue Caps with the guitarist Tex Davis and a drum sound that was just brushes.'

When the show moved on to Liverpool in March, there was another guitarist in the audience, although this one was yet to be discovered. 'I saw a few shows, the best being the Eddie Cochran one,' recalled George Harrison. 'I remember Eddie Cochran well; he had his black leather waistcoat, black leather trousers and raspberry coloured shirt. He came on doing 'What'd I Say' and as the curtain opened he had his back to the audience, playing the riff. I was watching his fingers, to see how he played.'

In the year in which *Saturday Night And Sunday Morning* was banned from British cinemas – albeit briefly – because of its 'beer and sex' content and the films *Pyscho* and *A Man For All Season* each made a huge and lasting impact, British television was offering up comedian Harry Worth's show alongside the adventure series *Danger Man*. At the same time an average teenager was earning around £10 a week and had about £7 to spend after contributing to the weekly household budget.

Britain lost one of its longest running music shows from the small screen in early 1960 when *Cool For Cats* came off the air after four years, but gained its first ever 'official' Top 50 singles chart and Top 20 albums chart when *Record Retailer* was launched in March as the UK's first music trade paper. Adam Faith and 'Poor Me' topped the new extended singles chart while

Freddy Cannon's *The Explosive Freddy Cannon* held the top spot on the initial album listing – but only for one week before normal service was resumed.

The US rock singer's debut album interrupted *South Pacific*'s 70 week run at the head of the previous *Melody Maker* album chart and the film soundtrack was back at number one (in the new official chart) a week later and it stayed there for a further 19 weeks – and beyond. In fact *South Pacific* was the bestselling album in Britain for an extraordinary total of 115 weeks, between 1958 and 1961.

After a couple of years away from the recording studio and the film set, Elvis Presley got his discharge papers from the US Army and on his way home from Germany made a brief but memorable stop-over at Prestwick Airport in Scotland. He left the plane to step onto British soil for the only time in his life and chatted to fans through the airport fence. The spot is marked with a plaque and the occasion is also remembered thanks to the airport's Graceland bar.

Their seemingly never-ending tour round Britain was taking its toll on Vincent and Cochran, who told the press that while everything was 'fine', he had a preference for how the tour was set up. 'I would say that I prefer doing one-night stands as opposed to whole weeks at one theatre. It's just that I like a change.' And then there was the question of souvenir-hunting fans. 'Guitar picks. I've handed out a whole stack of them,' recounted Cochran. 'Shirts too. Now and again a fan asks for one of my shirts as a keepsake and I don't like to say no. Also on average we signed between 200 and 300 autographs each week.'

For Vincent, the biggest problem was the travelling between the towns and cities of the UK. 'Most of our journeys are by train ... but I must say I don't like British trains. They're not comfortable, there's no way to relax; travelling just becomes boring and sometimes unbearable.' Interestingly, musician Slater, who played on shows or sessions with the likes of Carl Perkins, Jerry Lee Lewis, Duane Eddy and The Everly Brothers, also accompanied Vincent on train journeys in the UK.

'I'd get on the train with Gene and he'd go straight into the first-class carriage even though we didn't have first-class tickets,' says Slater. 'Then he'd throw his bad leg with the caliper on, down the length of the seat and that way nobody ever came into the carriage.' While he describes Vincent as 'scary but harmless', Slater also recalls that the leather-clad rock singer rarely went anywhere unarmed.

'He always carried a gun, but we never knew whether he brought it into the country with him or got it here.' Stories from other musicians suggested that when people asked Vincent if his gun was actually loaded, he would reply, 'What's the point of having a gun if it ain't loaded?'

As the Cochran/Vincent caravan was drawing to a close — and 'My Old Man's A Dustman' by Lonnie Donegan became the first single by a British act to enter the UK chart at number one — more American stars were descending on the British Isles. The Everly Brothers, fresh from signing a ten-year, one million dollar deal with Warner Bros, which guaranteed them $100,000 per annum, arrived with The Crickets on the back of Duane Eddy and Bobby Darin beginning their tour.

Having accepted an offer to return and continue their tour, Cochran and Vincent concluded the original ten-week booking with a show at the Hippodrome, Bristol on Easter Sunday, April 16 1960. The next day, the car carrying the two American singers to London Airport to catch a plane home skidded into a lamp post. Vincent suffered a broken collarbone and ribs while Cochran's girlfriend Sharon Sheeley broke her pelvis, but Cochran was thrown head first through the windshield and rushed to hospital in Bath where he died without regaining consciousness.

Two months later, 'Three Steps To Heaven' – the record Cochran made on the eve of his departure for Britain – topped the UK chart. According to Slater, who remembers Cochran as 'a really nice guy, very shy and really good-looking', we had not seen the best of the man from Los Angeles, who was just 21 when he died. 'His loss was a real tragedy as he had a great future ahead of him, with that great big guitar he used to play.'

When Cochran died, Duane Eddy was already a couple of weeks into his first-ever British tour with Bobby Darin and Clyde McPhatter plus best sellers Emile Ford and The Checkmates. With seven UK top

30 hits under his belt, Eddy was still second on the bill to Darin whose five British hits included the back-to-back chart toppers 'Dream Lover' and 'Mack The Knife'.

Arriving for the 22-date tour, Duane Eddy recalls the images he faced after arriving at London's Heathrow Airport. 'We got off the airplane – it was dark and we were all excited – and we saw a little mist and fog rolling about and thought 'it looks just like the movies'. Then somebody would say 'look there's an English taxi' and somebody else would spot a double-decker bus.'

Carrying his two guitars – 'my Gretsch and my Dan Electric bass string guitar and my amplifier' – Eddy and his touring party were soon off on their travels and experiencing a whole new road system. 'When we started out in the States we didn't have a highway system and I think your road system was about the same as ours back then, but I do recall that there weren't too many long straight stretches over here,' he says. And the venues – cinemas and theatres – were also different. 'They were smaller then the ones we played in the US, but we had bigger package tours there, with 12 to 14 acts.'

Journeying up and down the highways and byways of Britain, playing mostly one-nighters, left an impression on Eddy. 'We'd stop and look at an old church in some village and then there would be a lunchtime stop somewhere else but we didn't know where anything was. We did do a little sightseeing in Edinburgh when we played in Glasgow for a week and I went to see the

Castle while Bobby Darin went off to play golf.'

While there was little opportunity to get to grips with the music being made by British artists, Eddy does recall hearing cover versions of records made by his pals from America – the likes of Dion, Bobby Vee or Brian Hyland. 'I thought 'That's not right, they should put out the original versions'. But while US discs were being covered, there was no risk of anybody recreating Eddy's trademark 'twangy guitar' sound. 'Nobody really tried to copy me other than maybe Bert Weedon who was a good guy and came backstage to see me on the tour. He was a good entertainer and he could play.'

With Darin closing the show, Eddy was second-to-last on the bill, but on the opening night things didn't go to plan, according to the guitarist. 'Bobby was due on after me and halfway through the set there was polite applause and my sax player Jim Horn leaned over and said 'I don't think they like us' and I said 'Yeah it looks like it's going to be a long night'.' And even after they had thrown in a rousing version of 'Greensleeves' – 'these foreigners must know it and maybe they'll like it as it came from here' was Eddy's thinking – all remained calm and sedate until the end of the set.

'Then the whole place erupted – they stamped their feet, clapped their hands and shouted 'We want Duane!'. They kept it up for about ten minutes and Bobby couldn't get on,' recalls Eddy. 'I took about nine bows and Bobby had to wait and he was pretty upset about the delay.' The up-shot was that Eddy was moved to close the first half of the show with someone else going on before Darin – and that somebody could have been Emile Ford, who was considered to be the first British black pop star.

Eddy recalls that his tour manager – 'a black guy called Charlie Carpenter' – was astounded as he watched Ford perform from the wings of the theatre. 'I remember Charlie saying 'I can't believe it, he's a brother but he's got no soul'. Charlie thought a British black guy had to be as soulful as a black American kid.'

As Eddy and Darin continued entertaining fans around Britain, news arrived of Jack Good's new TV show to replace *Boy Meets Girls*, which had ended in early March. Titled *Wham!* (could it have served as an inspiration for Messrs Michael and Ridgeley over twenty years later?), it was set for a nine-week run with the *NME*'s resident record reviewer Keith Fordyce as the host. The featured artists on the first show were some of Good's regulars – Billy Fury, Joe Brown, Jess Conrad, Dickie Pride and Italian rock 'n' roll star Little Tony – but Marty Wilde, whose manager had earlier argued with Good over airtime, was conspicuous by his absence.

In addition to meeting with Weedon, Eddy also recalled that Cliff Richard and The Shadows were in the audience at either his Lewisham or Edmonton show in London at the start of the tour. 'I remember seeing this beautiful young man, who was about 17 years-old, with his group and thinking he'd be a good rival to Elvis.' But if meeting Richard was one thing, Eddy recounts another memorable moment. 'The nicest thing about that tour was that Tommy Steele sent me a little picture of himself with a message which said, 'Welcome to Britain Duane, have a great tour'. I set that up in my dressing room during the tour,' he says before adding, 'That was a classy thing to do, although I never actually got to meet him in person.'

The reaction of his British fans on that debut tour of Britain in 1960 is something that remains with Eddy to this day. 'On that tour I was made to feel like a bigger star than I had ever felt before. Some places they had to have police dogs out to hold back the crowds. One of the magazine headlines I saw said, 'Eddy Hit Of Darin Show' and although Bobby and I remained friends through it all, he was disappointed when he drew me to be on that tour with him.

'I was more rock 'n' roll than him and people told me that when we played it was the first time they had heard a band which sounded just like the record. I was touring with the same guys who were on the records – it was the best band I had ever on that tour.'

As a man who has sold over 100 million records worldwide, won a Grammy and been inducted into the Rock 'n' Roll of Fame, Eddy inspired his fair share of young musicians, including John Fogerty from Creedence Clearwater Revival who said, 'Duane was the first guy, the first rock 'n' roll God.'

The Kinks' Dave Davies saw one of the 1960 dates. 'Duane Eddy eventually appeared on stage and it was one of the most thrilling experiences of my life. The sound was amazing … he looked so cool, so nonchalant.' Later, Davies went a stage further in honouring his guitar hero when he and his brother Ray adopted the title of one of Eddy's US hit records as a new name for their Ray Davies Quartet. 'My devotion to Duane was not misplaced because using the name Ramrods seemed to do the trick. For the first time, we got signed by an agent.'

By the time the tour came to an end in Guildford on April 10, Eddy was devoted to Britain and had even learned to appreciate some of its cuisine. 'We loved it all. We had those little Wimpy things which were a bit like a letter from home and I loved your fish and chips. I also switched to tea during that tour – not because your coffee was bad but because your tea was that good.' But even so there was one thing that left him a tad disappointed. 'I'm not a big drinker and I thought your English beer was interesting when I first tried it … but it was warm.'

One of his abiding memories of being in Britain in 1960 is of how things looked and felt just 15 years after the end of World War II. 'Some things were a bit gray and a bit depressing,' he says. 'I was driven out to one part of London where they hadn't cleaned up after the war and the bomb damage was still apparent. It was a like a scene out of a World War II movie. I'd heard about it but seeing it first-hand set me to thinking 'My God, imagine if you'd been in there'.'

Interestingly, after that first visit to Britain, Eddy established an organisation called Circle of Friends rather than a straightforward fan club, which still gets together whenever he visits the UK – and sometimes there have been unexpected results. 'One of those friends who came to a get-together a few years back actually came to see me in concert with his mother in 1960 when he was just 12 years old.'

As part of their British tour in the early months of 1960, Don and Phil Everly hit Manchester for a show at the Free Trade Hall and in the audience once again were Nash and Clarke who by this time were appearing in local shows as the Two Teens (under the names Ricky and Dane). And their musical style had been influenced by the two American singing brothers. 'From the time I first heard the Everly Brothers, I knew I wanted to make music that affected people the way the Everlys affected me,' recalled Nash.

While the show was, according to Nash, 'fucking fabulous', there was another memorable moment awaiting the two aspiring Mancunian singers when they traced the Everlys back to the Midland Hotel and waited on the hotel steps for close to three hours to get a glimpse of their heroes. And when the two stars arrived, Nash stepped forward and introduced himself and his mate with the words, 'We sing like you – we copy your style.' When Don Everly asked if they were any good, Clarke replied 'We think we are' and the evening ended with Phil Everly telling the two local teenagers, 'Hey Graham and Allan, keep doing it. Things'll happen.'

Having left the US Army, Presley returned to the business of making records and playing concerts but both the circumstances and the reaction of fans had changed after two years out of the limelight. Colonel Parker set a new non-negotiable fee of $150,000 for Presley's concert performances while fan Reginald Cundell wrote to the *NME* about a track from Presley's first post-military recording session which was issued as a single.

Speculating that Elvis' popularity might be on the wane, Cundell, in his letter to the paper's *From You To Us* column, warned, 'If Elvis continues to make records like his inaudible and tuneless 'Stuck On You' ... he had better watch out.' In fact, Presley didn't have to worry as the track 'Stuck On You', which peaked at number three in the UK and was the singer's first ever stereo single, made it to number one in America on the back of advance orders of 1.2 million.

A year after the TV show *Oh Boy* had had its first airing in the US, Don and Phil Everly admitted that they were two people who saw the show during its brief time on US television. Watching in Nashville, Tennessee, they said, 'We thought they were excellent and of course we saw Cliff and Marty on them,' before they questioned exactly how up-to-date the shows were. 'Weren't the tele-recordings quite old by the time they reached us?' In fact, in 1960, they were watching episodes of *Oh Boy* that had been made two years earlier.

EMI's Abbey Road studios – home to hits by Cliff Richard and The Shadows, Adam Faith, Russ Conway and Michael Holliday – had two major rock 'n' roll visitors in May 1960 when Gene Vincent dropped in to record the top 20 hit 'Pistol Packin' Mama' with The Beat Boys (featuring Georgie Fame on piano), and Johnny Kidd and The Pirates made 'Shakin' All Over'. While his backing group adopted appropriate pirate outfits, Kidd, a former member of skiffle group The Nutters, opted to wear an eyepatch on stage as he helped push his record to number one in the UK chart.

Having spent two years training to be an architect and only playing the odd rock show at the weekend, Ricky Sarstedt decided it was time to pursue a career as a solo singer. His first step was a talent contest organised by Cadbury, the chocolate manufacturer. 'My girlfriend at the time spotted this advert in *Melody Maker* or *NME* from Cadbury, who were just promoting their new Drinking Chocolate, and wanted somebody to do commercials and become the Chocolate Time Troubador,' recounts Sarstedt. Although he was reluctant to be branded as the Chocolate Time Troubador, Sarstedt was keen to be heard. 'I though it might be a means to an end – a way to get people to listen to me playing my three chords.'

The contest took place in the Classic Cinema in Chelsea's King's Road and in the audience was a record producer named Phillip Waddilove who, with his business partner Michael Barclay, had made records for Lonnie Donegan and Petula Clark at Pye Records. 'I won the contest and Phillip saw me and called up Michael and said 'I think we've found our boy'. It was in the days of the man with the big cigar who discovered unknown acts,' explains Sarstedt.

As the Chocolate Time Troubadour, Sarstedt's job was to visit coffee bars and clubs with girls who handed out samples of drinking chocolate while he played his guitar and sang. Once his new managers had negotiated Sarstedt's way out of his Cadbury's contract, they set about finding material for him to record, but it was one of Sarstedt's own songs which became his first record.

'I wrote a song called 'Hot Chocolate Crazy' – 'my baby don't care about my kissin' because she's chocolate crazy' – which I thought would be used in the campaign,' says Sarstedt. 'It wasn't but it did become my first record for Pye in August 1960.'

Determined to turn him into a pop star, managers Waddilove and Barclay decided that Ricky Sarstedt wasn't a name to compete with the likes of Billy Fury, Adam Faith or Cliff Richard. As Barclay's favourite film was Orson Welles' *Citizen Kane*, that took care of a surname and it was left to Waddilove to come up with a first name. 'He said we needed something that was fairly unusual, looked good in print and on the marquees outside theatres and that was how Eden came along,' says Sarstedt. 'I was thinking 'Call me whatever you want!' – I had arrived on another planet and it was all exciting.'

May 1960 saw BOAC launch its first regular Boeing 707 service from London to New York and American Air Force pilot Gary Powers and his U2 plane were shot down over Soviet airspace by USSR jets. At the same time, up in Liverpool, a venue and a group were both moving on in pursuit of bigger audiences.

A couple of weeks before the Cavern hosted its first-ever rock night – May 25, with Cass and The Casanovas and Rory Storm and The Hurricanes on the bill – the former Quarry Men were auditioning as The Silver Beetles for a job as the backing group to local hero Billy Fury. 'Larry Parnes came to town auditioning,' recalls Paul McCartney. 'He was the big London agent. He was looking for backing groups and someone told him there were a few groups around Liverpool.'

On May 10, McCartney, John Lennon, George Harrison, Stuart Sutcliffe and stand-in drummer Johnny Hutchinson assembled at the Wyvern Social Club to try out for Parnes, alongside rival bands including The Casanovas, Gerry and The Pacemakers, Derry and The Seniors and Bob Evans and His Five Shillings. According to Harrison, The Silver Beetles started out at a disadvantage. 'We were very poor and never had any matching clothes but we tried to put together a uniform. It was a bit of a shambles.'

And the future lead guitarist with The Beatles also recalled the reaction to his group from the man from London. 'Larry Parnes didn't stand up saying that we were great or anything like that. It felt pretty dismal.

But a few days later we got the call to go out with Johnny Gentle.' The Silver Beetles – with another temporary drummer Tommy Moore – were in fact booked to accompany Gentle on a seven-date tour of Scotland which opened in Alloa on May 20.

For Liverpudlian and ex-Quarry Man Rod Davis, the fact that the Cavern stayed true to the music it had started out promoting was encouraging. 'The last skiffle group played at the Cavern in May, so it went on for a long time despite there being less and less hit records from the likes of Chas McDevitt, Johnny Duncan and Lonnie Donegan.' Arguably it was Donegan who had had Britain's last skiffle hit in December 1958, with the American folk-tinged song 'Tom Dooley'.

While ABC-TV confirmed that they had no plans for a new show after the end of *Wham!*'s run in mid-June, the BBC's Light Programme opted to extend its Sunday morning pop show *Easy Beat* to one hour and named guitarist Bert Weedon as the new leader of the house band, in succession to John Barry. And while *Easy Beat* and its sister show *Saturday Club*, continued to attract sizeable audiences of interested teenagers at the weekend, the music papers entertained their readers with details of the lifestyles of the new stars.

The *NME*'s 'Life Lines' section was intended to give fans an insight into what made their heroes tick, and two of Britain's brightest hitmakers were featured in May 1960 editions of the newspaper. Adam Faith named The John Barry Seven (led by the man who acted as arranger on Faith's records) as his favourite band with tea and coke as his preferred drinks and, while he opted for casual Italian-styled clothes, Faith listed his 'Miscellaneous Faves' as 'girls, fast cars, bullfighting and radical thinking people.'

Billy Fury confided that red was his favourite colour, his top foods were chicken, beef and melon and his best pet was his boxer dog Crackers. He also explained that his ambition was to take up motor racing.

The seemingly never-ending interest in music – either pop or rock 'n' roll – even had an impact on those closest to it. 'Pop music in the late 1950s and into 1960 swept everything away,' says Marty Wilde. 'You couldn't ignore it and more and more records got played on Luxembourg and the BBC, where even *Two Way Family Favourites* became popular with young service people in Germany and their families in Britain.' In fact the programme, with presenters in London and Cologne, boasted an audience of over six million in 1960.

On the back of his success on tour with Duane Eddy, Emile Ford was presented with a gold disc for a million sales of 'What Do You Want To Make Those Eyes At Me For', which had opened the year at number one. By the end of June 1960, a further five British artists – Michael Holliday, Anthony Newley (twice), Adam Faith and Lonnie Donegan – had topped the chart alongside Americans Johnny Preston, The Everly Brothers and the late Eddie Cochran.

And during the second half of the year, Cliff Richard, Johnny Kidd, The Shadows and Ricky Valance had all held the top spot in the company of US stars Jimmy Jones, Roy Orbison and Elvis Presley. These chart listings were also essential information for the young Bob Harris, who was busy preparing for things to come by making his own radio show in his parents' back room using a reel-to-reel Grundig tape machine, microphone and Decca stereogram.

Long before he worked on radio or TV, Harris studied where an auto-changer record player dropped the needle onto a disc and assiduously counted the lead-in and fade-out times. He calculated that the 14 seconds from the fade to the start of the next track was, 'Enough time for me to back-announce the record, talk about the music and introduce the next song.' He also explained that he had one main source of information. 'I got all my info about tours, new releases and gossip from *New Musical Express*. I used to cut out the Top 30 singles chart and underline the records that I owned, compiling my own weekly Top 20, which became the basis of the show.'

After having played on a dozen hit records as Cliff Richard's backing group, The Shadows decided it was time to start making records without their star singer and in April they visited Abbey Road studios to record a track called 'Apache' – plus a version of the familiar sing-along-a-coach-trip song 'Quartermaster's Stores'.

Written by Jerry Lordan, 'Apache' was produced by

Norrie Paramor, the man who made all of Richard's records, and Bruce Welch recalls that the process was the same irrespective of who was in the studio. 'We'd run through things for about five minutes to give the engineer a chance to get a level. Then, when the red light went on, we just got on with it and put it down in one take.'

Despite the fact that Paramor was in absolute charge of proceedings – 'Norrie was the boss in the studio and you never argued with him' says Welch – the group got together when the session was over and steeled themselves to tell their producer that they preferred 'Apache' to the song he had suggested. 'So Norrie did what he always did with his recordings; he took them home to play to his kids and because they liked 'Apache' it came out as the A-side.'

By August 'Apache' had ousted Richard's 'Please Don't Tease' (which also featured The Shadows) from the number-one spot and justified the group's decision to record without a singer, although this was originally inspired by an American guitar legend. 'Duane Eddy gave us the right to play instrumentals because he was having enormous hits,' explains Welch.

Part of the success of 'Apache' was down to coverage in the media and, as Welch recounts, the Shadows' record company hired one of the music industry's top PR men to help out. 'Les Perrin was hired by EMI to plug 'Apache' and he went round sticking arrows in the desks of various music writers – Les always liked a stunt.'

But the band also played their part in promoting their debut solo hit, according to Welch. '*Melody Maker* was the jazz paper and *NME* was the rock paper and was enormously important to us and to the public. We were friends with people like Derek Johnson at *NME* and we always kept in contact and would ring up to get advance news of our chart placings from them.'

The Shadows' success, coupled with Richard's continuing influence, saw them both booked for a three-month season at the London Palladium, while Larry Parnes put together a package involving Billy Fury, Joe Brown and Gene Vincent to go out on tour in memory of Eddie Cochran with part of the proceeds going to the late singer's dependants.

At the same time America was revelling in the distinctive sounds emanating from the second Newport Folk Festival, which was held on Rhode Island and featured the likes of Joan Baez, Pete Seeger and The Clancy Brothers alongside Blues stars John Lee Hooker and Muddy Waters.

Ten years after the release of their first long-playing records (LPs) in Britain, Decca Records announced that in the past decade they had released a total of 300 albums and, in a 1960 look-back at the format, *Record Retailer* referred to sleeves as 'envelopes' but admitted that the idea of printing notes on the back was 'one of the happiest innovations the LP brought in its train.'

While Elvis Presley topped the British album chart for the first time in July 1960 with *Elvis Is Back* and

Roy Orbison made it in the singles chart with his single 'Only The Lonely' – a song which was turned down by both Presley and The Everly Brothers – an Australian entertainer named Rolf Harris hit the top 20 with a ditty entitled 'Tie Me Kangaroo Down Sport' which came complete with something called a wobble board.

The 1960 summer Olympics were held in Rome and while British athlete Don Thompson triumphed in the 50km walk and the future King Constantine of Greece won gold in sailing, a young America boxer named Cassius Clay won the light heavyweight division and took his first steps towards eventually becoming both Muhammad Ali and 'The Greatest'.

Back home in the UK, it was revealed that just one in ten drivers was a woman, although the arrival of the Mini in 1959 had in part changed the outdated attitude that it was humiliating for a man to be driven anywhere by a woman. However, the new Jaguar car launched in 1960 was not targeted at the woman driver. The E-Type was proclaimed as the fastest production car ever made with a top speed of 150mph and it was embraced – mainly by men – as one of the flashiest and sexiest cars ever made.

Two new names also appeared on the recording scene in 1960 – and they came from completely opposite sides of the tracks. While Top Rank records – a division of the famous film company – hired independent producer Joe Meek to make records with the likes of Michael Cox, The Flee-Rakkers and a budding actor named John Leyton, a company called Melodisc signed an even more impressive artist. Pope John XXIII became the first Pontiff to make a record, when his blessing Urbu et Orbi was coupled with a hymn sung by the choir of St Peter's Rome.

Using the name The Beatles for the first time, the group from Liverpool took up a residency of more than 100 nights in Hamburg – playing at the Indira and Kaiserkellar clubs – between August and November. And while Lonnie Donegan earned his first ever gold disc – after five years of trying – for 'My Old Man's A Dustman', a new dance craze was appearing on the horizon in America.

Chubby Checker – who was born Ernest Evans in South Carolina – was invited to record the Hank Ballard song 'The Twist' by the host of *American Bandstand,* Dick Clark on the back of a sudden surge of interest in the dance. On August 6, Checker debuted his version on Clark's show and within weeks he was at the top of the US chart with sales of over a million. As an added bonus, every copy of the disc came with instructions on how to do 'The Twist' – 'imagine you are stubbing out a cigarette with both feet while drying your back with a towel.'

Reflecting on his immediate and enormous success in America, Checker simply explained, 'Timing had a lot to do with it.' Expanding on Neil Sedaka's theory surrounding the circumstances of his own success, Checker added, 'Buddy Holly had gone down. Elvis Presley had gone into the army, Chuck Berry had been ostracized for transporting a minor across state lines,

Jerry Lee Lewis had married his cousin and he was ostracized. Little Richard had gone to the seminary. It was a down period. It was like rock 'n' roll had died.'

In Britain, 'The Twist' showed no great lasting appeal as it climbed to number 49 for a week in September and then re-appeared five places higher a month later, before disappearing after another one week stay on the chart. This was despite Keith Fordyce telling the readers of the *NME*, 'It's a steady rocker with Chubby Checker vocalising about a new kind of dance step.' The same paper's reaction to Cliff Richard's new album *Me & My Shadows* was, however, altogether more enthusiastic. Under the banner headline 'No Home Should Be Without This Album', the reviewer suggested that the music 'banishes gloom and is guaranteed to restore that happy wide-awake feeling.'

The label launched in Detroit by Berry Gordy in 1959 finally came to Britain in September 1960 when the first Motown Records – issued through the independent UK label Oriole – appeared featuring The Contours, Mary Wells and The Marvelettes. Gordy spent time explaining that his first label was named after Detroit – the Motor City or Motor Town – and the sister Tamla imprint was inspired by the Debbie Reynolds hit Tammy. Either way it would be a further four years before a Motown act – The Supremes – would finally hit the UK chart ... on the Stateside label launched by EMI as a home for American repertoire.

NME's Poll for 1960 featured Elvis Presley ahead of

Cliff Richard as World Male Singer and Connie Francis in front of Brenda Lee as Top World Female, while The Everlys were again Best World Group and Duane Eddy took the title of Top Music Personality. Britain's Top Male was Richard in front of Adam Faith, while Shirley Bassey edged out Alma Cogan as Top Female, Emile Ford was named Best TV Singer and Apache by The Shadows was named Top British Disc.

As the year drew to a close, news was published giving details of the tours lined up for 1961 with Brenda Lee, Roy Orbison, Johnny and The Hurricanes and Brian Hyland all being among those set to visit Britain in the opening couple of months of the new year.

But before these US stars arrived, there was Christmas and that meant panto season. Among those booked for the traditional festive entertainment were Adam Faith (*Dick Whittington* in Wimbledon); Michael Holliday (*Mother Goose* in Gloucester); Gary Miller (*Humpty Dumpty* in Manchester); Lonnie Donegan (*Cinderella* in Nottingham); The Dallas Boys (*Babes In the Wood* in Stockport); and Ruby Murray (*Cinderella* in Torquay).

Not appearing in pantomime and back home in America after their debut UK tour and record-breaking number one 'Cathy's Clown' – eight weeks in the top spot in Britain and worldwide sales of three million copies – The Everly Brothers were content to reflect on their musical style. 'We're not Grand Old Opry … we're obviously not Perry Como … we're just pop music. But you could call us an American skiffle group.'

On October 27 1960 a major censorship trial began at London's Old Bailey court when book publishers Penguin were charged under the Obscene Publications Act following their decision to publish D.H. Lawrence's book *Lady Chatterley's Lover*, which had been banned from sale in the UK since 1928.

At the end of a six-day trial – during which the prosecuting counsel had asked the jury if this was a book 'You would want your wife or your servants to read' – Penguin were found not guilty and, on the first day after the end of the trial, over 200,000 copies of the book were sold in shops across the land.

At the other end of the scale – as America elected John F Kennedy as its 35th President – the two biggest hitters in British pop both set new records. While Elvis Presley was busy notching up best-ever UK advance sales of over 540,000 for 'It's Now Or Never', Britain's very own Cliff Richard recorded total career sales in excess of 5.5 million up to the end of 1960 – just as Richard's fourth British number one, 'I Love You' took over from 'It's Now Or Never', Presley's fifth UK chart topper.

Chapter 8

1961: More Pop Than Rock

A 14-year-old girl from London's East End who would be dubbed the 'bouffant-haired teen queen of pop', made a sensational arrival on the British pop scene in 1961, having stepped into Abbey Road studios in January to make her first record.

Helen Shapiro went from singing school to the studio for her artist's test, and her rendition of 'Birth Of The Blues' left producer Norrie Paramor confused, as he didn't believe that the singer was either 14 – or even a girl. 'I had to go to his office and sing for him,' says Shapiro. Having convinced Paramor, Shapiro then went into studio one to make her first single 'Don't Treat Me Like A Child', which took her to number three in the UK chart. 'I remember going into the control room and hearing my voice for the first time through loudspeakers. It sounded like me but better.'

Before the year was over Shapiro would become the youngest female chart-topper when 'You Don't Know' reached number one and she followed up with 'Walkin' Back To Happiness', which became her second successive million-seller and even spent a week in the US Top 100. 'Virtually everything was done in one take and I was known as 'one take Charlie',' recalled Shapiro as she explained how things were recorded back then. 'The way we worked was to choose a song, somebody would do an arrangement and I just came in and did it.'

While Shapiro was on the verge of becoming the latest British sensation, American singing superstar Frank Sinatra set up his own Reprise Records and immediately signed his pal Sammy Davis Jnr. to the label because, as he explained, 'I want to avoid having bad rock 'n' roll artists associated with my new Reprise label.' At least Ol' Blue Eyes was consistent, as he had earlier described rock 'n' roll as 'The most brutal, ugly, degenerate, vicious form of expression it has been my displeasure to hear.'

And it seemed that the Hollywood Women's Press League were equally unimpressed with rock stars, as they dismissed Elvis Presley as the 'least co-operative actor.' However in February, Presley took time off from acting – and annoying the ladies of the press – to return to the stage for the first time in three years with a concert in Memphis in front of 10,000 people. It raised over $50,000 for local charities and, during the performance, Presley was given a plaque by RCA Records to recognize total sales of 76 million records.

Across the Atlantic, a five-piece group made their debut as The Beatles at the Cavern Club in Liverpool during a lunch-time show on February 21. They were paid £5 before going on to play two more gigs at different venues on the same day.

In an unprecedented move, producer Paramor decided to 'experiment' and release The Shadows' single 'Kon-Tiki' in the US before the UK. 'It will be interesting to see if, by the time it is issued here, it is an American hit', he explained. It wasn't. But that didn't stop 'Kon-Tiki', when it did come out, hitting the number-one spot in Britain although the group had to sit and watch as a Danish guitarist named Jorgen Ingmann reached number two in the US with a cover of their debut UK hit 'Apache'.

While all the signs were that rock 'n' roll was on the way out in favour of ballads and catchy pop numbers, a couple of British groups continued to fly the flag for the music condemned by Sinatra as 'brutal, ugly, degenerate and vicious.' Vince Taylor and The Playboys and Dick Rivers and Les Chaut Sauvages managed to kick off what was described as a 'full-blown riot' in Paris when their performances at the Palais des Sports resulted in a punch-up between fans and the local gendarmes.

Belfast-born Van Morrison was among those who recognized that popular music was moving in different directions. 'There were two branches of rock 'n roll when I was brought up – the Elvis branch, a straight commercial thing that included Presley, Ricky Nelson, Roy Orbison. The other branch was Jerry Lee Lewis, Little Richard, Fats Domino, people who were a little less commercial than Elvis,' explained Morrison, who maintained a particular fondness for the man known as 'The Killer'. 'Jerry Lee seemed to have a lot more going on. He covered a lot of territory, so I used to listen to him.'

Shadows guitarist Bruce Welch also spotted that the public were becoming split over the music they wanted to listen to and buy. 'There was an audience that wanted harder American rock 'n' roll – the Teds still wanted Gene Vincent, Eddie Cochran and Jerry Lee – and there was an audience that wanted softer pop rock like Neil Sedaka and Bobby Vee and The Everlys.'

And, by his own admission, Welch and The Shadows were also moving in a new direction. 'By the early 1960s we were no longer a rock 'n' roll act – we had moved on to become all-round entertainers.' Reflecting that The Shadows were successful 'because of instrumentals and because we could play rock 'n' roll', Welch added, 'Our manager Peter Gormley and Norrie Paramor advised us and they suggested that rock 'n' roll was not going to last.'

David Hughes was one of the fans who noticed the change but he wasn't overly concerned about the new music. 'It was a seamless move from hard rock 'n' roll to softer stuff like Bobby Vee and Del Shannon,' he says. 'But no one was putting music into any sort of boxes – you were just listening to everything you could.'

However Hughes, later to become Marketing Director with EMI Records, was unimpressed by the British cover versions of the hits from America which record producers in the UK seemed intent on making. 'Producers like Wally Ridley heard the latest releases when they got a box of discs in from RCA or CBS in America and then decided which songs Dickie Valentine or Ronnie Hilton or Mark Wynter would cover.'

And future award-winning British music radio executive Tony Hale agrees. 'People in this country who were on record back then were given this stuff from America to record and it didn't really change until Lennon and McCartney arrived to write their own songs.'

For teenagers like Hughes and thousands more, America was the 'golden land' which delivered the stuff of dreams. 'I knew nothing about America except that it had to be better than us because all that stuff had come a long way and it was so good; and they talked with a great accent and made great records.'

After the UK motor trade celebrated the one millionth Morris Minor rolling off the production line, the USSR went more than one stage further and sent the first man – Yuri Gagarin – into space on April 12 1961, just three weeks ahead of American astronaut Alan Shepherd orbiting the earth.

Britain's newest pop music show *Thank Your Lucky Stars* first aired on April 1 but the debut show had a familiar air of respectability about it, as host Pete Murray introduced Anne Shelton, The Dallas Boys and Hughie Green. According to Hale, this was an example of a major reaction to some of the stuff that had gone before. 'The end of the rock 'n' roll thing was the establishment saying we don't want any of that – we want clean-cut boys and girls who behave.'

America was also experiencing change with soul

and R&B singer Ray Charles cleaning up at the 1961 Grammy Awards with wins for Best Album, Best Vocal Single, Best Pop Single and Best R&B Performance, while at the same time a teenager from Minnesota was taking up residency in a New York club. Bob Dylan's debut in Greenwich Village in April was at Gerde's Folk Club. He also reflected on the changes that had taken place in music. 'Little Richard, Carl Perkins and Jerry Lee Lewis were the people I listened to before I got into folk music. But their scene wasn't happening anymore. It was over.'

While the end of the British Board of Trade's ban on the import of goods from America meant that more and more guitars came into the UK marketplace, the established non-US brands fought to hold onto business. German company Hofner put on offer a range of five guitars including one bass guitar, with the top-of-the-range Hofner V3 priced at 50 guineas (£52.50p), while Czech manufacturer Futurama had their Futurama 3 model on sale for 45gns (£49.25p).

But budding musician Terry Slater had his on eye on something altogether more lavish.

Having bought a Hofner from one of the shops in London's Soho district – 'you'd spend your weekends just looking in awe at the guitars in the shop windows in Denmark Street and Charing Cross Road' – Slater moved on from his £20 model to the latest in American imports. 'The early Fender Stratocasters were about £125, which was an awful lot of money in those days and I can't remember how I got the money to afford a Strat. But I know I just wanted one.' Alongside the latest in guitars, there was also an innovation in the area of listening devices, with Grundig offering a breast pocket-sized transistor radio for 25gns (£27.25p).

Two hopeful young British performers issued interesting third singles in April 1961 as Pye Records launched their new Piccadilly label. Joe Brown's 'Crazy Mixed Up Kid' failed to chart despite his two earlier hits, and Jess Conrad, again on the back of a couple of minor hits, released 'This Pullover', which also flopped. In fact, in 1977 it was voted the sixth 'worst song ever' by listeners to Capital Radio.

But while there was a seemingly never-ending list of young men determined to break into the record business in Britain during the early 1960s, the dearth of successful female pop singers prompted the *NME* to publish a feature asking the question 'Can Girls Really Rock?'

While US stars Brenda Lee, Connie Francis and Skeeter Davis were listed alongside UK best-seller Helen Shapiro as artists that had 'made it', and the article reckoned that Brits Anita Scott and Janice Peters could follow suit, it still reached very conservative conclusions: 'We're not particularly anxious for the girls to take over the rock scene. We'd much rather they remained just – well – just girls.' Not a view they'd be brave enough to put in print a decade or so later.

During their tour of South Africa in March, Cliff

Richard and The Shadows elected to play shows for 'coloured audiences' in Cape Town and in Salisbury (re-named Harare) in Rhodesia (now Zimbabwe) with box-office receipts going to local charities. On his return to Britain, Richard declared, 'When we go back to South Africa, we'd like to do more shows for the non-Europeans.'

By May 1961, record producer George Martin had notched up more than a handful of hit records with the likes of Dick James, Eve Boswell, Eamonn Andrews and Peter Sellers (with and without Italian actress Sophia Loren), but he had still to make a disc that reached the coveted number-one spot on the chart. All that changed, thanks to an unlikely group called The Temperance Seven which had been co- founded by Brian Innes, a near neighbour of Martin. 'I went along to see them and liked their sound: it was interesting, mellow and steeped in nostalgia.'

And when he came to make the chart-topping record 'You're Driving Me Crazy', Martin deliberately tried to create an old-time feel. 'We even put scratches on the record and tried using single mikes, and (singer) Paul McDowell used a megaphone in the studio to achieve that particular vocal sound.'

Martin's first major chart success in the new era of pop and rock also compensated in some way for the runaway success of one of his rival EMI producers. 'I did envy Norrie Paramor enormously because he had a young man who was originally called Harry Webb, who became Cliff Richard, and it didn't matter what he recorded – it could have been 'God Save The Queen' – it became number one.'

And as he didn't have a major pop star signed to his Parlophone label, Martin contented himself with making what he called 'oddball records' with people like Peter Ustinov, Charlie Drake and Bernard Cribbins, but he still had his eyes and ears set on other styles. 'I wanted to have something that would be easy to make instead of the difficulty of making comedy records. And I wanted to beat Norrie, who had the most number one records,' said the man who would eventually take the record with Elton John's 1997 version of 'Candle In The Wind' – Martin's 30th chart topper.

At the same time, the British Songwriter's Guild reported some interesting data which showed that, of the 104,000 records played on UK radio during 1960, 39% of them were British, and the BBC played a total of 20,000 discs. In addition, by the middle of 1961, British radio, including Radio Luxembourg which had opened a London studio in the 1950s, would have featured all ten of the discs which topped the UK singles chart during the first six months of the year.

The list, of course, included the ever-present Elvis. His third UK number one in the first half of the year 'Surrender' (after 'Are You Lonesome Tonight?' and 'Wooden Heart') set a new record by leaping from number 27 to number one in the chart with advance orders of 460,000. Next came two-time chart toppers

The Everly Brothers plus six first-timers – Johnny Tillotson, Petula Clark, The Marcels, Floyd Cramer, The Temperance Seven and Del Shannon.

Meanwhile, four of the biggest rock/pop stars of the day busied themselves with a range of projects including a film, a musical, a theme park and some iffy lyrics. As Cliff Richard settled into filming his new movie *The Young Ones*, so Marty Wilde took to the stage to play Elvis Presley in Manchester in the pre-London West End run of *Bye Bye Birdie*, which was described as a 'Presley spoof' musical.

Over in America, US star Chuck Berry decided to invest his hard-earned record royalties in a 30-acre amusement park near St Louis which he named Berry Park. Meanwhile, Lonnie Donegan focused his attention on changing the lyrics of an old-time American blues ode to cocaine called 'Have A Whiff On Me' to the much more acceptable 'Have A Drink On Me'.

The change of title worked, as the record peaked at number eight, but it represented Donegan's third run-in with the broadcasting authorities as he had been forced to change the word 'ruddy' to 'bloomin' in his 1959 hit 'Battle Of New Orleans', while his even earlier effort 'Diggin' My Potatoes' – it was considered to be a blatant reference to sex – had been classed as obscene and banned from the airwaves.

Life was altogether more joyous for former England football captain Billy Wright, who was 'captured' at Abbey Road studios for the TV programme *This Is Your*

Life by host Eamonn Andrews. Wright, the first player to win 100 England caps, was in the studio to hear a playback with his wife Joy (one of The Beverly Sisters) plus Russ Conway and Dorothy Squires.

Football also featured in a release from Oriole Records in May 1961 entitled 'The Spurs Song' which celebrated (albeit a week or two early) Tottenham Hotspur's FA Cup Final win over Leicester City. At the same time Pye put out an EP of Raymond Glendenning's BBC radio commentary of the game.

Although he had not topped the British charts, Neil Sedaka had racked up half a dozen hits by the time he made his first trip to the UK in May 1961. And although 'Little Devil' was still in the top ten, he elected to sing the follow-up on his debut TV show. 'My first visit was to play *Sunday Night At The London Palladium* and perform my new record 'Happy Birthday Sweet Sixteen'. Adam Faith – who was very good looking – and Helen Shapiro – she was wonderful – were on the show.'

As one of the first composers from New York's famous 'song factory' – which was based in the Brill Building off Broadway – to record his own songs, Sedaka was an established writer and performer by the time he arrived in Britain as a 22-year-old. 'It was one of my first trips abroad and Britain was very civilized and very polished and everybody sounded very intelligent,' he recalls. 'I don't remember it as being very dingy or having bad food but I was just a youngster. I was very impressed by the architecture and the parks – and the people liked me so I liked them.'

While he was here, Sedaka also found time to meet up with Britain's number-one popular music star. 'I do remember meeting Cliff Richard, who they told me was very revered as your Elvis of England.' And, it seems, Britain was somewhere Sedaka discussed regularly with his fellow American artists. 'I was a friend of Gene Pitney and we often spoke about his success in Britain (he wrote the hits 'Rubber Ball' for Bobby Vee and 'Hello Mary Lou' for Ricky Nelson), and I talked to Bobby Vee and Connie Francis about the British market. We were watching your charts very carefully because it was an important market for me and other artists,' says the man whose total record sales exceed 30 million.

Betting – on horse and greyhound racing plus football – came out of the back alleys and dingy corners of public houses and appeared on the streets of Britain in May when betting shops were legalised. Other entertainment on offer in the year included the films *Oliver*, *Catch 22*, *A Taste Of Honey* and *West Side Story*, while *Dr Kildare*, *The Avengers* and comedians Morecambe and Wise all appeared on TV for the first time. And if you fancied something a bit more cultured, star ballet dancer Rudolf Nureyev became more accessible after he jumped the barriers at Paris airport and defected to the West from the USSR.

In an effort to make people 'think of me as a singer

and not more specifically as a rock singer', Billy Fury recorded 'Halfway To Paradise' and was rewarded with his first top-three chart hit. The Liverpool born singer's debut album *The Sound Of Fury* – which included songs he composed under the alias Wilbur Wilberforce, was produced by Jack Good and featured Joe Brown on guitar – also made it into the UK Top 20.

By the middle of the year, four months after coming second in the Eurovision Song Contest, Britain's entry 'Are You Sure', which peaked at number two in the UK chart, had reportedly earned singers and composers the Allisons – Brian Alford (John Allison) and Colin Day (Bob Allison) – a cool £12,500 in record and publishing royalties. And it was estimated these earnings would double through live, radio and TV appearances.

Among a clutch of new British singers intent on pushing their way to the top were Shane Fenton, Paul Raven and John Leyton. Both Fenton (later to become Alvin Stardust) and Raven (who would turn into Gary Glitter) were signed to EMI and recorded in Abbey Road studios, but only Fenton met with any success which came as a welcome bonus to engineer Norman Smith.

Bizarrely Fenton, who was inspired to pursue a career in rock 'n' roll by a chance meeting with Buddy Holly backstage at the Doncaster Gaumont during the American singer's UK tour in March 1958 – when he also jammed backstage with Holly and the Crickets – took on his first professional identity at the request of the heartbroken mother of Johnny Theakston.

Theakston was the original Shane Fenton and had led both Shane Fenton and the Beat Boys and Shane Fenton and the Fentones before dying from rheumatic fever aged 17. With the chance of a BBC audition, his mother asked the band to stay together in memory of her son and band roadie Bernard Jewry moved on to become the band's lead singer under the name Shane Fenton.

Working with producer Ron Richards, he then made 'I'm A Moody Guy' which, as Smith recalls, was Fenton's first taste of success. 'We had a minor hit with 'Moody Guy' which boosted my wages a bit because at that time engineers were paid bonuses if they worked on hit records – but strangely enough producers only got a flat salary.'

John Leyton was an actor who in 1961 was starring in the TV series *Harpers West One*, playing a rock singer called Johnny Saint-Cyr. During one of the shows, he performed a song called 'Johnny Remember Me', which somehow caught the attention of producer Joe Meek who had previously engineered Lonnie Donegan's number-one hit 'Cumberland Gap'.

Recorded in Meek's famous 'bathroom' studio in his flat in London's Holloway district, 'Johnny Remember Me' eventually took Leyton to number-one despite the panel on *Juke Box Jury* voting it a resounding 'miss'. He had failed a year earlier with his version of 'Tell Laura I Love Her' but would still go on to star in the blockbuster movie *The Great Escape*.

Also produced by Meek was popular rocker Cliff Bennett and his group The Rebel Rousers who focused on playing Presley, Vincent and Cochran covers until they recorded 'You've Got What I Like' in 1961 – although it would be another three years before Bennett finally hit the charts with a song written by the team of Lennon & McCartney.

Another established favourite of serious rock 'n' rollers was Vince Taylor, who earned his best reviews for 'Brand New Cadillac' in the summer of 1961, when it was cited as the best British-made rock record since either Richard's 'Move It' or Kidd's 'Shakin' All Over' but, despite getting a thumbs-up from the critics, chart success continued to elude the American-born, British-based singer.

When the first edition of a new magazine called *Mersey Beat* appeared in Liverpool, launched by art student Bill Harry, it was intended to promote the city's growing rock 'n' roll scene. At the time, the word 'beat' was rarely used as a musical term but it was considered appropriate in the context of an area covered by a local policeman. The first issue came out on July 5 1961 and included an essay on the 'dubious origins of Beatles' written by John Lennon, a fellow student of Harry's at the Liverpool Art College.

The second edition of the 3d (1p) magazine carried the front page headline 'Beatles Sign Recording Contract' and referred to the band's debut release with singer Tony Sheridan of 'My Bonnie' for the German

Polydor label. It was a request for this record in Brian Epstein's NEMS record store which led to the Liverpool businessman visiting the Cavern in November to see The Beatles for the first time.

An increase in purchase tax plus higher manufacturing costs pushed up the price of records with singles increasing by 5d (2p) to 6s 9d (33½p) and top line albums costing 37s 2d (£1.86p), up from 35s 9½d (£1.78p). Pye also took the opportunity to, confusingly, increase the price of their Golden Guinea series – set at the traditional guinea price of 21s (£1.5p) – to 21s 6d (£1.7½p).

With his new managers and a new recording contract – plus a new identity as Eden Kane – Rick Sarstedt also had to settle into a new lifestyle. 'They groomed me, did a kind of makeover thing and said 'now that you're Eden Kane you're going to have be this character' which had nothing to do with me being myself.' He also needed a new song to record and that came courtesy of established songwriter Johnny Worth, who also composed under the alias Les Vandyke.

'He had written 'What Do You Want' and 'Poor Me' for Adam Faith and he came up with a song, although there was a suggestion that I record a country song called 'Before I Lose My Mind',' explains Sarstedt. But it was Worth's song 'Well I Ask You' that won the day and became both Kane's debut chart entry and also his only number one. Recalling that the song was neither a ballad nor a rocker, Sarstedt says, 'There is no explanation for some things, especially why a song that was so different from what was happening should be a hit. However, it did have a great feel and needed a certain kind of performance, but once we'd done a couple of takes and found the right groove it was easy.'

Although Sarstedt doesn't remember anyone at the session saying, 'That's a hit', 'Well I Ask You' finally displaced The Everly Brothers' 'Temptation' at number one after two months on the chart. Looking back, Sarstedt does however recall that being a chart-topper did bring him 'money, fame and fans', although he admits, 'respect was a little harder to come by.'

And reaching number one when his heroes – such as Billy Fury, Marty Wilde and Eddie Cochran (while he was alive) – had failed gave Sarstedt something to reflect on. 'It's a statistic and a matter of timing. I enjoy the fact that I had a number one and I'm very proud of it, but that's as far as it goes.' And there is another 'not a lot of people know that' statistic surrounding Sarstedt – his brothers Peter and Robin also had solo UK top-three hits.

BBC TV's *Juke Box Jury* programme took a surprise turn in August 1961 when Cliff Michelmore, Derek Hart, Fyfe Robertson and Kenneth Allsopp – the team of presenters from the popular news magazine show *Tonight* – were invited to make up the panel, but their appearance was overshadowed by the decision taken by the rulers of East Germany to build the Berlin Wall and split the former capital city of Germany in half.

And as The Dave Brubeck Quartet took jazz into the top ten with 'Take Five' so Adam Faith opted to spread his wings and moved onto the cabaret circuit, making his debut at The Room At The Top (above a furniture store in Ilford High Road), and Bob Dylan signed a contract with Columbia Records in New York after playing the harmonica on a recording by folk singer Carolyn Hester.

For between 7s 6d (37½p) and 17s 6d (87½p) pop fans could buy a ticket to see the likes of Cliff Richard, The Shadows, Adam Faith, The Temperance Seven, Gene Vincent, Billy Fury, Eden Kane, The Brooks Brothers and Jess Conrad on stage at the Empire Pool Wembley on September 10 in *NME*'s Big Stars of 1961 Show.

Record sales were now such big business that newsagents W.H. Smith were busy expanding this area and in a full-page advertisement announced the opening of two new 'modern record departments' in their stores in Gloucester and Bognor Regis, which brought their total number of record outlets to 27, including seven in London. This was followed soon after by an advertisement from the Co-op, which declared that record departments were 'an important enterprise amongst the societies', as 11 stores from Birmingham to York opened record outlets. And it wasn't just in Britain that records were doing big business.

During the last week of September 1961, it was reported that no less than 18 UK discs were bestsellers in 11 'overseas countries', including 'lands as far afield as Israel and South Africa.' Among the big international hits were records by Cliff Richard, Petula Clark, Helen Shapiro, Lonnie Donegan, Eden Kane and John Leyton plus, surprisingly, Scottish singer Andy Stewart's hit 'Donald Where's Your Troosers'?

The final album chart for September 1961 featured The Shadows at number one, as they became the first group to top the chart, although George Mitchell's Black And White Minstrels (which was more a choir than a group) had enjoyed six weeks at number one earlier in the year. A couple of months later, Cliff Richard followed his backing group to the top with '21 Today', to become the first British solo singer to have a number-one album.

The latest Larry Parnes' promotion – his Star Spangled Nights tour – went out on the road in October with Eden Kane joining Fury, Brown, Tommy Bruce, The Allisons, The Karl Denver Trio and Peter Jay and The Jaywalkers. Looking at a poster for the show from Sunday October 29 1961, Sarstedt (Kane) reflects, 'It says 'Book now, one night only' and tickets cost 3s 6d (17½p), 5s 6d (27½p) or 7s 6d (37½p). Billy Fury was the star of the show and topped the bill, while I closed the first half, but you couldn't help but stay and watch Billy.'

Although they were rivals in the charts, Sarstedt has nothing but praise for fellow singer Fury. 'He was definitely the most magnetic performer, he had rock 'n' roll magic and when he came on it was something special.' Confirming that virtually the entire cast wore suits and ties – 'nobody wore jeans on stage and only a couple wore leather', Sarstedt reminisces about the crowded bill. 'There were so many people on the show that I would probably end up doing about six songs – it was the hit plus a B-side and an opening and closing rocker, maybe a Chuck Berry or Gene Vincent song. But it all depended on the number of acts and how much time you had.'

Having spent most of his early career travelling to shows by car or even on the bus, Sarstedt said that by the time he had a number-one record and a follow-up top ten hit things had improved. 'By this time finances were a little better so we went by train sometimes and things were generally pretty good with plenty of work.' And like most of his contemporaries, Sarstedt was happy to leave the business side of things to his managers. 'After all I was doing better than I was before. I was thinking 'this is good – 20 quid a week' and I was living the life of Riley ... until I had to go home to my mother's house.'

Around this time, former big band and dance hall singer Dick James decided to retire from the singing business and become a music publisher. The man who turned the TV theme 'The Ballad Of Robin Hood' into a Top 20 hit in 1956, launched Dick James Music in September 1961 and listed among the company's first published songs was a composition called 'Double

Scotch', which credited George Martin as its composer.

As 1961 drew to a close, so a new liberated age loomed on the horizon. If the freeing-up of the book *Lady Chatterley's Lover* for publication had swept away some of the establishment barriers, the launch of the satirical magazine *Private Eye* – with its enthusiasm for mocking and exposing the high and mighty and the famous and infamous – appealed to a new, young and less restricted generation, while the introduction of a female contraceptive pill opened up the gates to an age of sexual freedom.

But the year was not quite over in terms of music. *The Young Ones* – the new film from Cliff Richard and The Shadows – was generally welcomed with open arms by the media with the *NME* describing it as the 'Best Teenage Romp Ever!' and over in America legendary cowboy singer Tex Ritter hit on a novel way of promoting his record *Hillbilly Cowboy*. He recorded over 100 different versions, each with an individual name check for the most influential disc jockeys who, in turn, were sent a personalised copy of the disc.

The annual *NME* Poll once again had Elvis Presley as Outstanding World Male ahead of Cliff Richard, with Connie Francis voted Outstanding World Female over Helen Shapiro and The Everly Brothers retaining (again) their title as Outstanding World Group. And while Richard and Adam Faith were again numbers one and two in the Best British Male category, Helen Shapiro pushed Shirley Bassey into second place as Best British

Female. The Springfields emerged as Best British Group and John Leyton's 'Johnny Remember Me' was chosen as Best Disc ahead of Billy Fury's 'Halfway To Paradise'.

The same paper's charts listing – based on points for positions – had Presley at the top with 1487, Richard in second place on 1009 while Shapiro, the Shadows and The Everlys filled the next three places. Way down at the bottom of the pile – with just one point for just one week in last place on the chart – were Max Bygraves, Johnny Mathis, Al Saxon and Bob Wallis.

Even though Presley topped both *NME*'s popularity and points charts, 1961 was in fact the best ever year for British number ones with ten of the 21 chart topping records coming from UK artists including, in the second half of the year, Eden Kane, John Leyton, Helen Shapiro(twice), Shirley Bassey, The Shadows, Frankie Vaughan and Danny Williams.

However it wasn't any of the established big-name, chart-topping, award-wining British or American artists who made the final headlines of the year. Described as the biggest 'popular music phenomenon' since 'Rock Around The Clock', 'The Twist' was a record by Chubby Checker that had first made the UK top 40 twice in 1960. It was back and this time it was at the heart of a revived Twist dance sensation, although it was his follow-up record 'Let's Twist Again' which made it to number two in December 1961.

Bizarrely, it had taken nearly two years for the craze for the Twist to have a serious impact on British audiences following Checker, a former chicken-plucker from Philadelphia, first hitting number one in the States. But once the Twist returned, it went from strength to strength with films such as 'Hey Let's Twist', 'Twist Around The Clock' and 'Don't Knock The Twist' being released in quick succession.

At the time movie producer Sam Katzman admitted that his film *Twist Around The Clock* had cost just $250,000 to make and added, 'In less than six months it had grossed six million – so of course I'm gonna make more *Twist* movies.' The London showings of *Twist Around The Clock* were accompanied by dance demonstrations by the Lionel Blair Dancers, while Checker was signed up to make a make a very odd TV show with Chris Barber's Jazz Band called *Trad With A Twist*. In France, Johnny Hallyday topped the charts with his French-language version of 'Let's Twist Again' while in America, Checker became the first artist to top the chart twice with the same record when 'The Twist' returned to number one in the opening month of 1962, when it also peaked at number 14 in the UK.

So as one year ended and a new one began, the Twist was still the hottest new craze in Britain and at least three established stars sang its praises. 'It knocks me out' said Cliff Richard and Helen Shapiro reckoned it was 'tremendous', while Frankie Vaughan went slightly overboard and dubbed it 'the greatest musical thing to hit England since rock 'n' roll.'

Chapter 9

1962: The Sixties Begin To Swing

While the Twist may well have been all the rage in Britain, in America and around the rest of the world at the start of 1962, the first rumblings of an ambitious home-grown musical movement were being heard in a studio in north London owned by a famous, establishment record company.

Decca Records, created in 1930 by Sir Edward Lewis, had agreed to give a test recording session to four enthusiastic young men from Liverpool, who turned up at the company's studio in Broadhurst Gardens, Hampstead on January 1 1962.

The Beatles – John Lennon, Paul McCartney, George Harrison and Pete Best – arrived at 11am and ran through 15 songs in three hours, including three songs written by Lennon and McCartney, before driving back home. Eventually, however, the group and their manager Brian Epstein learned that they were not going to be offered a contract by Decca's talent scouts, who turned instead to the London-based group Brian Poole and The Tremeloes.

Epstein claimed that the Decca executives told him: 'We don't like your boys' sound. Groups are out: four -piece groups with guitars particularly are finished'. But there was speculation that Poole and his group got the nod as they came from east London and not the north of England, which made meetings and recording easier and cheaper. In fact the five-piece group from Dagenham had already built up a steady following on the club circuit and been featured on the BBC's *Saturday Club*.

At the same time, the Beeb brought the popular *Pick Of The Pops* back to the airwaves in a new extended format which ran from 4pm to 5pm on a Sunday afternoon and quickly became the BBC's most popular music show. And there was some consolation awaiting The Beatles back in Liverpool when they topped the first ever *Mersey Beat* popularity poll – beating rivals Gerry and The Pacemakers by filling in coupons and voting for themselves.

In early 1962 Elvis Presley was still making headlines even when he didn't actually do anything. As the government of Thailand banned all his films on the back of riots during a showing of *Blue Hawaii*, manager Tom Parker upped the ante once again and announced that the price for a one-hour Presley TV special now stood at a whopping $400,000.

On the other hand Cliff Richard was happy to celebrate 500,000 advance sales of his new record 'The Young Ones', while in America a brand new group arrived with the sounds of sea, sand and California in their records – surf music arrived on the US chart with the Beach Boys' debut single 'Surfin'.

At the same time, following the release of his record 'Tribute To Buddy Holly', British singer Mike Berry received a letter from Holly's parents in which they told him that his song was a 'wonderful, sincere tribute to their son.' But, while the single reached number 24 in the UK chart, it was not even released in America.

In their new year round-up of tips for the top in 1962, *NME* listed the likes of Pierce Rodger, Lena Martell, Anita Harris and Iain Gregory alongside US acts Ann-Margaret, Barry Mann and John D Loudermilk. The music paper also carried news of the big tours set for Britain in early 1962 including Cliff Richard, The Shadows and The Dallas Boys; Adam Faith, The John Barry Seven and Desmond Lane; Helen Shapiro, The Brook Brothers, The Four Jays and Dave Allen plus Bobby Vee, Tony Orlando and The Springfields.

The details of bookings for Britain's ever popular summer season shows were also published with Danny Williams heading for Blackpool; The Springfields appearing in Weymouth; The Mudlarks and The Brook Brothers also headlining in Blackpool; Lonnie Donegan visiting Yarmouth; and The Beverly Sisters topping the bill in Llandudno.

Meanwhile Richard's 'The Young Ones' was the first number one of the new year. It debuted in the top spot and was tipped to become the fastest million-selling single in the UK after 830,000 copies were shifted in four weeks. Britain's top star was chasing the million-selling record of six and half weeks set by arch rival Elvis Presley's 1960 hit 'It's Now Or Never', but in the end he had to settle for seven weeks and second place.

However, after a wait of five weeks, Presley eventually followed Richard to the top with 'Can't Help Falling In Love' which was certified in America as his 29th Gold Disc and then, after a month, it was the turn of The Shadows to top the chart for two months with 'Wonderful Land'.

For guitarist Bruce Welch the release of 'Wonderful Land' – The Shadows' third instrumental number one – came at a time when recording techniques were beginning to change. 'The biggest change was going to two-track, which meant we could overdub and put another guitar on. I was beginning to understand some of the technical stuff by then but couldn't understand, and never had the bottle to ask, how people like Buddy Holly, The Everly Brothers and Neil Sedaka could sing with themselves,' he says.

Admitting that the group had recorded 'Wonderful Land' some time before it was released, Welch added, 'We had it in the can for years because we weren't happy with it but we didn't know what was wrong. Norrie (Paramor) went off and put strings on it when two-track came in and just presented it to us without ever telling us what he was going to do. We were knocked out with it.'

Cliff Richard and his backing band also continued to scale new heights with the singer voted Show Business Personality of the Year by the Variety Club of Great Britain, while The Shadows became the first group to top the bill at the celebrated Paris Olympia. Two other firsts achieved in March 1962 were Helen Shapiro becoming the first British act to top the Japanese chart – with 'You Don't Know Me' – and The Beatles making their radio debut in Manchester on the BBC programme *Teenager's Turn*.

And just in case anyone wondered, the Twist was still attracting big sales with four Twist- related titles in the US top 30 in March and three – Checker's 'Let's Twist Again' and 'Slow Twistin' plus 'Teach Me To Twist' (his duet with Bobby Rydell) – in the British Top 30. But before the year was out the Minister of Education in Malaysia told schoolteachers not to teach the Twist as it was 'an unhealthy and non-eastern culture', while the US Embassy in Saigon was raided by police and a secretary charged with allowing guests to dance the Twist. Earlier, a spokesman for the US President had denied that 'Twist dancing' took place in the White House.

The other big news from the USA was that astronaut John Glenn became the first American to orbit the earth, while items also filtered through to say that Ricky Nelson had officially renamed himself as Rick Nelson and that a debut self-titled album had been released by Bob Dylan who, in turn, officially changed his name from Zimmerman to Dylan.

Almost two years after he survived the car crash which killed his friend Eddie Cochran, Gene Vincent set out on his seventh tour of the UK, alongside Brenda Lee.

While somebody observed that he was a 'curly-haired shy character with a perpetual air of despondency', his performance brought the observation that 'the crude rock 'n' roll he revitalized brought the crowds in.'

Just as The Shadows were feted as the first British 'small instrumental group' to earn a gold disc – for a million sales of 'Apache' – so their bass player Jet Harris played his last show at the *NME* Poll Winners Concert in April before going solo and eventually linking up with former Shads drummer Tony Meehan. At the same time *NME* boasted a double celebration as, ten years after being re-launched as the *New Musical Express*, the music paper's circulation topped the 200,000 mark.

Back in the country for the first time since his ill-fated and short-lived appearance in 1958 with his 13-year-old wife (and second cousin), Jerry Lee Lewis was given a surprisingly warm welcome as he toured with Johnny Kidd and The Pirates and Vince Eager. Meanwhile, down in deepest Kent, Keith Richards and Mick Jagger were busy, according to Richards, 'record hunting' in advance of creating their own band. Although they had been at junior school together in Dartford, the pair lost touch until a chance meeting on a railway station in 1961 confirmed their love of the same music.

'Did we hit it off? You get in a carriage with a guy that's got 'Rockin' At The Hop' by Chuck Berry on Chess Records and *The Best Of Muddy Waters* also under his arm, you are going to hit it off. He's got Henry Morgan's treasure,' is how Richards remembered the encounter.

While Richards and Jagger shared a love for R&B stalwarts such as Jimmy Reed, Howlin' Wolf, John Lee Hooker and Bo Diddley, the future guitar-playing founding member of the Rolling Stones was less impressed with what else was going on in Britain at the time. In a letter to his aunt Patty, written in April 1962, Richards observed, 'Of course we've still got the old Lags here, y'know Cliff Richard, Adam Faith and 2 new shockers Shane Fenton and John Leyton SUCH CRAP YOU HAVE NEVER HEARD.' Somewhere, with the passing of time, Richards seemed to change his opinion of Fenton, as he was later quoted as describing him as 'the godfather of British rock 'n' roll.'

However, the new EMI recording artist Ray Cathode was someone who was never going to feature on Richards' list of 'old Lags' as he didn't actually exist. It was a made-up name printed on a Parlophone disc produced by George Martin entitled 'Time Beat', which featured sound effects built around the BBC time signal.

Another innovative technical contraption made its debut appearance in the Moka coffee bar in Soho's Frith Street – where the first Gaggia coffee machine in London had been installed in 1953. Costing £1250, the Cinebox was an early visual jukebox which featured 40 film clips of acts such as Eden Kane, Bobby Rydell

and The Viscounts, which were projected onto a 21"
screen.

Over at the BBC, in an attempt to head off any
accusations of payola – which involved record
companies or music publishers or managers or
artists paying disc jockeys for plays on the radio –
the Corporation reiterated its year-old policy which
stipulated that all the records played would be chosen
by the BBC Gramophone Department rather than
individual presenters. The broadcaster explained that
the policy was in place to 'ensure the presentation
of entertaining and well-balanced programmes',
rather than to discourage song-pluggers or any other
interested parties.

While 15 year-old Helen Shapiro became the
youngest British act to top the bill at the London
Palladium, The Beatles' manager Brian Epstein was,
on May 8 1962, just a stone's throw away at the
HMV store in Oxford Street where he was making a
demonstration record of his group that he could send
to record companies.

The man who cut the disc was impressed with what
he heard and called an executive from the music
publisher Ardmore & Beechwood, whose offices were
above the shop. He also liked the demo and he offered
to set up a meeting between Epstein and Parlophone
label manager George Martin, despite the fact that
EMI, who owned Parlophone, had rejected The Beatles
a year earlier.

EMI in-house producers Norman Newell and Wally Ridley had been asked to review the Beatles' first recording with Mike Sheridan for Polydor, which had been sent in by Epstein, and they subsequently turned them down on the basis that it sounded like 'a bad recording of the Shadows.' Coincidentally, EMI also owned the music publishers Ardmore & Beechwood and the HMV store where they were based.

As the largest record store in the country, HMV Oxford Street insisted on a dress code for its staff in the early 1960s, with female personnel required to wear 'court or semi-court shoes with heels and with stockings at all times, while paying special attention to hair grooming and general appearance.' For the men it was regulation black shoes, dark suits and white shirts, while special attention had to be paid to creating a 'general appearance as befitting a West End showroom.'

Despite rejecting The Beatles (and even having doubts about Elvis Presley) the staff producers at EMI were amongst the most successful record makers in the UK pop business, with Newell and Ridley working in competition with Martin and Paramor as they produced records for the company's HMV, Parlophone and Columbia labels.

Originally employed as a conductor/arranger, Norrie Paramor's stock had risen thanks to the hits he made with Ruby Murray, Michael Holliday, Cliff Richard and The Shadows and he added another chart topper in the summer of 1962 when Frank Ifield, a former policeman in Coventry, returned from his new home in Australia to start making records in Britain. After three minor hits in 1960, Ifield went back into the studio in an attempt to save his career.

'Frank had had a bit of lean time and was probably close to being dropped altogether,' recalled Abbey Road engineer/producer Bob Barrett, who was in the control room with Paramor and Norman Smith. 'At the end of the session Norrie said he had a feeling about one particular track and felt it could be a hit. I said 'I wish had your confidence Norrie, I don't really see it as a hit record'.' The record was 'I Remember You' which went on to reach number five in America and pass the one-million sales mark, as well as being the first of four UK number-one records for Ifield in less than a year.

Among the other record makers during the summer of 1962 were actress Pat Phoenix who played Elsie Tanner in the ITV soap opera *Coronation Street* and the actor Leo McGuire, who was Alex Gordon in the rival BBC series *Compact*. But neither McGuire's 'Cryin' For The Moon' nor Tanner's 'Rovers Return', which was produced by a budding Australian music entrepreneur named Robert Stigwood, made any impression on the chart.

Interestingly the British singles chart up to the end of June 1962 threw up only six number-one records – the lowest number since 1954 when there were just four chart-toppers in the first half of the year. And, following Richard, Presley and The Shadows holding the top spot until the middle of May, B. Bumble and The Stingers reigned for a week with 'Nut Rocker', followed by Presley's 'Good Luck Charm' for six weeks, ahead of Mike Sarne's two week run with 'Come Outside', which featured a young Wendy Richard before she starred in *Are You Being Served?* and *Eastenders*.

With Prime Minister Harold Macmillan in his sixth and final full year in office, at a time when the average house price in Britain was £2620, the public were invited to the cinema to enjoy *Dr No*, the first James Bond film, starring Sean Connery as the hero spy, and the epic *Lawrence of Arabia* with Peter O'Toole – both of which came out ahead of the news that the ultimate movie sex symbol, Marilyn Monroe, had been found dead in Los Angeles.

On June 6 1962, The Beatles were finally invited to Abbey Road studios for a Parlophone record test. George Martin's first reaction when he heard their music was to say, 'They were pretty awful. I understand why other record companies turned them down'. But once they got together things changed. 'When I met them I liked them,' he said.

In fact, Martin was so convinced that 'they were star material as live performers', that he took the risk of signing them to his Parlophone label. The contract he offered, which was effective from June 4 1962 and ran for one year with three one year options, meant The Beatles would earn 2d (81p) per double-sided single – and this was to be split five ways between the group and their manager Brian Epstein.

Across north London in Tottenham at around the same time, The Dave Clark Five were celebrating the release of their first vocal record 'I Knew It All The Time' – they had issued an instrumental debut recording of 'Chequita' at the start of the year. Despite the fact that the group, which was formed in 1958 and were regulars on the Mecca ballroom circuit, had managed to put out two records in less than six months, Clark, a former stuntman, said, 'The Dave Clark Five was basically a live band. We failed a lot of record auditions but we packed them in.'

Acclaimed songwriter Carole King – who, with her husband Gerry Goffin, composed hits for the Shirelles ('Will You Still Love Me Tomorrow'), Bobby Vee ('Take Good Care Of My Baby') and the Chiffons ('One Fine Day') – opted to release 'It Might As Well Rain Until September' as her debut single. At the same time her family's babysitter Eva Boyd recorded and released the Goffin/King number 'Loco-Motion' under the name Little Eva. And while both records reached the UK top three, Eva's rendition of her employers' song topped the US charts.

As filming for Cliff Richard's third film, *Summer Holiday*, proceeded to Greece in the summer of 1962 – where The Shadows' Bruce Welch had to be rescued from the Mediterranean – the top-selling singer was awarded another accolade. He was named as one of Britain's Ten Best Dressed men, alongside TV and radio presenter David Jacobs, on a list created by the Clothing Manufacturers Federation.

Meanwhile, Richard and his backing group were also busy setting up a new joint venture record production company called Shad-Rich, and the first person they employed was ex-Shads drummer Tony Meehan who joined from Decca Records as their chief talent scout.

On July 12 1962 at the original Marquee Jazz Club in Oxford Street, before it moved to Wardour Street in 1964, a six-piece band which had taken their name from a 1950 Muddy Waters' song made their stage debut. Under the name The Rollin' Stones (the track was called Rollin' Stone), Mick Jagger, Keith Richards, Brian Jones, Dick Taylor, Ian Stewart and Mick Avory filled the gap left when Blues Incorporated were booked for a live BBC Jazz Club broadcast.

Asked to step into the breach by Blues Inc's leader Alexis Korner, Richards recalled the excitement of the evening. 'A gig! You're sitting with some guys, and you're playing and you go 'Ooh yeah!' That feeling is worth more than anything.' While the group's set that night consisted of a selection of blues songs, Jagger later explained that the Rolling Stones were more than an R&B band. 'Well we like rock 'n' roll as a much as we like rhythm and blues so even though we call ourselves a rhythm and blues band, at rehearsals we'll do anything from Elvis Presley to Buddy Holly to Richie Valens,' said the singer.

This was the time when Britain's blues scene began to take shape through Korner and the likes of Cyril Taylor, Long John Baldry, Dave Hunt and Georgie Fame who frequented London clubs such as the Marquee, the 100 Club, Flamingo and the Crawdaddy in Richmond and, while commercial success was neither earned nor expected, it would lead to a host of blues-based bands emerging down the line.

By 1962 singers Adam Faith and Anthony Newley had both branched out, with Faith being touted as the host of six 30-minute TV shows (imaginatively called *The Adam Faith Show*) which each week would feature one star name and an unknown artist. Newley had racked up 12 UK hit singles between 1959 and 1962 – including two number ones – before he set his sights on the world of musicals.

Collaborating with writer Leslie Bricusse, he created the stage show *Stop The World I Want To Get Off* which, according to American newspaper reports received 'the biggest ever US disc coverage of songs from a British show', with over 40 records being issued including versions of 'Gonna Build a Mountain', 'Once In A Lifetime' and 'What Kind Of Fool Am I?'.

The never-ending speculation as to whether Elvis Presley would ever visit Britain continued as British-based South African business man Sumed Areff reportedly offered The King £250,000 to play a series of 25 shows in Europe, including 15 appearances in the UK. Earning a lot less but more likely to show up were Brian Poole and The Tremeloes (billed as two separate acts) who, having been signed by Decca in preference to The Beatles, found themselves booked to appear on July 28 at Hatfield football ground in Hertfordshire as part of a Twist-Jive session.

New programmes on TV included *The Saint*, *Z Cars* and *Steptoe & Son*, while the *Sunday Times* went out on a limb and published the first newspaper colour supplement just as Ford launched their streamlined Capri model. And, while the first commercial Hovercraft service began between Rhyl in Wales and Wallasey in Lancashire, a revolutionary American communications satellite was launched in America on July 10 1962. Orbiting the earth every 2.6 hours, Telstar relayed live television transmissions between the US and Europe – and inspired a record producer in north London.

Joe Meek, who trained as a radar technician in the Royal Air Force, had already made hits for John Leyton and Mike Berry in the home-made studio in his flat in Caledonian Road, Holloway before Telstar was launched. Inspired by the world's first communications satellite, he then created an instrumental track which he produced with The Tornados who had worked as singer Billy Fury's backing band.

'Telstar' (the record) eventually reached number one in the UK in October 1962 – with sales in excess of 900,000 – and two months later topped the US chart, making The Tornados the first British group to achieve the coveted top spot on the American Hot 100. While The Tornados followed Acker Bilk as only the second UK act to top the US chart, the likes of Lonnie Donegan (with two top five hits), Marty Wilde, Helen Shapiro, Cliff Richard, Frank Ifield and Matt Monro were among the few British artists to actually feature in the America chart between 1955 and 1962.

Around the same time as he was creating 'Telstar', Meek was also working with Terry Slater's band The Flinstones and the producer's first move was to change their name. 'We were signed to EMI and they got Joe Meek to produce us but he changed our name to The Stonehenge Men. 'We didn't care so long as we got a record out,' says Slater. And sure enough the newly named Stonehenge Men made 'Big Feet' in the summer of 1962 in Meek's studio. 'It was around the same time as 'Telstar' and I remember going to Meek's studio. You went up the stairs where there was one big room and a toilet which was part of the studio and another small room with the mixing desk. You'd be up to your ears in wires with mikes all over the place.'

Recalling that Meek was 'fucking crazy', Slater found himself in the studio one day listening to a session. 'I was just tapping my foot to the music and there was this thumping noise coming through Joe's earphones and he couldn't work out what it was. He went crazy trying to work out where it was coming from and then he realised it was me tapping my foot on the floorabout 15 feet further along the same floorboard from the singer's mike. It was my tapping that was going through his microphone into Joe's earphones.'

Even though they were produced by Meek – and appeared on the same HMV label as chart-toppers Danny Williams, John Leyton and Johnny Kidd – The Stonehenge Men failed to find chart success, although they stayed together long enough to open for The Everly Brothers when they toured the UK in late 1963.

On August 15 1962 drummer Pete Best played what was to be his last show with The Beatles – an evening appearance at the Cavern Club – before being replaced three days later by Ringo Starr for a performance at an Horticultural Society Dance held in Hulme Hall in Port Sunlight, Cheshire. A month later this new line-up of Lennon, McCartney, Harrison and Starr returned to Abbey Road twice and, as engineer Norman Smith recalled, they brought more than just their talent.

'They brought in loads and loads of records from Liverpool to show us what sounds they wanted. They were so aware of what was going on in America,' says the man who went on to produce Pink Floyd and achieve pop chart success himself as Hurricane Smith. 'They brought in things like Carl Perkins and a lot of Motown stuff and (when we heard them) we thought the Americans must be cheating.' The end product of the two Beatles' sessions on September 4 and 11 were three songs written by Lennon and McCartney –

'Love Me Do', 'P.S. I Love You' and 'Please Please Me' – plus a version of a Mitch Murray song called 'How Do You Do It'.

When it came to choosing which track to release as the group's first single, The Beatles were adamant that it wouldn't be Murray's effort and as Martin thought 'Please Please Me' was 'too good a song to throw away' as a debut release, they all opted for 'Love Me Do'.

It wasn't just first-time chart toppers such as Helen Shapiro, Danny Williams and Eden Kane who broke through in 1962. US acts such as The Four Seasons, Dion, Tommy Roe, Jimmy Justice and Chris Montez all debuted on the UK charts, while over in America, *Cashbox* magazine's DJ poll voted Acker Bilk as Most Promising Instrumentalist with Kenny Ball's Jazzmen as second Most Promising Orchestra and, most bizarrely, 16 year-old child actress Hayley Mills as the 13th Most Promising Female Vocalist … 15 places ahead of Helen Shapiro.

With news of autumn tours by Del Shannon and Joe Brown; Little Richard, Jet Harris and Sam Cooke; and Bobby Vee, The Crickets and Ronnie Carroll – who had finished fourth in the 1962 Eurovision Song Contest with 'Ring-A-Ding Girl' – there was another attempt to get Elvis Presley to the UK but once again it was doomed to fail.

This time he was invited to appear on the Royal Variety Show, but Presley's manager Col Tom Parker declined and explained, 'We have pointed out to newspapers that call us that it is true we have not been able to make appearances in Britain but it is also true that we have not appeared elsewhere.' Adding that more people can see Presley in films than could ever see him on stage, Parker said, 'We are thinking in terms of the many rather than the few.'

If Presley was reluctant to visit the UK, Cliff Richard was more than happy to travel to America which he did in October 1962 to appear in seven cities and on the influential *Ed Sullivan Show*, but Britain's number one singer still failed to get a single US chart entry during the year. Returning to the stage and to Britain, however, was Little Richard whose UK tour included a show at the Tower Ballroom, New Brighton on October 26, when he was paid £500 by promoter Brian Epstein and was supported, surprise surprise, by The Beatles.

Three weeks before this show The Beatles' first single 'Love Me Do' had been issued by Parlophone and on the same day as they supported Little Richard, the new disc entered the *NME* chart at number 27. These two items of news earned the Liverpool group their first mention in an *NME* story which, under the heading, 'Beatles In Little Richard Concert', reported that it was 'a major booking for the 'Love Me Do' stars – in their home town.'

October was also the month when The Rolling Stones made their first studio recording in Highbury, north London when Jagger, Richards, Jones, Stewart and drummer Tony Chapman recorded versions of songs by Muddy Waters, Jimmy Reed and Bob Diddley which they distributed to record companies, but to no avail. Records which did come out however were Frank Sinatra's *Great Songs From Great Britain*, which he had recorded in London during the summer, and two early Elvis Presley albums which had been withdrawn in 1957 when RCA switched UK distribution from HMV to Decca.

The Presley LPs *Rock 'N' Roll No.1* and *Rock 'N' Roll No.2* were reissued in the UK on the back of an RCA executive spotting secondhand and home-taped copies selling for as much as £3.10s (£3.50p). 'I am doing this to prevent high price sales in secondhand and home-made tape recordings ...this is not fair on the fans,' he explained.

Also not fair on the fans was the BBC's decision to ban the novelty song 'Monster Mash' by Bobby 'Boris' Pickett and The Monster Mashers – it would be ten more years before the US number one, which the broadcasters deemed to be 'too morbid' to play, finally hit the UK chart.

Back in the UK in October 1962 were The Everly Brothers and, according to the brothers' friend and backing musician Terry Slater, it was somewhere they were always happy to be. 'The brothers saw England as a second home and they loved being here. All the British stars wanted to meet them and were in awe of them and hung on every thing they did and played.'

Even so when Don Everly collapsed and flew back to America, leaving Phil to complete the tour on his own, the promoters, according to Slater, were less than pleased. 'They only wanted to pay Phil half the money because they only had half an act.' Although he didn't go to see the Everlys, David Hughes was an ardent music fan and a regular at his local Granada cinema in Maidstone where he caught Lonnie Donegan, Gene Vincent (twice), Adam Faith and Little Richard during his 'back in the UK' tour.

'He did the whole act of getting on top of a grand piano, falling off it and lying on the stage with someone shouting for a doctor,' recalls Hughes. 'Then someone rushed on to help him and he got up and went straight into 'wop bop a lu-la'. The crowd went crazy but you couldn't hear it very well as they used the house PA system which wasn't very good.'

In the midst of all this rock 'n' roll activity, US President Kennedy was busy having a stand-off with his Soviet counterpart Khrushchev that took the world to the brink of nuclear war. With the USSR building missile bases in Cuba, Kennedy ordered a naval blockade of in-coming Soviet ships and threatened retaliatory action if it was broken. After six days the USSR ordered its convoy to return home and agreed to dismantle the Cuban bases.

With 'Love Me Do' slowly climbing the UK chart, The Beatles returned to the studio to finish recording the song that producer George Martin had earlier decided to 'leave for another time.' 'Please Please Me' was completed on November 26 and, after his first four sessions with them, Martin paused to analyse his new group. 'We re-exported American music back to America. A lot of things John and Paul did were dead copies of the things they'd heard. They would listen to American records, lift phrases and work out how they'd want to do it. If George mastered a Chuck Berry riff, he would come in very proudly and play it ad nauseam.'

When the annual *NME* Poll was published for 1962, the world's Outstanding Male, Female and Group were Presley (again), Brenda Lee and (again) The Everly Brothers, while the three British titles for Best Male, Female and Group were retained by Richard, Shapiro and The Springfields. And, while The Shadows were voted Best Small Group, The Beatles made a surprise entry in eighth place in the Best Group section – just a month after the release of their first record.

Returning to Britain in late 1962 was singer Mickie Most who, during his time in South Africa, had notched up a run of eleven number ones with his cover versions of US rock 'n' roll hits. But the man who would go on to produce Jeff Beck, Lulu and Herman's Hermits was not happy with what he found when he got back to his homeland.

'The British music scene was very sad then, very pathetic,' was how he summed it up. 'The American stuff was pretty much the same – there was a lot of

Bobby Vee and Del Shannon which was quite pleasant but it didn't really have the depth of say Elvis Presley or Chuck Berry or Little Richard.' The former Most Brother who went on to create Rak Records as the home to Hot Chocolate, Suzi Quatro and Mud, declared, 'The early Sixties were a down time.'

As 'Love Me Do' finally peaked at number 17 with sales of 17,000 which EMI boss L.G. Wood declared 'not all that good' (and amid rumours that manager Brian Epstein had somehow bought up to 10,000 copies), so Rick Sarstedt heard the new music coming from the array of emerging beat bands and realised things were about to change. 'When I heard 'Love Me Do' I thought , 'Wow this is like The Everly Brothers but it's not, it's more raw!' It was great stuff,' says the man who, as Eden Kane, would be tagged as 'The last teen idol before The Beatles.'

While Sarstedt admits that he 'screwed it up a little' because he failed to promote himself properly, he also believes that he was 'Beatled-out of the business' although he returned in 1964 with his fifth top ten hit 'Boys Cry'. Somebody who was just starting in the business in 1962 was Bob Dylan, who arrived to make his first ever UK appearance at the Pindar of Wakefield pub in London's Grays Inn Road.

The last month of the year saw Acker Bilk and 'Stranger On The Shore' finally drop out of the UK chart after a record-breaking run of 55 weeks and a peak position of number two. On the other hand

Presley ended the year with a grand total of 52 weeks at number one between 1957 and 1962 with thirteen separate releases while, in common with the first half of the year, there were just six chart-toppers between July and December 1962, including – of course – two more titles from Presley.

He hit the top spot with 'She's Not You' and 'Return To Sender' and was joined on the list by Ray Charles' 'I Can't Stop Loving You' alongside 'I Remember You' and 'Lovesick Blues' from Frank Ifield, plus 'Telstar' from The Tornados. While Connie Francis may not have had a number-one hit in 1962, she was still a big enough name to be asked to fly 6000 miles in a day – to Britain and back to America – in order to dub some dialogue onto her film *Follow The Boys*, which was being made at Elstree Studios.

Before the year was over, one of the leading lights in the discovery and promotion of rock 'n' roll found himself under arrest for payola and facing trial in a New York court room. Disc jockey and promoter Alan Freed was accused of accepting $2700 from two record companies in exchange for airplay on his radio programme and, after refusing to testify, he was found guilty, fined $300 and given six months probation. It marked the beginning of the end of Freed's days as a pioneering broadcaster

As Presley once again topped the *NME*'s points for chart positions list with 1463 points – followed by Richard (on 1131), Ifield, The Shadows and Acker Bilk

– Bob Wallis was again in last place with a single point alongside Dave MacBeth and Patti Lynn. And for those who suspected that the best days (and sounds) of rock 'n' roll had probably gone, there was a list of seasonal records which went some way to proving the point.

Christmas 1962 brought with it the puppets Pinky & Perky singing 'Give Us A Kiss For Christmas'; Belgian group The Waikikis offering 'White Christmas In Hawaii'; British heartthrob Craig Douglas urging everybody to 'Cuddle Up With Craig'; American singer Paul Evans with the story of 'The Bell That Couldn't Jingle'; Danish aristocratic folk singers Nina and Frederick crooning 'Silent Night'; while Paddy Roberts, a South African ex-lawyer and pilot-turned-songwriter and risqué performer, wished everyone 'Merry Christmas You Suckers'. If it hadn't been for Brenda Lee 'Rockin' Around The Christmas Tree', the festive season would have been a very dull time indeed!

The end of 1962 also marked the end of the chart careers of two inspirational British trend setters – Marty Wilde and Lonnie Donegan – alongside a host of other artists who, like Eden Kane, were about to be 'Beatled-out of the business.' Alma Cogan, The Allisons, Anthony Newley, Pat Boone, Jimmy Justice, B. Bumble, Peter Jay & The Jaywalkers, Conway Twitty, The Temperance Seven, Joan Regan, The Ventures, Russ Conway and Johnny and The Hurricanes would never again see themselves on a British chart listing.

But even as the likes of Cliff Richard, The Shadows, Adam Faith, Petula Clark, Elvis Presley, Frank Sinatra, Roy Orbison, Johnny Cash and Chuck Berry continued to claim a place among the bestsellers, a new sound and a new sensation arrived to deliver a major body-blow to the style of rock and pop music that had gone before.

Mersey beat and the swinging Sixties were not just around the corner, they were about to launch the most powerful and influential decade in the history of popular music. And it was led by Britain, which began to produce an unbelievable array of bestselling artists who quickly became the envy of the world.

But for all their success and influence, these revolutionary new acts, who represented a restless generation anxious to mark their territory, had their roots in the music of the Fifties. Whether they came from Liverpool or London, Manchester or Newcastle, Birmingham or Belfast, Cardiff or Glasgow, it was the music of America – and R&B and rock 'n' roll in particular – that sowed the seeds of the beat boom of the Sixties.

According to Keith Richards the Sixties began in black and white and 'exploded into technicolour.' But the black and white image which launched the Sixties was one that had developed in the mid-Fifties out of the drab grey picture of Britain as it emerged from a world war.

1963 saw England swing like never before as the

country threw a party and invited everyone to join in. It involved sex, fashion, drugs, politics, protest and — above all else — music. The poet Philip Larkin famously proclaimed: *'Sexual intercourse began in 1963 / (which was rather late for me) Between the end of the 'Chatterley' ban / And the Beatles' first LP'*

The first Beatles LP was *Please Please Me*, which came out in March 1963 and it included six tracks not written by Lennon and McCartney — they all came from America and had been part of an earlier, important musical era which laid the foundations for the creation of the most famous monument to rock and pop.

The Sixties may have been hip and happening but without what went before it would never have got off its arse and started dancing.

Chapter 10

1963 - 65: Beat, beat and more beat

After a decade dominating the world of popular music, rock 'n' roll began to totter and tumble in the early sixties as something called 'beat music' captured the attention of Britain's teenagers.

These youngsters had seemingly outgrown the music of the fifties and by the early sixties their heroes had lost their appeal and faded for different reasons. Bill Haley was too old, Elvis had calmed down, Jerry Lee Lewis went too far by marrying his 13 year old cousin, Little Richard gave himself up to the church, Chuck Berry went to prison and Buddy Holly was dead.

Now 1963 was when, for many, the modern world was born. While The Beatles were at the forefront of the new movement they were not alone in changing the face of Britain's music scene, although it was 'Mersey Beat' that captured the headlines as the foursome from Liverpool followed their brief foray into the charts in 1962 with number one albums and singles.

The fact was that although *Please Please Me* and *With The Beatles* shared the heights with the soundtrack album *West Side Story* and offerings from both Cliff Richard and The Shadows, they were already the new but as yet uncrowned kings. With over 30 weeks at the top of the UK album chart, The Beatles' arrival ensured that Cliff and his backing group would go another 14 years before hitting the top spot again.

But it wasn't just The Beatles who were making an impression, Liverpool groups such Gerry & the Pacemakers, The Searchers and Billy J Kramer with the Dakotas infiltrating the singles charts alongside Manchester's Freddie & The Dreamers and London's very own Brian Poole & The Tremeloes. In the background, groups such as The Dave Clark Five signed their first record deal and the Rolling Stones made their club debut in London, with long-standing members Mick Jagger, Keith Richards and Brian Jones joined later in the year by stalwarts Charlie Watts and Bill Wyman. As a member of the newly formed group The Detours before he helped launch The Who, Roger Daltrey sensed that all this chart action was the start of something. "From 1963 there was all this energy. It was happening, and it was happening because of music."

With Britain's attempt to enter the EEC blocked by France's President Charles De Gaulle and America experiencing the first stirrings of a civil rights campaign that would run and run, pop music was becoming a frenzied business. While The Beatles went out on four package tours of the country (headlining the final one in November), the likes of the Stones, Brian Poole and The Searchers were all darting around the country, usually as the support act to a major American star.

Depending on where you went to see these package tours, the price of a seat was anything from 10s 6d (52p) down to 3s 6d (17p) while bands with a hit record on their CV could earn between £25 and £15 a night depending on the size of the hall. On top of these expenses, a 45rpm single cost 6s 11p (35p) and a whole LP ran out at 30s 11d, while the necessary equipment such as a Brunswick portable record player cost 18gns (£18.90p) and a transistor radio 12gns (£12.60p).

The arrival of The Beatles and the fact that they sang songs they had written themselves – their first two albums had 16 songs (out of 28) written by them – signalled a new phenomenon amongst British pop musicians. "To have a band that wrote their songs was sort of unheard of back then, and it was an inspiration," recalls Graham Gouldman from 10cc, a man who was so inspired that he wrote hits for The Yardbirds, The Hollies and Herman's Hermits.

However in 1963 it wasn't just pop music that was making the news, as Britain spent, the summer reeling from a scandal known as the 'Profumo Affair'. The Tory Government's Secretary of State for War (there wasn't one for Peace) John Profumo admitted lying to Parliament over his relationship with the model Christine Keeler, who was also involved with a Russian naval attaché. While the Government survived, Profumo was forced to resign.

Meanwhile the new music being made in the UK was not just impressing British fans but was also making stars from across the water sit up and take notice. Little Richard told *NME*, "I've never heard that sound from British musicians before," while Tommy Roe admitted,

"I rave over The Beatles, who have a truly fantastic American sound".

America, however, didn't just sit back and let Britain's new music steal all the plaudits, as girl groups the Crystals, Chiffons and Ronettes all had debut hits alongside three brothers, a cousin and best friend from California called The Beach Boys, whose disc 'Surfin' USA' was a hit despite *NME's* reviewer suggesting that it was "unlikely to repeat its American success here because it's a geographical song that deals with several unfamiliar American locations".

While the Great Train Robbers were getting away with £2.5 million from a Royal Mail train in August and Jerry Lee Lewis was signing to Liberty Records for a reported $10,000 year for five years, The Beatles, who received £300 for their last ever show at Liverpool's Cavern Club, were described in the *Daily Mirror* as "Four Frenzied Little Lord Fauntleroys" earning £50,000 a week.

In the same year as Kelloggs introduced a cockerel on packets of Corn Flakes, yoghurt arrived in the UK (bilberry flavour) and *Dr Who* (William Hartnell) was launched on TV, The Beatles' second chart topper 'She Loves You' sold over 1.6 million copies, despite the reservation of EMI managing director L.G.Wood. "Our marketing manager had set the advance order at 350,000, which was an extraordinary number in those days. I told him it was too high but he stood his ground and eventually we compromised on 250,000 – we sold over a million!". In the midst of all this success somebody somewhere coined the phrase 'Beatlemania.'

As more and more groups got together, record companies, who were busy scouring the country for new talent, gave their support to talent contests. In Leeds in October there was a *Festival for the Young Ones* which invited over 60 groups to compete for "big time prizes and a chance for stardom" as Pye Records (home to The Searchers) were offering to "take tapes for possible record tests and TV auditions".

However all the excitement that was delivered by new music and new acts in 1963, could not take away from the tragedy that took place in America in November when President John F Kennedy was shot and killed during a motorcade through the city of Dallas. With Lyndon Johnson in place as their new President, America welcomed The Beatles in February 1964 when they flew in to appear on the top rated *Ed Sullivan Show* and attracted an audience of 73 million. Their first US number one – one of six that year – 'I Want To Hold Your Hand' was described by *Billboard* magazine as "a driving rocker with a surf on the Thames sound".

America was now warming to the new beat sound coming from Britain and groups including Gerry & the Pacemakers, Dave Clark Five, The Searchers, The Animals and the Rolling Stones all earned US chart placings. The so-called 'British invasion' reached its peak in April when The Beatles took all top five places on the *Billboard* Hot 100 singles chart.

Despite their disagreement on membership of the

EEC, Britain and France agreed in early 1964 to build a Channel tunnel, which would eventually open 30 years later, while the British charts set a new record as, for the first time, there wasn't a single American single in the top 10 as nine English acts were joined by Ireland's Bachelors.

The rivalry between The Beatles and the Stones was slowly building, with young fans opting for one act or the other, although some (your author was one) chose to support both. The Stones had been part of the BBC's new pop programme *Top of The Pops* when it was aired in January (four months after Associated Rediffusion launched *Ready Steady Go* with the catch phrase "the weekend starts here"). If The Beatles' 'mop top' appearance had shocked the establishment, the Stones were classified as "untidy rebels", with *Daily Express* writer Judith Simons (who years later would claim optimistically that the song 'Hey Jude' was all about her) suggesting that London's finest were "boys whom any self-respecting mum would lock in the bathroom".

And the group's Keith Richards had his own view of the rivalry. "We're not going to be the Fab Four, all wearing the same shit," while *NME* writer Richard Green, after hearing the Stones' debut album, declared, "If it doesn't take over from The Beatles at the top of the LP chart I will eat my record player". Fortunately for him it did, replacing *With The Beatles* for 12 weeks, although the Fab Four did hold the top spot for more than 30 weeks.

In an effort to break the BBC's stranglehold on UK

radio, Britain's first pirate radio station was launched in March, with Radio Caroline basing itself over three miles offshore in international waters. It was joined before the year was out by Radio London and between them they boasted an array of exciting and hip deejays, including John Peel, Emperor Rosko, Johnny Walker and Kenny Everett.

As they were 'pirates', the major record companies could not be seen to be supplying records but thanks to the magazine publisher Jocelyn Stevens, who was a supporter of the stations, promotions men could legally deliver records to his offices in London from where, mysteriously, they made their way to the boats.

Artists were invited to travel out to the stations, although it involved long train journeys from London to the Essex coast followed by a trip in a small boat across the three miles of open sea - and you had to remember to take your passport as once you had left British waters, you needed it to get back into the country. DJ Walker recalls "not many artists came out", adding that it was an arduous way to promote your new single. "The tender to Caroline took about 90 minutes each way and left most people sick."

A month later Britain experienced a series of seaside brawls as groups of mods (parkas and scooters) and rockers (motor bikes and leathers) set about each other in Margate, Clacton, Brighton and Hastings. Arrests were made and youngsters were sent to jail while the press labelled the two groups "vermin and louts". In other news, following the death of major politicians Lady Nancy Astor, who was the UK's first seated woman MP, and Pandit Nehru, Prime Minister of India from 1947, South African activist Nelson Mandela was sentenced to life imprisonment. Fortunately for his country he was released early.

Around the same time American folk singer Bob Dylan began to capture the attention of the British music press, with *NME* telling its readers that "he works in the folk field and himself plays guitar and harmonica (at the same time) as well as singing". His casual dress sense (jeans, crumpled shirt and work boots) prompted an executive at his American record company to comment "to look like that he must be a genius".

NME's annual Poll Winners Concert in 1964 highlighted the changing face of British music when the likes of Brian Poole, Manfred Mann, Billy J Kramer, The Searchers, the Stones and, of course, The Beatles dominated proceedings, although Cliff Richard (who performed at every *NME* concert from 1960 to 1970) and the Shadows got in on the act.

While it was beat from Britain that was dominating the charts and airwaves (both legal and illegal), America was making inroads thanks to a label born in Detroit in the late fifties. On the back of hits in the US from Mary Wells, Stevie Wonder and Marvin Gaye, *MM* ran a feature announcing, "Coming Your Way – Tamla Motown" and ran through a selection of the label's artists but somehow failed to mention The Supremes, who became the first act from the label, and the first all-girl group, to top the UK chart.

Among the seemingly never-ending conveyor belt of new British groups were Herman's Hermits from Manchester and London's The Kinks and both topped the charts in 1964, much to Kink Dave Davies' delight. "It was fantastic to knock stars such as The Beatles and Stones off the top of the charts".

Herman was in fact Peter Noone and his producer Mickie Most saw something oddly appealing in the youngster. "I saw a young John Kennedy in Peter Noone. I saw his picture on a postcard and wrote on the back 'Good for US market. Young Kennedy'. Have to find them a song." And he found the American hit 'I'm Into Something Good' as their passport to number one while The Kinks settled on 'You Really Got Me' which, in years to come, would be hailed as the forerunner of heavy metal and punk.

As the look and sound of Britain changed dramatically, *MM* took it upon themselves to analyse the country's music fans. They announced that pop fans peak when they "slip into their twenties" and buy records by Cliff Richard but "never Adam Faith or Marty Wilde." Jazz fans on the other hand were deemed to be usually male, living in London and "fiercely intolerant of other musical forms" while fans of the new beat music were reckoned to be between 14 and 26 years of age, buy three LPs a year and spend 15s (75p) a week on singles.

After their debut movie *A Hard Day's Night* premiered

in both London and Liverpool (where 200,000 people turned out to welcome them home), The Beatles began their first ever major tour of America while the Stones were banned from Ed Sullivan's TV show when fans went wild. Sullivan announced, "I promise you they'll never be back on our show. Now the Dave Clark Five are nice fellows, they are gentlemen." However, around nine months later Sullivan relented and the Stones were back on the show alongside Tom Jones and Dusty Springfield.

The Beatles were not just dominating the charts and the headlines with their records, tours and TV appearances but, according to sixties singing star Helen Shapiro, they were changing how music was created. "They were the first artists to go into the studio and say 'I've not quite finished yet' and then rehearse a song and add to it. This effectively put an end to the old concept of three hour recordings sessions."

As 1964 came to an end there was political change around the world. Harold Wilson became Britain's new Prime Minister when he won the election by just four seats and ended 13 years of Tory rule, while Nikita Khrushchev was replaced as the all-important leader of the USSR's (Union of Soviet Socialist Republics) Communist Party by Leonid Brezhnev and in America Lyndon Johnson won the US Presidential election.

At the same time *NME* listened to Dylan's album *Another Side of Bob Dylan* and told their readers, "his singing is often out of tune (sort of a singing Marlon

Brando) and his harmonica and guitar playing sounds as if he's still learning."

While 1964 saw the opening of the first 'spaghetti' Western A *Fistful of Dollars* and the TV debut of *The Likely Lads*, it was also the first year since 1957 in which Elvis Presley did not have a number one single in the UK while Cliff Richard, who failed to top either the album or singles chart, acknowledged the times were changing. "There's no doubt that they (The Beatles) took pop music into another realm. We were the pioneers and they came after, built upon that foundation and took it soaring away."

After passing on The Beatles' first four singles, America's Capitol Records began 1965 by announcing that the group's second album *Beatles '65* had passed the three million sales mark in just one month while disc jockey Alan Freed, the man credited with creating the phrase "rock'n'roll", died aged just 43 and virtually penniless. Meanwhile a new singer from Wales named Tom Jones appeared on the scene but *NME*'s reviewer dismissed 'It's Not Unusual' as "quite catchy" before adding "but I don't envisage this as chart material." Within a month it was number one!

Never everyone's favourites, the Rolling Stones continued to court controversy. After taking out an advertisement in *NME* in December wishing starving hairdressers a Happy Xmas, the group were urged by *Tailor & Cutter* magazine to wear ties and "save the nation's tie-makers from bankruptcy." But things got more serious for Messrs Jagger, Jones and Wyman later in the year when they were each fined £5 for insulting behaviour after urinating up a garage wall "without taking steps to conceal the act." Suggesting the band should have set a higher moral standard, the magistrate described Wyman as "a shaggy haired monster."

Not to be outdone The Beatles upset the great and the good when they were awarded MBE's in the Queen's Birthday Honours List, which resulted in protests and medals being returned to Buckingham Palace. One protester wrote "The British house of royalty has put me on the same level as a bunch of vulgar numbskulls." All this happened just a month after the Queen's sister, Princess Margaret had attended the premiere of The Beatles, second film *Help!*

While it was the boys who were leading the way as far as groups were concerned – although the Applejacks and Honeycombs both had girl members – *MM* focussed on what they dubbed "Girlie Groups" and highlighted the Supremes, Shangri-Las, Gingerbreads and Ronettes from America alongside – wait for it - the UK's very own Three Bells, Three Quarters and the Dollies.

For award-winning lyricist Tim Rice, seeing the Ronettes on *Ready Steady Go* perform 'Baby I Love You' was a genuine magic moment. "They were quite simply the most exotic ladies I had ever seen." Suitably besotted, he wrote to them inviting them to dinner on any night during the UK tour with the Rolling Stones. "Amazing to relate they wrote back but regretted that they simply did not have any spare time. It was a bitter pill to swallow," explains Rice.

Among the new boys on the block were The Who and they had their eyes set firmly on attracting a particular set of fans with their devotion to what was called 'pop art'. Pete Townshend went into great detail to explain the new phenomenon. "It's representing something the public is familiar with in a different way. We have a jacket made from a Union Jack flag, a jersey with an RAF insignia and I have a white jacket covered in medals. We stand for pop art clothes, music and behaviour."

After the 1965 *NME* Poll Winners concert featured no less than 10 groups – and just four solo singers – the Richmond Jazz & Blues Festival, established in 1961 and the forerunner of the Reading Festival, started to move with the times with jazz acts being relegated to the afternoon and groups such as The Who, The Yardbirds, The Animals and The Moody Blues headlining the evening slots.

In America the anti-Vietnam war movement was gaining ground with over 25,000 protesters marching in Washington DC and the same number assembling in New York, while race riots in Los Angeles saw 34 people killed and property worth $35 million destroyed. London and the rest of the world joined in the Vietnam protest movement, with marches involving hundreds of thousands of people.

Although he was no longer a regular chart topper, Elvis Presley was still seen as 'The King' and being granted an audience was up there on most people's wish lists. Herman's Hermits met up with him in Hawaii in August on the set of his film *Paradise Hawaiian Style* and singer Noone recalled the occasion. "Elvis looked exactly like he appears on film and was perfectly natural. He said how much he liked British groups. Colonel Parker protects him all the time, listens to everything he says and won't let him be photographed except by his own photographers."

Just over a week later Elvis agreed to meet The Beatles at his house in Bel Air, California, where they talked and jammed. "We all plugged in whatever was around and we played and sang," said John Lennon. And while this was going on, the two managers, Col. Tom Parker and Brian Epstein played pool in another room.

Newly emerging American group The Byrds – they explained that they used the Y instead of the I because "we didn't want to be confused with English slang for girls" – made an appearance in London and were rewarded with a review in *NME* which said, "The Byrds' biggest fault is this 'cool, couldn't care less' attitude on stage and off. The audience don't like it and neither do I." Hot on their heels an advert appeared in the *Hollywood Reporter* for "Folk and Roll musicians and singers for acting roles in a new TV series".

Over 400 people turned up for the auditions, including a young musician named Stephen Stills but NOT Charles Manson (later convicted in a spree of Hollywood killings and sentenced to life imprisonment) who was rumoured to have been among the hopefuls but was in fact in prison at the time. The final four were British child actor Davy Jones, folk singers Michael Nesmith and Peter Tork plus Micky Dolenz, a former child star in the TV show *Circus Boy...* and they became The Monkees.

America also delivered a new TV spy series called *The Man From Uncle* in which agents from the United Network For Law and Enforcement fought against an organisation known as THRUSH. Two years later *The Girl From Uncle* appeared on screens and she, rather insensitively perhaps, also fought against THRUSH. The BBC, meanwhile, were busy linking original French animation with English stories to create *The Magic Roundabout* which - with Brian the Snail, Zebedee, Dougal and Florence – ran for 441 episodes.

As the year came to an end, your author, then a cub reporter on a local paper, got to interview the up and coming group The Who when they played at Chelmsford Corn Exchange. Surrounded by instrument cases, alcohol, pills and groupies – and with their manager wielding a suitcase full of cash – Townshend gave me the exclusive news that the band had "contemplated a break-up" because they were bored and not making much money. I made it the headline to my interview story but over 50 years later – despite the death of original members Keith Moon and John Entwistle – they are still going.

I had made my debut as a 'rock reporter' some nine

months earlier when I interviewed the Rolling Stones at Southend and they too focussed on money with Keith Richards telling me, "We don't know how much we earn each week or each year and being number one makes no difference … our earnings are as much a secret to us as to you."

While the 1964 album chart featured only two acts – The Beatles and the Stones – the 1965 listings again featured the same two most successful British groups but this time they were joined by Dylan and the soundtrack to the film *The Sound Of Music,* featuring Julie Andrews, which outsold every other album and spent 20 weeks at number one.

Dylan's number one album was *Bringing It All Back Home* and for budding rock musician Bruce Springsteen it, along with *Highway 61 Revisited,* represented something special. "They were not only great records but they were the first time I can remember being exposed to a truthful vision of the place I loved. Bob Dylan is the father of my country."

Chapter 11

1966 -70: The new sound of America

A new year began with America, who had dispatched over 180,000 troops, mounting a major offensive in Vietnam while anti-war protests continued throughout 1966 both in America and Europe. In Britain Labour Prime Minister Harold Wilson turned his earlier four seat majority into a 96 seat General Election victory in the wake of Freddie Laker launching his no-frills low cost airline Laker Airways.

But waiting somewhere in the wings in 1966 were the likes of The Grateful Dead, described as "chemically enhanced musicians", Jefferson Airplane and The Velvet Underground and a new brand of rock music that would emerge as psychedelia.

Pink Floyd, originally called rather quaintly The Tea Set but re-named by founding member Syd Barrett in honour of American bluesmen Pink Anderson and Floyd Council, became regulars at the "Spontaneous Underground" Sunday afternoon shows at London's Marquee Club, while Phil Spector spent a massive $20,000 creating his "wall of sound" backing track for Ike & Tina Turner's 'River Deep Mountain High'.

When John Lennon made a passing remark to *London Evening Standard* writer Maureen Cleave that the Beatles "are more popular than Jesus" it was largely ignored in Britain but led to a storm of protests in America on the eve of the group's tour. Later, after radio stations had banned records and people set fire to discs and photographs, Lennon apologised and the band's tour continued to sell-out crowds.

In May the Fab Four made what would turn out to be their final concert in the UK at the *NME* Poll Winners show when the reviewer ended his report coincidentally but prophetically with the line "The Beatles were disappearing down a hatch and away, not to be seen again." Three months later they played their last ever gig at San Francisco's Candlestick Park and were "not to be seen again" … on stage at least.

While a further bevy of new American acts began appearing on the scene, including Buffalo Springfield, Big Brother & The Holding Company (with Janis Joplin), Quicksilver Messenger Service and the newly named Mothers of Invention, led by Frank Zappa, Dylan managed to upset his established folk fans by appearing in the UK with his electric band The Hawks – a fan in Manchester famously called the singer "Judas" during the show – while Cream, featuring Eric Clapton, Jack Bruce and Ginger Baker, were dubbed Britain's first "supergroup".

As England won their first (and only) football World Cup, beating West Germany at Wembley, The Beach Boys released their new album *Pet Sounds*, which was reviewed in *MM* by a panel of musicians. Clapton pronounced that it was "one of the greatest pop LPs ever released" while Spencer Davis said, "It's fantastic." On the other hand Keith Moon declared "there's nothing revolutionary in the album" and Scott Walker commented, "I don't like it as much as other Beach Boys albums."

After UK Prime Minister Harold Wilson had imposed a six month wage and prices freeze on the country, former bass player for The Animals, Chas Chandler arrived back from America with a young singer/guitarist in tow who he teamed up with Noel Redding and Mitch Mitchell to create the Jimi Hendrix Experience. Hendrix wasn't the only American musician to make headlines as *MM* featured what they called "The great American comeback" and highlighted psychedelia as the "new in word."

According to Radio Caroline's Walker, psychedelia prompted a new rivalry. "Psychedelic music was America's answer to The Beatles and there was enormous competition between US and UK acts." The new movement and its links with drugs had another impact on pop music. "Most of the people who wrote songs back then were hugely affected by marijuana and acid," says Beatles, Roxy Music and Sex Pistols producer Chris Thomas.

Drugs were becoming increasingly common and their impact on musicians was explained by The Hollies' Graham Nash when talking about his departure from the band and eventual move to America. "Their (the Hollies') perceptions about life were different to mine and the more beer they drank – and the more dope I smoked – the wider the division between us grew." While the Hollies carried on regardless, Nash was getting together with the great and good of America's new music scene, eventually joining David Crosby and Stephen Stills to form Crosby Stills & Nash. Monkees-reject Stills, perhaps influenced by the power of flowers, peace and love, had high hopes for the trio. "There was a time when I thought CS&N could rule the world. But I never said we could save it."

A *MM* feature headlined "the great American comeback" picked out groups such as The Monkees, Love, The Association, Left Bank and Count Five as new contenders and warned of a "trans-Atlantic singles strike" and they were proved right as, by the end of the year, for the first time, singles by US acts outnumbered those by UK artists in the British chart. The arrival of psychedelia, and America's new 'West Coast sound', had an impact on UK groups, as Noone recalled. "San Francisco basically blew Herman's Hermits out of the water. We were top of the bill there and the other acts were flower-power and they didn't like us. They were down on us because we were a pop act and didn't know where Vietnam was."

The emergence of Cream and Jimi Hendrix signalled a change in rock music for Bruce Springsteen, who recognised that "The era of the guitar god was in full swing. Long, intense, blues drenched jams were the order of the day and I was ready." He probably had less interest in the fact that British pop legend Cliff Richard announced that his fan club, boasting 432,000 members, would close down after nine years in order for the singer to take a course in divinity.

There was tragedy in Wales as 147 people were killed when a coal slag heap engulfed the village of Aberfan, shocking Britain to the core while floods in Florence claimed over 100 lives and destroyed major works of art. Over in America a former Hollywood actor named Ronald Reagan entered politics and was elected as Governor of California.

Something dubbed the 'underground' movement was quickly taking a hold on Britain's pop culture and, with financial support from Paul McCartney and US poet Allan Ginsberg, a new magazine called *International Times (IT)* was launched in October with an all-night rave in London's Roundhouse. It was heralded as a Pop/Op/Costume/Masque/Fantasy-Loon/Blowout/Drag Ball and featured Pink Floyd and Soft Machine.

Two days before Christmas, *Ready Steady Go* came off the air after over three years because of a Musicians' Union ban on miming on TV but there was a new pop show on the horizon as *The Monkees* was broadcast by BBC TV, four months after its US debut, the foursome notching up two number one singles and a chart topping album in America. Despite being seen as rivals to The Beatles, The Monkees, according to Michael Nesmith, "were not a musical act". He went on to explain, "We had very little to do with the music business and absolutely nothing to do with rock 'n' roll. None of us had any concept of making records or writing music or playing in a band."

And on the night this new pop TV special was first seen by the nation – New Year's Eve 1966 – George Harrison was banned from the London nightclub Annabel's for not wearing a tie. Undeterred the Beatle, along with his wife Patti Boyd, Eric Clapton and Brian Epstein, made their way to a slightly less glamourous Lyons Corner House where they saw in the New Year.

For pop fans around the world 1967 was the year of love and peace and "flower power" as the focus of attention shifted from Britain and beat music to America's West Coast and the allure of kaftans, beads, bells and tie-dye t-shirts, although some so-called psychedelic groups were reluctant to accept the new 'in' word.

Floyd's Nick Mason announced that the band did not call themselves psychedelic but explained, "It's just that people associate us with this and we get employed at the freak-outs and happenings." The Move, from Birmingham, were another group whose outrageous appearance and stage shows linked them with the new movement but singer Carl Wayne dismissed the notion. "Psychedelic music is a load of shit and we get quite nasty with anybody who calls us psychedelic."

While they didn't want to be branded as 'psychedelic' both Floyd and The Move brought a new excitement to their stage shows, with Floyd adding giant lava lamps, slide shows and lighting effects while The Move set off fireworks, smashed television sets and even destroyed an effigy of Prime Minister Harold Wilson. Groups were also learning all about amplification and turned to bigger and better amps and speakers to up the decibels when it came to performing live.

The emerging guitar hero Hendrix was another who liked to play loud and perform some never seen before on-stage antics, but he paid a price in March 1967, on the first date of his UK tour with The Walker Brothers, after burning his hands when he set fire to his guitar and ended up in hospital. The publicity stunt, which involved lighter fuel, brought some headlines and the threat of a ban from the theatre owners but the new guitar hero carried on regardless. One man who was not put off by the stunt was future Queen guitarist Brian May who was on the entertainment committee at Imperial College London when they paid Hendrix £1000 to perform a couple of months later.

In addition to playing with his own band that night – "I actually played 'Purple Haze' when Hendrix was there and it's rumoured he came down and saw me" – May recalls that a thousand people paid to see Hendrix. "We all crammed in and it was magical beyond belief, the warmth and huge-ness of his sound was mind-blowing". Even though he booked him, May never actually got to meet his hero. "The closest I got was him walking from the changing room to the stage in a cloud of smoke and asking 'where's the stage man?', and we all nodded our heads in the direction of the stage."

Outside music there were other events taking place, as the first ever American Football Super Bowl, when the Green Bay Packers beat the Kansas City Chiefs, was played out in January in front of a TV audience of over 60 million. In the same month three American astronauts – Gus Grissom, Ed White and Roger Chaffee -were killed in a fire during a simulation exercise on the launch pad at Cape Canaveral.

Considered by many to be the greatest double A-side single ever released, The Beatles' 'Strawberry Fields Forever' and 'Penny Lane' bizarrely ended the group's run of 11 consecutive number one singles when it peaked at number two – behind Engelbert Humperdinck's 'Release Me'. At the same time Buffalo Springfield ("no relation to Dusty" said *NME*) released 'For What It's Worth', which was dubbed "uninspired and monotonous" but became an anti-Vietnam war anthem.

Three brothers named Gibb, who were born on the Isle of Man, returned from Australia to begin forging a career as The Bee Gees, just as The Monkees became the first American group to top the UK albums chart. The American quartet were now big business and made a suitable impression on music writer and publisher David Roberts, who was a schoolboy at the time. "The music was great, the songs were brilliant and they were valid. None of us gave a second thought as to whether they played on their records or not."

Hippies were now at the forefront of American society and 10,000 of them gathered in New York's Central Park to protest about war, censorship and politicians, but *NME* was still to be convinced as they described The Grateful Dead's debut album as "mostly an ace drag unless you happen to be stoned, then you might be tempted to utter 'yeah'." However, the fancy for new way-out clothes saw boutiques spring up nationwide and London's fashionable Lord Kitchener's Valet offered naval bell bottom trousers for 45s (£2.25p), police capes for 60s (£3) while Continental versions - with piping - were a tad cheaper at 50s (2.50p) and Union Jack t-shirts for 15s (75p).

While Elvis Presley was busy marrying Priscilla Beaulieu – who he had met at a US Army Base in Germany when she was just 14 – in front of 100 guests at the Aladdin Hotel in Las Vegas, London was hosting two concerts which reflected the changing of the guard in pop music. The annual *NME* Poll Winners show featured no Beatles but Cliff Richard was there once again alongside The Move, Cream, Lulu, Dusty Springfield, The Beach Boys and Small Faces, but just over two weeks later a so-called Technicolour Dream was held at Alexandra Palace with Pink Floyd and Soft Machine. Over 7000 people attended what was described in *MM* as the "first serious attempt at a Human Be-in in England."

After his problems with his burning guitar, Hendrix found himself banned from Kew Gardens because, they said, "people in fancy dress aren't allowed" but Procol Harum, fresh from supporting Hendrix in concert, found themselves at the top of the charts with 'A Whiter Shade Of Pale' and initial sales of over 350,000.

Love and peace was established as the 'in' theme in pop music as The Beatles recorded 'All You Need Is Love' for a satellite TV broadcast watched by 400 million people, the Rolling Stones followed with 'We Love You', then came The Troggs with 'Love Is All Around' and finally American singer Scott McKenzie topped the charts with his anthem to all things hippy – 'San Francisco (Be Sure To Wear Flowers In Your Hair)'.

The Beatles' revolutionary new album *Sgt. Pepper's Lonely Hearts Club Band*, which cost a record-breaking £25,000 to produce and took over 700 hours of studio time, was topping the charts on both sides of the Atlantic in June. By the end of the year *Sgt Pepper* had spent 25 weeks at number one in the UK chart, a position it shared with The Monkees, who racked up a total of nine weeks with two albums, and once again *The Sound Of Music,* which boasted another 13 weeks in the top spot and its third successive year as the best-selling album in Britain.

Peter Asher, half of the hit duo Peter and Gordon and brother of McCartney's then girl-friend Jane Asher, was closer than most people to the progress of *Sgt Pepper.* He had heard parts of it during his visits to Abbey Road Studios but was in for a surprise when it was finished. "He (Paul) brought round an acetate and played it to the whole family. I was astonished and he left a copy at our house."

For future hit maker Tom Robinson the album was "a huge achievement" as, in his words, The Beatles "managed, as the biggest band in the world, to locate themselves at the heart of the underground scene." Less impressed was Sex Pistol-in-waiting Glen Matlock, who received the album as a Christmas present when he was just 11 years old. "I think it's a bit daft to be honest." And *NME* didn't get carried away either, telling readers that it was "a very good LP that will sell like hot cakes" while *MM* declared the album to be "remarkable."

While all this was going on, the first major pop festival was taking place in Monterey in California. It was brought together with the help of a band of 'governors' including McCartney, Jagger, Brian Wilson and Donovan who all, weirdly, did not appear at the three-day event which did feature The Byrds, The Who, Simon & Garfunkel, Jimi Hendrix, Mamas and Papas, Jefferson Airplane and The Grateful Dead. Jann Wenner, who would launch *Rolling Stone* magazine four months later, was on the spot and reported that it was "a superb moment for rock 'n' roll".

Despite the best efforts of a new generation to change the ways of the world, love and peace was not on the agenda everywhere. America was still fighting in Vietnam and world boxing champion Muhammad Ali found himself stripped of his title and sentenced to prison (later quashed) for refusing the US Army draft.

At the same time Israel and Egypt embarked on what became known as the 'Six Day War.'

Britain's three year flirtation with the pop pirates came to an abrupt end in August 1967 when the Labour Government introduced the Marine Offences Act which made the pirate radio stations illegal, claiming they interfered with European radio wavelengths and paid no royalties on the records they played. Within a month the BBC had introduced Radio One as their new pop station, with ex-pirate presenters such as Kenny Everett, John Peel and Tony Blackburn on board. The plan was for it to broadcast pop music to a host of hopeful teenagers for 18 hours a day.

But there were dissenters about the Government's new law, the closure of the pirates and the rather hasty appearance of a new BBC 'pop' station. Walker was one and he made his point by staying on at the Caroline North station, moored in international waters off the Isle of Man (which refused to acknowledge the new UK law) until 1969 and BBC Essex presenter Dave Monk, then a 16-year-old schoolboy, was another. "I listened to Caroline religiously after all the others had closed down. There was something dashing about sticking two fingers up at the legislation."

Just three days before the death of manager Brian Epstein, The Beatles began to spend time with the Maharishi Mahesh Yogi at his meditation centre in Wales, with McCartney telling the world, "Young people who take drugs should give them up and start meditating instead." A student in America at the time, Paul Gambaccini was moved by something completely different as a controversial new musical called *Hair* opened in New York. Featuring nudity, swearing and a racially integrated cast, he recalls it as "one of the transformation musicals of my lifetime."

Following the first heart transplant, performed in South Africa by Dr Christian Barnard, the shooting of revolutionary Che Guevara in Bolivia and the death in a plane crash of soul singer Otis Redding, the BBC in Britain took *Juke Box Jury* off the air after nine years and 1,432 shows and broadcast The Beatles' coach tour extravaganza called *Magical Mystery Tour* on Boxing Day, with the *Daily Express* reviewer saying he had never seen "such blatant rubbish."

In a year when the films *Bonnie & Clyde*, *To Sir With Love* and *How I Won The War* (featuring John Lennon), hit the cinema, it seemed that psychedelia, flower power and all that went with it was coming to a disappointing end. Graham Nash said simply, "Flower power is dead – killed by all the people who just weren't genuine" while *MM* mourned the passing of "one of the sincerest and major steps forward for the pop world".

And those at the heart of a movement that was both embraced and criticised, said their own goodbye in October 1967 when the good folks of San Francisco organised "the death of a hippie", a mock funeral to mark what was seen as the crass commercialisation of the love and peace message.

Britain's Prime Minister Harold Wilson began the new year by giving his support to the 'I'm Backing Britain' campaign, which was aimed at getting people to work for an extra 30 minutes a day for no extra pay, and within four months that pay could have included the country's first decimal coins as the new 5p and 10p pieces were introduced.

The assassination in America of Senator Robert Kennedy in June was the second major tragedy in three months following the shooting of civil rights activist Martin Luther King. On the up-side, peace talks began in Paris to end the Vietnam War – although it would run for a further eight years - but a move to liberalise Czechoslovakia was abruptly ended when 250,000 Warsaw Pact troops from USSR, Poland, Hungary and Bulgaria marched into the country and restored communist rule.

While The Beatles celebrated another number one with 'Hey Jude' – the first record on their own Apple label and the only UK release to top the US charts in 1968 - Cliff Richard, still on EMI after a decade, notched up his first chart topper for three years with 'Congratulations'. The Beatles had, following the death of Epstein, decided to launch a series of new businesses, with Lennon explaining, "We decided to play business for a bit."

But their Apple operations – a boutique plus film, publishing and electronics – were not destined for a bright or long future, with McCartney confirming,

"The main downfall was that we were less businessman and more heads," while rock photographer Gered Mankowitz commented, "It was all pretty stoned, hippy and lovely for a few minutes and then somebody pointed out that it was a business."

In the midst of all this activity it seemed that the British pop charts were in for an overhaul – amid accusations of hype and skulduggery – as the British Market Research Bureau began compiling singles and album charts with the help of record shops, record companies and something called a computer.

In the wake of America's Monterey jamboree, Britain got into the pop festival business in August 1968 with an event on the Isle of Wight billed as the 'Great South Coast Bank Holiday Pop Festival'. Featuring The Move, Tyrannosaurus Rex and Jefferson Airplane, who arrived with 30 technicians and five tons of equipment, it was held in a 40 acre field on Britain's most southerly island and was a fund-raiser for a local swimming pool.

Whatever had come and gone in pop music over the previous few years, there was a familiar sound to the end of year celebrations as the Beatles ended 1968 (for the fifth time in six years) with a number one album, *The Beatles*, although they shared the top spot that year with a previously unheard of 13 other acts and (once again) *The Sound Of Music*, which appeared at number one for the last time.

Close on the heels of Richard Nixon being elected President of America, three US astronauts – Frank

Borman, Jim Lovell and William Anderson – became the first humans to travel around the earth's satellite and see "the dark side of the moon", five years before a certain multi-million selling album was conceived and released. Seven months later Neil Armstrong and Buzz Aldrin took things on a pace in the space race when they became the first men to walk on the moon, while Michael Collins went round and round in space waiting to pick them up.

1969 also saw Elvis return to the top of the UK album chart for the first time in seven years, The Who introduce *Tommy*, a creation that was dubbed a "rock opera", and Scottish songstress Lulu share the title "Eurovision winner" with acts from France, Spain and Holland in a bizarre four-way tie, while the festival of all festivals took place in New York state.

Over four days in August, at the Woodstock Music & Arts Fair, a crowd estimated to reach 450,000 at its peak gathered to listen to over 30 acts and experience three (non-violent) deaths, two births and four miscarriages plus countless conceptions and a record-breaking amount of drugs and alcohol. It all ended with Hendrix playing 'Star-Spangled Banner' at nine o'clock in the morning.

Just over a year after his performance at Woodstock, when he received a record-breaking fee of $125,000, Hendrix was found dead in London. Tony Bramwell, who booked him to play the Saville Theatre in 1967, recalls his last conversation with the guitarist in the summer of 1970. "He phoned me and asked if he could play the Saville again. I told him it had closed down and he said, 'I would have loved to do that gig again, it was my favourite.'"

While major sixties groups such as the Rolling Stones, The Who, The Kinks and The Hollies stayed together – despite a few rows, bust-ups and the untimely death of the Stones' Brian Jones – The Beatles were coming to the end of their global domination of pop music. Both George Harrison and John Lennon (with Yoko Ono) released solo albums in 1968 while *Abbey Road,* the last album the group recorded, topped the charts in 1969 – followed by *Let It Be* in 1970 – but on the last day of the seventies Paul McCartney filed a law suit to dissolve the partnership known as the Beatles & Co.

One man who was at the very heart of The Beatle' break-up was EMI chairman Sir Joseph Lockwood, who acted as a go-between in the feud between Lennon and McCartney. "I tried to stop it falling apart and had no trouble with Paul, but Yoko was a problem and there seemed to be no solution other than for The Beatles to break up. She came into my office with John for lunch one day. I put her down the end of the table and she put a tape recorder on the table and taped the whole lunch."

And as things went from bad to worse, and maybe in an effort to warn the world of what was coming, the final song on the group's final recording was titled 'The End'. With that, music moved on to embrace a host of new musical genres including, metal, folk rock, heavy metal, 'prog' rock, something called 'soft' rock and the 'concept' album. In the words of Doris Day's 1964 hit it was time for us all to 'Move Over Darling' and let a new crowd onto the dance floor, where they could do the Hustle, the Bump and even the Funky Chicken.

Bibliography

A to Z of British Radio by Seán Street (Scarecrow Press 2006)

Abbey Road by Brian Southall (Omnibus 1997)

All Shook Up by Joseph Connolly (Cassell & Co 2000)

The Beatles Anthology (Cassell & Co 2000)

Bermondsey Boy by Tommy Steele (Penguin 2007)

Born To Run by Brice Springsteen (Simon & Schuster 2016)

Eric Clapton The Autobiography (Century 2007)

From The Bomb To The Beatles by Juliet Gardiner (Collins & Brown 1999)

Inside Out A Personal History of Pink Floyd by Nick Mason (Weidenfeld & Nicolson 2004)

Jerry Lee Lewis His Own Story by Rick Bragg (Cannongate 2014)

Kink by Dave Davies (Boxtree 1996)

Life by Keith Richards (Weidenfeld & Nicolson 2010)

London Live by Tony Bacon (Balafon 1999)

My Life My Way by Cliff Richard & Penny Junor (Headline 2008)

Not Fade Away by John Gribbin (Icon Books 2009)

Off The Record by Joe Smith (Pan Books 1990)

O, What A Circus by Tim Rice (Hodder & Stoughton 2000)

Rockin' At The 2Is Coffee Bar by Andrew Ings (Book Guild 2010)

Radio Luxembourg: The Station Of The Stars by Richard Nichols (Comet 1983)

Rock & Pop Year By Year by Luke Crampton & Dafydd Rees (Dorling Kindersley 2003)

Sex & Drugs & Rock'n'Roll: The Life Of Ian Dury by Richard Balls (Omnibus 2011)

Stoned by Andrew Loog Oldham (Secker & Warburg 2000)

Thanks A Lot Mr Kibblewhite by Roger Daltrey (Blink Publishing 2018)

The Whispering Years by Bob Harris (BBC Worldwide 2001)

Three Steps To Heaven by Bobby Cochran with Susan Van Hecke (Hal Leonard 2003)

Wild Tales by Graham Nash (Penguin Viking 2013)

Dreamboats & Petticoats Bringing On Back The Good Times the album out now and catch the brand new musical on tour from 2022 to book tickets go to kenwright.com

Dreamboats & Petticoats Music That Lives Forever the album out now and see the concert tour featuring Marty Wilde, Eden Kane and Mark Wynter from 2022 to book go to my www.flyingmusic.com